the
GOD-MAN

A GUIDE TO UNDERSTANDING THE GODHEAD

A LOOK AT THE TWO NATURES OF JESUS THE CHRIST
EXPLORING HIS ABSOLUTE DEITY & HIS
ABSOLUTE HUMANITY

GOD AND MAN WORKING TOGETHER
TO SAVE MANKIND

ROBERT SPEARMAN

The God-Man
A guide to understanding the Godhead
A look at the two natures of Jesus the Christ
Exploring His absolute deity and His absolute humanity
God and Man working together to save mankind
by Robert Spearman

Published by:
Pentecostal Publishers
1057 D Ave., No.6
Douglas, AZ 85607
Email: robertqpm@aol.com

Scripture versions cited:

Amp   The Amplified Bible, Grand Rapids: Zondervan (1965)
GNNT   Good News New Testament, New York: American Bible Society (1976)
KJV   King James Version
Msg   The Message, Colorado Springs: Navpress (2002)
NASB   New American Standard Bible, Anaheim, CA; Lockman Foundation (1997)
NIV   New International Version, Colorado Springs: International Bible Society (1984)

Library of Congress Cataloging in Publication Data
Spearman, Robert, 1930–
The God-Man: a guide to understanding the Godhead:
a look at the two natures of Jesus the Christ:
exploring His absolute deity and His absolute humanity:
God and Man working together to save mankind / by Robert Spearman
   p.cm
   Includes bibliographical references.
   ISBN 0-9769188-0-3
   1. Jesus Christ—Divinity. 2. Jesus Christ—Humanity
   3. Jesus Christ—Person and offices.
   I. Title

   BT216.3.S64 2006   232'.8
                    QBI05–600192
ISBN: 0-9769188-0-3
Library of Congress Control Number:

Publication date: December 3, 2006
Jacket design by Mary Morgan

I dedicate this book to my son

ALEXANDER SPEARMAN

God made him [the Son of Man] who had no sin
To be sin for us,
So that in him we might become the righteousness of God
2 Corinthians 5:21 (NIV)

Table of Contents

Part 2

Conclusion

INTRODUCTION

ISAIAH CHAPTER 53

Isaiah received an incredible vision from Yahweh. The vision was incredible because it revealed the Messiah as a suffering servant, as opposed to a liberating force, contradicting all contemporary conceptions of the Messiah. The Old Testament Jew envisioned the Messiah to be a man set apart by Yahweh to free Israel from political bondage.

Indeed, because the vision was incredulous, Isaiah begins chapter 53 by asking himself, who will believe this report? Who will understand this deviation from the accepted norm? Who will believe this message?

Of course, the Hebraic mind-set was formed by the Hebrew Scriptures which recorded mainly the physical power of Yahweh. The creation in six days, the curse and expulsion from the garden of Eden, the flood, deliverance from bondage in Egypt, the giving of the Law, sustenance during the wilderness journey, and the conquest of Canaan exemplified the physical influence of Yahweh. Yahweh's spiritual influence was little known in Old Testament times. Yahweh had not yet poured out His Spirit.

Yahweh's Spirit was missing from the Hebrew Scriptures. The Old Testament had rendered the hearts of the Jews insensitive, their ears dull, and their eyes dim to the power of Yahweh's Spirit (Isaiah 6:10). Except in a few cases the working of Yahweh's Spirit was without weight in the Old Testament. Little did the Old Testament Jew know that the full strength of Yahweh's spiritual power would be embodied in a Man (Colossians 2:9), a Man who had no kingly pomp.

Imagine a sad looking Man, burdened by the cares of the world, walking over rocks and pebbles in Israel, stopping to write in the sand to convey a message to onlookers. Now imagine Him having two natures, one divine and one human. Imagine Him being both God and Man, not half Man and half God, but fully God and fully Man. Imagine all the fulness of Deity (Spirit) dwelling in Him, enveloped by all the fulness of flesh (body, soul, spirit). This Man is God's messenger, God's ambassador to the world, Yahweh's right hand Man. Only a few recognized Him as God manifested in the flesh (1 Timothy 3:16).

Isaiah saw the arm of the Lord as a tender plant with its roots embedded in the desert; that is, in a starving spiritual environment, growing up in view of His Father in servile poverty. There was nothing extraordinary about the Man and nothing that attracted attention to Him. The Lord's power was mysteriously hidden in this Man's baffling commonality. His footsteps were as secret paths (Psalm 77:19).

He had no stately form or majesty that we should look upon Him in wonder, nor appearance that we should be attracted to Him. On the contrary, He was a Man of sorrows and acquainted with grief. And He was despised by men who scoffed at what He said. He was oppressed and afflicted by those who hated Him for His non-traditional doctrine. They brought about His crucifixion.

Yet, when His oppressors had Him put to death He did not open His mouth. Like a lamb led to slaughter, like a sheep that is silent before its shearers, He said nothing in self-defense. By oppression and judgment He was taken away from the land of the living-dead.

But why did He voluntarily give up His life when He had the power to destroy His enemies? The answer lies in the atonement. By his death He defeated the devil (death) and made the way of salvation possible and rolled away the curse from guilty men and women and opened the kingdom of heaven to true believers.

Contrary to Hebrew thinking all this is included in Isaiah's remarkable vision. The Christ was nailed to a tree and pierced through for our transgressions. He was chastened and crushed for our iniquities. Our sins fell upon Him and by His scourging we are made pure. He Himself bore our griefs and guilt. Our sorrows He took upon Himself and Yahweh cast our shame upon Him.

Indeed, all of us, like sheep, have strayed from the path of righteousness. Each of us has turned to his own way, seeking to do his own thing. All of us are sinners. Yet, by His grace, Yahweh's plan of salvation was designed to cast our wickedness upon Him, the Messiah.

It was the divine purpose of Yahweh that the Christ die for us, "For God so loved the world that He gave His only begotten Son, that whoever believes in Him should not perish but have eternal life" (John 3:16, NASB). He unwillingly yet willingly made Himself an offering for sin, accepting its penalty - death. Yet, because He was sinless, Yahweh raised Him from the dead. Now He sees the fruit of His work, His spiritual offspring, those made righteous by His righteousness, and He is satisfied and His days are eternal. And because the sinless Man Christ Jesus rendered Himself a sin offering on behalf of transgressors Yahweh is glorified.

A PRELIMINARY WORD

TWO IMPORTANT TRUTHS

Two important truths emerge from the New Testament regarding the God-Man. One is the reality that a virgin gave birth to a Manchild (Luke 1:35). Hence, God was the Father. Two is the fact that God is Spirit (John 4:24). God is not a man. (It goes without saying that God's Spirit is Holy.) Why are these two biblical truths important? Because they help us to properly understand the God-Man's dual nature.

These two truths are related. God (Spirit) brought about the birth of a Man. That is, Spirit impregnated the womb of the virgin Mary. Thus, God was the Father of the Son. Deity was the Father of humanity. And, for 33 years plus, Deity dwelt in humanity (Colossians 2:9). Hence, the two natures of the God-Man: Deity and humanity.

Mary was not the mother of God but the mother of the Christ, Christ the Man. The child that was nourished in the womb of the virgin was the Christ-child, not Deity. What God begets is God. What the virgin Mary gave birth to was God's Son - a Man. The Father dwelt in the Son.

Human generation necessarily embodies the origination of a new person not hitherto existing. The person generated involuntarily assumes the characteristics of the father and the mother. In the case of the Christ's human generation He assumed all the characteristics of humanity (body, soul, spirit) from His mother. In the case of Jesus' divine generation, the Father, who is Spirit, voluntarily assumed His Son's body. That is, God the Father did not become a Man but voluntarily dwelt in a

Man (2 Corinthians 5:19; Colossians 1:19). Through the virgin birth God entered time and history in a personal way in the form of a Man. Jesus' divine nature is eternal. But His human nature was limited. He was born (He did not pre-exist His birth) and He died.

GOD DID NOT "BECOME" A MAN

Despite the shades of doctrinal difference dividing the diverse denominations that make up the Christian religion, all of Christianity is of one accord regarding the two natures of the Lord Jesus Christ. All Christians agree that Jesus Christ, when He walked the earth, was fully God and fully Man. One nature being completely Spirit and the other nature was completely human. Humanity enveloped Deity. And there was no overlapping of the two natures. Each nature was distinct and separate from the other. Deity had no beginning and has no end and lives forever. Humanity was born and died.

However, God did not become a Man. Instead, by the virgin birth all the fulness of God dwelt in the body of a Man. Two thousand years ago God came down to earth and wrapped Himself in the flesh of the Lord Jesus Christ. Because He was miraculously begotten by God and born of a virgin mother Jesus Christ had two natures, one divine and one human. God did not become a Man because God does not change. God IS (Hebrews 11:6). The principles of divinity are the same yesterday, and today, and forever (Hebrews 13:8).

To become, according to accepted definition, means to undergo change or development. Change and development imply modification, transformation, substitution, and loss of original identity, things that are foreign to God's majestic oneness. God is Spirit and casts no shadow, a divine principle without variance. God is always the same and does not become anything other than what He is. Jesus Christ embodied all the fulness of God who is Spirit. *God's Spirit did not become flesh,* but God's Spirit dwelt in the flesh of the Lord Jesus Christ.

THERE IS BUT ONE GOD

The Bible states categorically that there is but one God (Deuteronomy 6:4 with Mark 12:29; Romans 3:30; Ephesians 4:6). God is undivided. No truth is more deeply embedded in the Hebrew and Christian mind.

Yet because all of God is summed up in the person of Jesus Christ, and because the Christian church accords Him that honor, we are led to suppose there are two divine beings. But, "In Him the whole fulness of Deity (the Godhead), continues to dwell in bodily form - giving complete expression of the divine nature" (Colossians 2:9, Amp). That is, God continues to be undivided, dwelling in the Man Christ Jesus. Thus, there are not two divine beings but one God.

Moreover, the Holy Spirit, another candidate for the office of divine being, is identified by the Lord Himself as His own Spirit. Speaking of His Holy Spirit, His divine nature, the Christ said, "I will not leave you as orphans; I will come to you" (John 14:18, NASB). After His death and resurrection He guarantees His disciples that He will come back in the invisible form of His Holy Spirit (see John 14:17). And Paul also identifies the Spirit of the Lord, His divine nature, with his Holy Spirit. "Now the Lord is Spirit, and where the Spirit of the Lord is, there is freedom" (2 Corinthians 3:17, NIV). God continues to be undivided. There are not three divine beings but one divine being.

THE VIRGIN BIRTH

The New Testament unequivocally asserts that in Jesus Christ all the fulness of God was personally manifested. (See John 1:14; Philippians 2:5-8; Colossians 1:19; 2:9; 1 Timothy 3:16; Hebrews 2:14.) Jesus Christ was fully God and fully Man. One person embodied two natures, Deity and humanity, actualized by the virgin birth. By the virgin birth all the fulness of Deity dwelt in humanity. Two separate natures resided in one person - for a time. Deity had to leave humanity at the Christ's death, however, for Deity cannot die.

The virgin birth was prophesied in the Hebrew Scriptures. "Therefore The Lord Himself will give you a sign: Behold a virgin will be with child and bear a son, and she will call his name Immanuel"(Isaiah 7:14; NASB). Immanuel is an Old Testament name meaning "God among us."

MATTHEW EXPLAINS HOW THE
VIRGIN BIRTH CAME ABOUT

"The birth of Jesus took place like this. His mother, Mary, was engaged to be married to Joseph. Before they came to the marriage bed, Joseph discovered she was pregnant. (It was by the Holy Spirit, but he didn't know that.) Joseph, chagrined but noble, determined to take care of things quietly so Mary would not be disgraced. While he was trying to figure a way out, he had a dream. God's angel spoke in the dream: 'Joseph, son of David, don't hesitate to get married. Mary's pregnancy is Spirit-conceived. God's Holy Spirit has made her pregnant'" (Matthew 1:18-20, Msg).

Matthew then goes on to quote Isaiah 7:14 ("Behold, a virgin will be with child and bear a son, and she will call His name Immanuel")for a couple of reasons. First, to show that Isaiah's prophecy had been fulfilled. But most important Matthew doubtless understands that the name Immanuel denotes that the Messiah is really "God among us" and that the divine nature of God is united, in some supernatural way, with the human nature of the Christ and that the body of the Messiah is begotten directly by the power and Spirit of God.

Indeed, the book of Hebrews lays stress on the fact that God prepared a body for the redeemer so that sin might be done away with once for all.

> The old plan was only a hint of the good things in the new plan. Since that old "law plan" wasn't complete in itself, it couldn't complete those who followed it. No matter how many sacrifices were offered year after year, they never added up to a complete solution. If they had, the worshipers would have gone merrily on their way, no longer dragged   down by their sins. But instead of removing awareness of sin, when these animal sacrifices were repeated over and over they actually heightened awareness [of sin] and guilt. The plain fact is that bull and goat blood can't get rid of sin. That is what is meant by this prophecy, put in the mouth of Christ: "You don't want sacrifices and offerings year after year; [therefore] you've prepared a body for me for a sacrifice" (Hebrews 10:1-5, Msg).

Because animal sacrifice was not the final solution for the sin problem God prepared Himself a body to expiate sin. Indeed, God Himself came to earth and assumed a human body through the virgin birth. By His grace He did this to eliminate sin and also to defend His honor and credibility - for God cannot arbitrarily abolish sin.

Part 1

Humanity 1

THE MYSTERY

Jehovah kept His Son a secret. Jehovah's authority and power were manifest in the creation but His love and mercy were concealed. Then God revealed His heart. In His Son He expressed His moral nature - grace, love, and mercy. Salvation, reconciliation, redemption, justification, sanctification, resurrection - previously unknown - were made manifest when God revealed Himself in His Son.

Before the Messiah's birth God's gospel was obscure, hidden in animal sacrifice. Notably the gospel was kept remote from the Gentile world. Then God revealed Himself to the entire world - not just to the Jews. Jesus Christ revealed "the mystery kept secret for so long..." (Romans 16:25). God's secret in Jesus Christ "is now disclosed and through the prophetic Scriptures is made known to all nations..." (Romans 16:26, Amp).

Paul wrote, "...we speak God's wisdom in a mystery, the hidden wisdom which God predestined before the ages..."(1 Corinthians 2:7, NASB). In the administration of the mystery Paul includes his present and future coworkers. "So then let us [apostles] be looked upon as ministering servants of Christ and stewards (trustees) of the mysteries - that is, the secret purpose - of God"(1 Corinthians 4:1,Amp).

It is worthy of note that mystery and revelation are, biblically speaking, closely associated. Indeed, mystery and revelation are virtually synonymous. One depends on the other. The idea of mystery and its parallels - hidden, secret, sealed, concealed - is often used in conjunction with the idea of revelation and its parallels - revealed, made known, manifested, expressed - in the New Testament. That is to say, *all* the mysteries of God are exposed in the revelation of the gospel of Jesus Christ.

The mysteries of Christianity are its doctrines revealed in the work of the Messiah and administered by His disciples. Both the Christ and Paul contrast God's mysteries and divine revelation with the wisdom of worldly philosophy. The contrast made is that God's mysteries are the result of divine revelation and spiritually discerned while the so called wisdom of worldly philosophy is the result of intellectual exercise.

> Jesus said, "Thank you, Father, Lord of heaven and earth. You've concealed your ways from sophisticates and know-it-alls, but spelled them out clearly to ordinary people. Yes, Father, that's the way you like to work"(Matthew 11:25,26, Msg).

> Paul wrote, "You'll remember, friends, that when I first came to you to let you in on God's master stroke, I didn't try to impress you with polished speeches and the latest philosophy. I deliberately kept it plain and simple: first Jesus and who he is; then Jesus and what he did - Jesus crucified"(1 Corinthians 2:1,2, Msg).

When God revealed Himself in His Son the mysteries that God had held in His heart from eternity were unveiled. With the coming of the Christ men are able to see the manifestations of God's will, "Making known to us the mystery (secret) of His will - of His plan, of His purpose"(Ephesians 1:9, Amp).

God's decision - His will - to manifest Himself in His Son was sovereign. The things God purposed in His Son originated in God's heart - without extra counsel. God sovereignly kept the birth of His Son hidden in His heart until He chose to make His true nature - His grace, love, and mercy - known to the world.

God gave Paul the revelation of the mystery of the gospel and appointed him administrator of the mystery, "to bring to light what is the administration of the mystery which for ages has been hidden in God..."(Ephesians 3:9, NASB). God kept His Son secret until the fulness of time. "But when the time had fully come, God sent [begot] his Son, born of a woman, born under the law, to redeem those under the law..."(Galatians 4:4, NIV).

Paul asks for prayer. He writes, "And don't forget to pray for me. Pray that I'll know what to say and have the courage to say it at the right time, telling the mystery [of the gospel] to one and all, the Message that I, jailbird preacher that I am, am responsible for getting out"(Ephesians 6:19, Msg).

Paul magnifies God for the revelation of the mystery of the gospel in Christ.

> This mystery has been kept in the dark for a long time, but now it's out in the open. God wanted everyone, not just the Jews, to know this rich and glorious secret inside and out, regardless of their background, regardless of their religious standing. The mystery in a nutshell is just this: Christ is in you, therefore you can look forward to sharing in God's glory. It's that simple. (Colossians 1:25-27, Msg).

Paul summarizes the revelation of God's mystery in Christ.

> I want you woven into a tapestry of love, in touch with everything there is to know of God. Then you will have minds confident and at rest, focused on Christ, God's great mystery. All the richest treasures of wisdom and knowledge are embedded in that mystery and nowhere else. And we've been shown that mystery!(Colossians 2:2, Msg).

That the Messiah was coming was no mystery to the Jews. But God withheld the real reasons for His coming. The Jews expected the Messiah to be a secular prince who would deliver them from foreign domination, one who would retake the throne of David. As a result they would live happily ever after.

However, little did the Old Testament Jew know of the fulness of salvation, reconciliation, redemption. Every year, once a year, year after year, he depended on animal sacrifice to ease his conscience. Yet, the guilt and shame of his sin remained.

Atonement came but once a year. Redemption was unknown because there was no redeemer. Justification was a foreign concept because sin had not yet been abolished. Sanctification - set apart by God - was felt by the Jews but did them no good. Indeed, it made them arrogantly proud.

A final mystery that God held in His heart from eternity was His intent to make of Jew and Gentile a whole new body. That is, in Christ the distinction between Jew and Gentile disappears. By faith in Christ all nations become heirs to the promises that Jews thought were exclusively their own. (See Romans 11:11ff.)

A place in heaven is reserved for those who believe that mystery and revelation have been united in Christ, that in Christ all spiritual truth has been summed up. One final mystery remains, however, and that is the great mystery of the God-Man. How was it possible that a Man be both God and Man? This great mystery is revealed in the virgin birth.

THE GREAT MYSTERY

Paul, the main administrator of God's secret in Christ, employs the word mystery twenty times in his epistles. But only twice does he describe the mystery as "great." The first time is in his letter to the Ephesians and the second time is in his first letter to Timothy. In Ephesians the great mystery is the spiritual union of Christ and His Church - being in Christ - a union that resembles the marriage connection: "This mystery is great; but I am speaking with reference to Christ and the Church"(Ephesians 5:32, NASB).

Paul's exposition of the great mystery that concerns us, namely the doctrine that God manifested himself in the flesh of Jesus Christ, is contained in 1 Timothy 3:16. It should be noted that many valid translations render this verse in the following lyrical format, leading some expositors to conclude that early Christians made it into a hymn.

Undeniably great is the mystery of Godliness:
That God was manifested in the flesh;
Was vindicated by God's Spirit;
Beheld by angels;
Proclaimed among the nations;
Believed on in the world;
And taken up in glory.

GOD MANIFESTED HIMSELF IN THE FLESH OF A MAN

The unfolding revelation of God which began in Genesis 3:15 was completed in the birth of the Messiah approximately four thousand years later when God manifested Himself in the ministry of Jesus Christ. The Messiah is the revealed mystery of Godliness - the Godhead. That is, God revealed Himself in human form in Jesus Christ. He clothed Himself in the flesh of the Messiah.

The revelation of the God-Man is the most extraordinary event of all time and indeed a great mystery - nonetheless a revealed mystery. The embodiment of God in a Man constitutes the fundamental doctrine of the Christian message. This amazing announcement in 1 Timothy 3:16 - God manifested in the flesh - makes the five following declarations worthy of attention. These five statements reveal what happened as a result of the God-Man's ministry on earth.

VINDICATED BY GOD'S SPIRIT

By resurrecting Him from the dead God - or God's Spirit - vindicated the Christ of all trumped-up charges brought against Him by the religious people of His day. The resurrection cleared the Christ of all man made accusations. God's Spirit of holiness, by the resurrection, furnished evidence that Christ the Man was God's Son, that He was sent on a divine mission, that He was God's ambassador on earth(Romans 1:4; 8:11).

By raising Him from the dead God's Spirit justified the righteousness of all claims the Christ made about Himself and His assigned task. After all, God would not sanction the doings and doctrines of an impostor. Moreover, by the resurrection, God's Spirit exposed the depraved and debased hearts of men.

BEHELD BY ANGELS

These are Old Testament angels who discovered, to their surprise, they had just become New Testament angels. Old Testament angels acted as God's messengers. They were spiritual agents who executed God's orders. God used Old Testament angels as mediators between His Spirit and the spirit of men, mainly the prophets, since God's Spirit had not yet been poured out.

The Christ ushered in a new kingdom and a new chain of command. God's Spirit, that is God's mediation through the Christ, now speaks directly to the spirit of men and women. In the New Testament the mediation of Old

Testament angels was terminated by the intervention of God Himself in the Christ, once, for all, and forever.

Now New Testament angels watch the lot of men (1 Peter 1:12) and rejoice in their salvation (Luke 15:10). Now they join with God in the manifestation of His love. They are active participants in the results of God and Man working together to save mankind. They are no longer messengers. Now they are "...ministering spirits, sent out to render service for the sake of those who will inherit salvation"(Hebrews 1:14, NASB).

The statement, "Beheld by angels," implies that angels beheld from a distance what God was doing in the Christ; that is, they were not active participants. In fact they probably didn't know what God was doing. Presumably angels do not have foreknowledge of God's plans. Whether God informed angels beforehand of His plans and purposes in the Christ is questionable. Most likely they did not know what God was doing until after He had done it.

When God clothed Himself in a human body, stepped into space and onto earth, the angels were most likely astonished. The union of His Spirit with one of His own creatures probably left the angels with their mouths open and perhaps made them blink in amazement. In reality, when God manifested Himself in the flesh of the Christ, He was delivering a message to His messengers: He was telling them to stand back and behold the glory of God, that is, God at work by His Spirit.

PROCLAIMED AMONG THE NATIONS

This statement, though it seems harmless and neutral, confirms another revealed mystery of the Godhead. It proclaims the unification of Jew and Gentile, making Gentiles, in essence, spiritual Jews. In God's economy, before the Christ's birth, there were two classes of people: Jew and Gentile. And each class occupied its own nation. Over the years, however, because they were the chosen people of God, the Jews had built up a wall of partition that divided the two peoples. The Jews regarded the Gentiles as excluded from their covenant with God.

But Paul points out, because of the Christ's ministry, the Jew had no special advantage before God just because he was a Jew. The Christ revealed that no man or woman is excluded from the grace of his or her maker. The God-

Man broke down the wall of partition that separated the Jew from the Gentile nations. He showed that the Gentiles were no longer shut out from God's kingdom, "For He Himself...broke down the barrier of the dividing wall, by abolishing in His flesh...the law...that in Himself He might make the two [Jew and Gentile] into one new [spiritual] man..."(Ephesians 2:14,15, NASB). Thus, by God's Spirit, because of the God-Man's work, the new covenant is proclaimed in all nations.

BELIEVED ON IN THE WORLD

This statement tickles the imagination. What is so extraordinary about this declaration? What does it have to do with the great mystery of the Godhead? How does it stand alongside "God was manifested in the flesh"?

The first consideration is the strong improbability that such an incredible doctrine would be believed. The dual nature of the God-Man is incomprehensible. That God, who is pure Spirit, would clothe Himself in the body of a Man and subject Himself to the flesh's limitations goes beyond human understanding. That God would descend to earth and dwell in a servant's frame seems irrational. Why would God do such a thing?

Yet this natural improbability has been supernaturally overcome and men have believed. Already in the first century, inside and outside the Jewish state, the doctrine of "God manifested in the flesh" obtained credence in the world. The new covenant was being ratified in the hearts of men in many nations.

The second consideration, which again revolves around the strong improbability that God's message would be believed, arises from the wickedness of men's hearts. Men are followers of Satan, lovers of self and the world, reluctant to believe any message from God. Indeed, the Jews rejected the prophets and put them to death (see Matthew 23 and Acts 7) and they finally had their Messiah killed. In the human soul there is nothing to excite faith in God. Unbelief is the norm.

Yet, in spite of overwhelming odds against it, the message respecting the God-Man was believed on in the world - from Rome to Jerusalem and beyond. Paul regarded the belief of the Jews and Gentiles another revealed mystery of the Godhead: Faith conquered the natural reluctance to confide in God; Faith overcame the natural feelings of the human heart. Acceptance of this great revealed mystery - God manifested in the flesh - clearly shows that more than human effort was operating in the world

TAKEN UP IN GLORY

"Taken up in glory" is a statement of godliness - of the Godhead - because it declares the power of God and the purity of the Man Christ Jesus. It was God who took the Messiah from earth to be with Him in heaven because He had not sinned. "After he finished the sacrifice for sins, the Son took his honored place in the heavens right alongside God..."(Hebrews 1:3, Msg).

But the statement - "Taken up in glory" - suggests more than this. It indicates that there is someone - a man like us - in heaven who represents us, mankind. God appointed Him our High Priest.

Now that we know what we have - Jesus, this great High Priest with ready access to God - let's not let it slip through our fingers. We don't have a priest who is out of touch with our reality. He's been through weakness and testing, experienced it all - all but sin(Hebrews 4:14, Msg).

During the Levitical priesthood, however, "...there were a lot of priests, for they died and had to be replaced. But Jesus' priesthood is permanent. He's there from now to eternity to save everyone who comes to God through him, always on the job to speak up for them"(Hebrews 7:24,25, Msg).

Such a high priest meets our need - one who is holy, blameless, pure, set apart from sinners, exalted above the heavens. Unlike the other high priests, he does not need to offer sacrifices day after day, first for his own sins, and then for the sins of the people. He sacrificed for their sins once for all when he offered himself. For the law appoints as high priests men who are weak; but the oath, which came after the law, appointed the Son, who was made perfect forever(Hebrews 7:26-28, NIV).

The Son, the Christ, the risen Man who sits at the right hand of God has obtained eternal redemption for His people and appears before God on our behalf. Christ the Man, the Messiah offered Himself for our sins - not an animal - so God took Him up to heaven and appointed Him our High Priest - our never ending intercessor. "He did not enter [heaven] by means of the blood of goats and calves; but he entered the Most Holy Place [heaven] once for all by his own blood, having obtained eternal redemption"(Hebrews 9:12, NIV).

This is the essence of the glory of the Godhead - salvation - Man working with God and God working with Man for our benefit.

CONCLUSION

One of the definitions of the word mystery in Webster's Seventh New Collegiate Dictionary is this: "A religious truth that man can know by revelation alone and cannot fully understand." The religious truth that concerns us is the mystery of the God-Man - two natures, one divine, one human in one person. As Paul says, this is a great mystery.

That God planted the seed of His Son's generation in the womb of a virgin - though a revealed truth - is nonetheless a mystery. That all God's divine nature entered the womb of a woman to provide Himself a body is hard to believe. Yet, when God wills a thing the order of nature is overturned.

In the Hebrew Scriptures the mystery of the God-Man was unclear. Messianic references were made to "the seed of a woman"(Genesis 3:15), and "a virgin would bear a child"(Isaiah 7:14), and "a child will be born..."(Isaiah 9:6), but how the child would be conceived was not specified. However, in the New Testament God clearly explained Himself. He said His Spirit will come upon a virgin and she shall bear a Son (Luke 1:35). Thus, God who is Spirit, fathered His Son who was flesh and bones - a great mystery indeed.

The great mystery of the Godhead embraces the New Testament truth that the Son who was born of a virgin embodied two natures - one divine and one human. And each nature was complete in itself. The divine nature was pure Spirit; that is, all the fulness of God. The human nature was all the fulness of humanity - body, soul, spirit - including its limitations - physical death. Jesus derived His divine nature from His Father. The human nature of the Son came from His mother. It should be clear that Deity assumed a human body.

Paul calls Deity dwelling in humanity - two natures embodied in one person – "God's secret wisdom that has been hidden and that God destined for our glory before time began" (1 Corinthians 2:7, NIV). God held the secret of Jesus Christ's dual nature in His heart from the beginning. If those in authority at the time of Jesus' ministry had understood the two natures of the Son of God - that He was the God-Man - "they would not have crucified the Lord of glory" (1 Corinthians 2:8, NIV).

THE END

Those that belong to Jesus will be resurrected when He comes the second time (1 Corinthians 15:23). He comes the second time to judge the world and to destroy all worldly rule and authority. Then He will hand over the kingdom He established - life eternal, the final defeat of death - to God the Father. "After that comes the end" (1 Corinthians 15:24, Amp).

The end, of course, is the end. The mediatory reign of Christ the Man is over. Everyone is finally redeemed or sent to hell. Everything that was intended to be accomplished by the incarnation and the work of atonement is finished. God will now administer the affairs of the universe as they were administered before the beginning - before the creation.

> "When everything and everyone is finally under God's rule, the Son will step down, taking his place with everyone else [in heaven], showing that God's rule is absolutely comprehensive - a perfect ending!" (1 Corinthians 15:28, Msg), "...so that God may be all in all" (1 Corinthians 15: 28b, NIV).

This is a glimpse through successive future ages into the endless end of things as we know them, when the world God created shall have entered its final stage, when the sun has grown dim and there are no more people on earth, no more birds, animals or fish. The devil's reign is finally over. Salvation and reconciliation are issues of the past. There is no more need for the law or the "Word." It's a time when there is no time - eternity is reinstated. It's a time like the time before the foundation of the world - or better, after its demise.

After this "world" experiment who knows what God will do next? Or even, what He's doing now? And what form it will take? More people?

HUMANITY 2

CONCEPTION

God is not bound by natural law. Indeed, He often does things contrary to natural law. Thus, a bush burns and is not consumed; water piles up to allow the Hebrew children to pass over the Red sea; the sun stands still; a fiery furnace does not harm live bodies cast into it; iron floats; an ass speaks. Likewise, when God's Spirit conceived the Christ He suspended natural law: He planted a divine seed into the womb of an inviolate virgin. Her pregnancy brought about the formation of the fetus that was to be the Christ child, born at the fulness of time (Galatians 4:4).

According to natural law conception takes place when the father's seed is implanted in the womb of the mother. The semen of the father comes together with the seed of the mother to form new life. The Christ's conception occurred when all the fulness of God's nature (Colossians 2:9) - His mind, heart, will, thought, word, purpose, design, plan, love, grace, mercy, judgment - was implanted in the womb of a virgin.

The Christ's body was procreated in the womb of a virgin by the direct power of God. According to God's plan to redeem the world back to Himself it had to be so: The Redeemer had to be pure and free from the corruption of the fall; yet, at the same time He had to be human. That is, one of us - not God. God therefore prepared Himself a pure and holy body (Hebrews 10:5).

In the Hebrew Scriptures, 740 years before the birth of the Christ, Isaiah prophesied that a virgin will be with child and will give birth to a son (Isaiah 7:14). In the same verse he specified that the child will be called Immanuel, meaning God among us. In just a few words this prophecy establishes three things: 1) the humanity of the child (born of a woman); 2) the deity of the child (born of a virgin); 3) the joining of humanity and deity in the child (God with us).

Isaiah's prophecy that a virgin will be "with child" required divine insemination; no man was involved. A parallel to divine insemination is found in the first chapter of Genesis when God created the universe and all that is therein out of nothing. He hovered over the waters and spoke the word and the universe came into existence. Merely by vocal expression God "inseminated" the void and created the cosmos. In like manner the angel Gabriel told Mary that God will come upon her and the power of the Most High will overshadow her (Luke 1:35). As a result the Christ was conceived.

Thus, when God implanted the fulness of His divine nature into the womb of a virgin, deity and humanity came together. The child conceived was divine as well as human. The child that was born received life from His Father, who is divine, as well as from His mother, who was human.

Similarly, in the beginning, the first Adam was formed from the dust. Then God breathed into his nostrils the breath of life and Adam became a living being (Genesis 2:7). That is, God the Father and mother earth brought about the birth of Adam.

Jesus Christ, the last Adam, got His divine nature from God His Father. From where did He get His human nature? Entirely from the substance of a pure virgin, made pure - sanctified and consecrated (Luke 1:30) - by her faith in God's word (Luke 1:38). Biologically Mary's human nature came from the stock of Adam.

How did such a thing happen? How did God invest the fulness of His divine nature into the womb of a virgin? Nobody knows. The element of mystery and miracle that surrounds human reproduction, however, should relieve the curious mind. In the final analysis it can be said that God assumed a human body through the agency of the virgin Mary (1 Timothy 3:16).

BEGOTTEN

The apostle John refers to the Christ's conception as "begotten" or "only begotten" (John 1:14, 18; 3:16, 18; 1 John 4:9), *Monogenes* in Greek. No other New Testament writer applies this term to the conception of the Savior. Luke uses the word *sullambano* which means "conceive"(Luke 1:31; 2:21). Luke also quotes the angel Gabriel who says God will "come upon" (*eperchomai* in Greek) the virgin Mary and the power of the Most High will "overshadow" (*episkiazo* in Greek) her (Luke 1:35). Matthew and Mark make no reference to the Christ's conception. Matthew simply says the virgin Mary "was found to be with child" (Matthew 1:18). If a virgin is found to be with child it has to be a miracle.

"Begotten" is the past participle of the verb "to beget." To beget means "to procreate, to father, to sire" according to Webster's Seventh New Collegiate Dictionary. In other words God the Father "procreated, fathered, sired" His Son. To beget also means "to generate" or "to cause to be." That is, God "generated" or "caused the Son to be."

ONLY BEGOTTEN 1

"Only begotten" has been translated from two Greek words, *mono* and *genes*. The apostle John combined them and made one word, *monogenes*, roughly translated "one and only generated." No doubt John coined the word to show that God had only one Son. God's other sons and daughters are adopted.

Being born of a woman made the Son of God human. Spirit was the Father but the Son was a Man. New Testament writers lay stress on the humanity of the Lord.

- The Word [of God] became flesh and blood (John 1:14).
- The sacred writings contain preliminary reports by the prophets of God's Son. His descent from David roots him in history (Romans 1:3).
- Since the children are made of flesh and blood, it's logical that the Savior took on flesh and blood in order to rescue them by His death (Hebrews 2:14).
- As the sacrificed blood of Jesus, God's Son, purges all our sin (1 John 1:7).
- Everyone who confesses openly his faith in Jesus Christ - the Son of God, who came as an actual flesh-and-blood person - comes from God and belongs to God (1 John 4:2).

- There are a lot of smooth-talking charlatans loose in the world who refuse to believe that Jesus Christ was truly human, a flesh and blood human being (2 John 7).

Because "there are a lot of smooth-talking charlatans loose in the world" who subtly disguise the Christ's humanity, John wanted this truth - that the Son was fully human - to be prominently recorded. No doubt John wanted to reveal the fulfillment of prophecy, specifically Genesis 3:15, which states that the Messiah will come into the world through the seed of a woman. By using the term "only begotten" John alludes to this prophecy's fulfillment. In addition, The prophecy of Genesis 3:15 suggests that without the seed of a woman the Messiah would not have come into existence for there would have been no agency to make Him a Man.

The terms Father and Son suggest a relationship of authority and obedience - humanity obeying deity. Our salvation hangs onto that relationship. Because the Son obeyed the Father's plan of redemption - we are redeemed.

"Only begotten" determines a relationship between Father and Son *that began in time*. We are only "begotten" once. In the Hebrew Scriptures the relationship between God the Father and His Son had not yet started. The Son's ministry had a beginning. The Christ was born to fulfill His mission at the fulness of time (Galatians 4:4). The Christ (not God!) became a person at conception. Not before. Before conception He was not a person.

He was born and experienced childhood. The child continued to grow, His humanity growing spiritually strong, increasing in wisdom, and the grace of God was upon Him (Luke 2:40). Then, when He was twelve years old the Christ removed Himself from the spiritual covering of His earthly parents and placed Himself under His heavenly Father's care (Luke 2:41-52). Even today there is a ceremony in Judaism known as *bar mitzvah*, pushing a Jewish boy into manhood, making him an adult responsible for his own sins.

BEGOTTEN IN TIME

Begotten in time means the Son was not eternal. He was conceived at a definite point in time - thus destroying the notion that His human nature might be eternal. His human nature had a beginning and an end. He was born, lived, and died. Thanks to the resurrection, however, His human nature is now ever-lasting. The point is, nonetheless, His human nature had a beginning, just like ours.

The Son's Father, on the other hand, is eternal. God the Father -Deity dwelling in the Son - had no beginning and has no end. The living God - the Son's divine nature - lives forever. Indeed, if the concept of "Father" brings to mind eternal-ness, the concept of "Son" implies a beginning and contradicts eternalness.

Old Testament prophets acknowledged that the Messiah had not yet man-ifested Himself. They predicted He would come sometime in the future. In fact, Daniel specified a particular point in time when He would come. "So you are to know and discern that from the issuing of a decree to restore and rebuild Jerusalem, until the Messiah, the Prince, there will be seven weeks [of years] and sixty-two weeks [of years] (Daniel 9:25, NASB).

Balaam, a messenger of God, Prophesied that the Messiah will be born in Israel. "I see Him but He is not now [living]; I behold Him, but He is not near; a star shall come forth out of Jacob, and a scepter shall rise out of Israel" (Numbers 24:17, Amp).

The second Psalm declares that the Man Christ Jesus will be born on a specific day. "You are my Son. Today I have become your Father" (Psalm 2:7, NIV).

Isaiah spoke of the birth of the Messiah and included a reference to His dual nature. "A girl who is presently a virgin will get pregnant. She'll bear a son and name him Immanuel (God-With-Us)" (Isaiah 7:14, Msg).

Isaiah, speaking for Jesus, prophesied that salvation would come to the world through a Man. "[T]he Lord has called me from the womb, from the body of my mother He has named my name" (Isaiah 49:1b, Amp).

Then, at the proper time, John the Baptist came declaring the reign of God was coming. "Repent for the kingdom of heaven is at hand. For this is the one referred to by Isaiah the prophet..." (Matthew 3:2,3, NASB).

Finally, Jesus Himself entered the scene, saying, "Time's up! God's king-dom is here" (Mark 1:15, Msg).

The Christ was begotten in a moment in time. His Father was divine, His mother was human. As a result He personified two natures. That He was born of a virgin indicates that He embodied a nature other than that which was derived from His mother.

"But when the fulness of the time came, God sent forth His Son, born of a woman, born under law" (Galatians 4:4, NASB). Why did Paul specify that the Christ was born of a woman? Isn't everybody born of a woman? Paul could have eliminated "born of a woman" and it would not have changed the meaning of the announcement.

It would sound strange to say that George Washington was born of a woman on February 22. By what other means would he have been born? Undoubtedly, the reason Paul specified that the Christ, the Son of God, was born of a woman was to emphasize His humanity.

"Born under law" also gives special consideration to the Christ's humanity. As a member of the human race He was subject to the law of God. As a Man He was bound by it requirements. The Son of God took His place under law to free mankind from its curse.

ONLY BEGOTTEN 2

God is invisible. No man has ever seen Him. Yet, the only begotten Son has made Him known. "This one-of-a-kind God Expression, who exists at the very heart of the Father, has made him plain as day" (John 1:18, Msg).

The Man Christ Jesus revealed the heart of the eternal Father. The Christ spent His life translating the Father's heart to a needy world. God's Son, in continual communion with the Father, interpreted God's inherent beauty to a people in need of love and deliverance from sin.

At conception the Christ became God's only begotten Son. His existence began in the womb of a virgin. Before conception He did not exist in shape or form. Before conception He was a plan in God's mind. At conception God's plan, God's Word, God's heart took on a body of flesh and blood.

Conception takes place only once - at a point in time. However, the Son was always inside the Father's eternal conscience. "He was chosen and foreordained, destined and foreknown, before the foundation of the world, but He was brought out to public view - made manifest - in the last days - at the end of the times" (1 Peter 1:20, Amp). Two thousand years ago, at the beginning of the last days, God revealed His heart.

Jesus is "the name of the only begotten Son of God" (John 3:18, NASB). In this verse "name" and "only begotten" supply evidence of Jesus Christ's dual nature. How so? The name "Jesus" refers to His deity. The name Jesus means, "Jehovah saves." "Only begotten" refers to the Son of God's humanity - a Man born in time. In other words, Jehovah (Jesus) saves because of the work of His Son the Savior. Deity guarantees salvation based upon a Man's sacrificial death.

God sent His love into the world, manifesting it in His Son. "This is how God showed his love among us: He sent [begot] his one and only Son...that we might live through him. This is love: not that we loved God, but that he loved us and sent [begot] his Son as an atoning sacrifice for our sins" (1 John 4:9,10, NIV). That is, God's *love* was made flesh and blood when He begot His Son.

In short, the ultimate manifestation of God's love took place in a moment in time two thousand years ago when the virgin Mary conceived the Father's Son. At His birth the Christ *became* the Father's only begotten Son. The star of Bethlehem established the time. And the kingdom of God was ushered into the world, letting the latter times begin.

HUMANITY 3

OBEDIENCE AND SUFFERING

That Jehovah required obedience was established in the garden of Eden. The idea of obedience first came to light "in the beginning" when Jehovah commanded Adam, "You can eat from any tree in the garden except from the Tree-of-Knowledge-of-Good-and-Evil" (Genesis 2:17, Msg). Adam disobeyed, was thrown out of the garden, and disobedience - his sinful nature - was brought into the world of people.

Suffering is another reality that was created "in the beginning." When Adam disobeyed, when he sinned against Jehovah, all his offspring inherited his sinful nature. Adam's tendency to sin - his sinful nature - was passed on to us, his descendants. Disobedience is the norm. So, as a result of everyone's sinful nature, all the inhabitants of the world are bound to suffer. Suffering and pain are the consequences of sin. Suffering and pain, whether emotional or physical, are built into the human condition because of Adam's disobedience.

LEARNING OBEDIENCE

How does the Christ fit into this picture of the human condition? He was a Man. He was a human being. And, He was obedient - even to death on a "torture stake" (Philippians 2:8).

Because He was born without a sinful nature, free of the corrupting influences of the fall, the Son knew nothing but obedience to His Father. Because He was sinless, disobedience was foreign to Him. As God's Son He was never out of accord with His Father's will. Why then does Scripture say that He *learned* obedience? "Though he was God's Son, he learned trusting-obedience by what he suffered, *just as we do*" (Hebrews 5:8, Msg, *italics mine*).

What this verse means is that the Son of God learned experientially and practically what the difficulty of obedience means - to us. To Him, obedience was natural. He could not be persuaded to disobey.

It cannot be supposed that He did not *know* what obedience was, or that He was inclined to disobey God, or that He had a rebellious nature that had to be subdued by suffering. On the contrary. What He learned - personally - was the nature of *our* suffering because of *our* obedience. If we are to obey we are to die to self. By the Christ's suffering He learned what obedience *really* means - *not the suffering brought on by sin but the suffering caused by obedience in a sinful world.*

Having learned - through suffering - what is involved in our obedience, "having arrived at the full stature of his maturity and having been announced by God as high priest in the order of Melchizedek, he became the source of eternal salvation to all who believingly obey him" (Hebrews 5:9,10, Msg). Another version of the Bible says, "having been made perfect [by learning obedience], He became to all those who obey Him the source of eternal salvation" (Hebrews 5:9, NASB).

"Having been made perfect" means that the Messiah was fitted in all respects to redeem men. Suffering was necessary to complete His character as Savior of men. "Having been made perfect" doesn't refer to the Christ's moral perfection, for He was always without sin. Being made perfect means that He is the perfect Man to represent mankind before God. "In bringing many sons to glory, it was fitting that God [Deity], for whom and through whom everything exists, should make the author of their salvation [humanity] perfect through suffering" (Hebrews 2:10, NIV).

COULD THE SON OF MAN SIN?

Both Adam and the Christ were men. Adam, before the fall, was innocent and sinless like the Son of Man. And, like the Son of Man, Adam was humanly perfect, being formed and given life by God's Spirit. Yet, Adam sinned. Therefore, as some might ask, could the Christ have sinned? As a Man endowed with free will, could He have gone against God's will?

Actually, the question is misleading if not trifling. He did not sin (Hebrews 4:15). Thus, any answer is academic and speculative. Nonetheless, the question is associated with the Christ's obedience. He battled with Satan in the desert (Matthew 4:1-11) and struggled with His human will in Gethsemane (Luke 22:44). The question - in the interest of divulging the Christ's full humanity - therefore merits a word in reply.

Certainly, Jesus' divine nature - God - could not sin. Neither could His divine nature be tempted to sin (James 1:13). On the other hand, the Christ's human nature, considered by itself, could have sinned. Supposedly, like Adam, He could have gone against God's will.

However, in the comparison of Adam and The Son of Man - as men - there is a difference. In the case of Adam, Jehovah communed with him from above, from heaven. Jehovah and Adam were two separate beings. In the case of Jesus, on the other hand, God communed with Him from within, from His innermost being. God "dwelt" in the Christ (Colossians 2:9). The two natures - divine and human - were bonded together. Only death separated them. While He was alive the Christ's divine nature and His human nature were one (John 10:30).

During His earthly ministry (He now ministers from heaven) the Christ's human nature voluntarily and absolutely submitted to His divine nature. In reality, then, because of His *total* submission to the authority of His indwelling Spirit, the Son of Man could not sin. He allowed God to maintain *complete* dominion over His life and actions. He let His Father, the Holy Spirit that conceived Him, stay in control. A Spirit controlled man does not, indeed, cannot sin.

Since the Spirit led Man, Christ Jesus, could not sin does this indicate that His battles and struggles were without significance? Was His fight to obey God mere shadow boxing? Were His temptations meaningless? On the contrary. He overcame temptation, not as God, but as Man. His battles with the devil were real. By appropriating the power of God available to Him He was enabled to overcome the lies and deceptions of the devil and defeat the actions of demon-led people.

Absolutely convinced that the devil and his demons were no match for God, the Christ hung on to and followed the leading of His Spirit. His unquestionable faith in God overwhelmed the lies of the devil and his cohorts. With God's Spirit as His guide He knew He would be victorious - no matter what. In the face of death - a Man with ten thousand angels at His disposal - He stood firm. Because His purity wouldn't allow Him to sin, by His struggles and sufferings He came to know, by experience, how we feel when faced with what seem to be big problems.

HIS HUMAN NATURE WAS REAL

The Son of Man was born without a sinful nature. Because God was His biological Father He did not inherit Adam's tendency to sin. He was above sinning. He valued life with God more than life with the world. He did not have the inclination or the compulsion to sin as we do.

Consequently, it might be thought that He was some kind of "superMan." It might be conceived that the Christ's struggles were artificial and contrived. Or perhaps that His physical feelings played no role in the Christ's intercourse with the world. Some might imagine His wranglings with the flesh and the devil were not real but in appearance only. After all, when He walked the earth Jesus embodied all the fulness of God.

But His flesh was real, too. His human nature was just as real as His divine nature. In the flesh He had to deal with the hypocrisy and the testing of the Scribes and Pharisees. The devil taunted His mind and promised Him everything the world has to offer. That is, power as a means to righteousness.

Human feeling and emotion filled His soul. Hunger was a need after fasting 40 days. He wept at Lazarus' tomb. He showed anger at the money changers in the temple. Among His last words on the cross was concern for His mother. In the Sermon on the Mount He dealt with real life. His parables were down to earth. He was not immune to the pain of being whipped severely. As a Man He faced the reality of a cruel death. Fear was not foreign to Him. The Christ's humanity was like ours in all respects except in the matter of original sin - disobedience.

In spite of the fact that the devil had no power over Him the specter of death and the tug of natural instincts were real. Real indeed - because He knew that in His flesh there was no power to overcome the attacks of the devil. So He looked to God for strength.

Though the Christ knew He would overcome the pull of flesh through God - strengthening His spirit - that knowledge did not alter the reality of testing and suffering. Like everyone He really experienced human distress. But He obeyed God's leading and did not waver.

Indeed, the Christ experienced over three intense years of enduring the machinations of worldly men and the devil. Yet, He overcame them all and even conquered death, the devil's most trusted partner. Now the Christ has been placed in a highly exalted position in heaven. Now the victor helps us - the vanquished - by His Spirit. Now the Son of Man, who felt the most dreadful assaults of men and the devil, provides relief to fallen humanity because He stood His ground as a Man.

CONCLUSION

The Christ came to do God's will. That was God's purpose in begetting (sending) Him. Yet, the Christ did not want to die. He prayed, "My Father, if there is any way, get me out of this. But please, not what I want. You, what do you want?" (Matthew 26:39, Msg). God sent Him to the cross. And He obeyed.

Learning obedience was not easy for the Christ. Learning obedience meant suffering - dying to self, subduing His human nature. But the result was resurrection from the dead. Thus, through the Christ's obedience and suffering, we learn that moral growth - the resurrection - comes by way of affliction. Indeed, affliction drives us to the foot of the cross - surrender and obedience to the Master.

Because of Adam's disobedience the sinful nature and death were brought into the world (1 Corinthians 15:21). Yet, because of the Christ's obedience, "everybody comes alive" (1 Corinthians 15:22). "For just as through the disobedience of the one man many were made sinners, so also through the obedience of the one man the many will be made righteous" (Romans 5:19, NIV).

Obedience, then, is the supreme test of faith in God. Comparing the penalty of Adam's disobedience (death) with the blessing of the Christ's obedience (eternal life) it becomes clear that obedience is the most vital standard in God's household. For this reason God created obedience in the beginning.

HUMANITY 4

FATHER - SON

"Son" is a title that refers strictly to the Christ's humanity - body, soul, spirit. "Son of God," on the other hand, is a title that *implies* all the fulness of God residing in the Son. But the term "Son," by itself, indicates that the Messiah was a Man - flesh and blood, born of a woman, living on earth. And He died, the first man to be resurrected from the dead - never to die again.

Prior to His conception and birth the Messiah did not exist in heaven except in God's heart. There is no flesh and blood in heaven. The concept of the Son was embedded in the Father's heart from the beginning but the reality did not take place on earth until the fulness of time had come. "But when the right time finally came, God sent [begot] his own Son. He came [was born] as the Son of a human mother..." (Galatians 4:4, GNNT).

Father and son are two notions that are inseparable. However, the Bible does not make reference to producing offspring in heaven. On the contrary, genetical reproduction happens on earth only. Biological reproduction is a physical event. The title "Son" does not include the divine concepts of Deity, Spirit.

When properly used the term "Son" involves the humanity of the Christ and includes humanity's limitations. The Son did not know the time of His second coming (Mark 13:32). He could do nothing of Himself (John 5:19). He needed food and water (Matthew 11:19). He suffered (Matthew 17:12). He wept (John 11:35). He died (Romans 5:10), concluding evidence that the Son was human. But the Father (Deity residing in the Son) did not die.

"Father" is a title that is an acceptable term to portray (a portion of) God's nature - Creator, Authority, Caring. God is also Father because He sired the Man Christ Jesus (Luke 1:35). Moreover, upon acceptance of His Son into our hearts, God becomes our Father by adoption (Romans 8:14). But it is a mistake to think that the word "Father" sufficiently expresses the whole character of God.

God is "Father" because He had (to have) a Son. If God is to be called Father He must have a Son. And, as far as salvation is concerned, the Son had to be a Man. Only a man is qualified to be the Savior of men. Spirit cannot arbitrarily provide salvation to mankind - composed of flesh and blood. God needed a Man to do the job, to free mankind from sin, to pay the penalty for sin. So God begot His Son.

According to Webster's Seventh New Collegiate Dictionary the definition of father is "a man who has begotten a child." Thus, a man who has not begotten a child is not a father. By the same token, if God fathers a child He is called "Father." Without a Son God cannot be called Father.

In the Old Testament The son of the Father was the nation of Israel (Exodus 4:22). In the New Testament the Son of the Father is the Christ. In both cases the terms "son" and "Son" determine that the offspring was flesh and blood and not Spirit.

SON OF GOD

"Father" is an expression that alludes to Deity residing in the Christ. "Son" alludes to the Christ's humanity. But what is the significance of the title "Son of God"? It brings to mind Jesus Christ's two natures - Deity and humanity. But most of all it emphasizes His divine nature. Had Jesus told the Jewish hierarchy He was the "Son" without adding "of God" there would have been no problem. But when He called God His Father, when He called Himself the Son of God (John 10:36), the Jewish authority knew He was identifying Himself with Deity and tried to kill Him (John 5:18). In a word, the title "Son of God" acknowledges the humanity of the Christ while demanding observance of His Deity - two natures in one person.

When Jesus called Himself the Son of God He was not referring to Himself as a separate person of God but the physical manifestation of The Father. In the Son is seen the image and likeness of the Father (Colossians 1:15), the sole expression of the Father (Hebrews 1:3). No one has seen the Father. So He made an exact image and likeness of Himself in the flesh of His Son. The Father (Spirit) revealed Himself in His Son (flesh) so we might know Him.

SON OF MAN

Though He knew Himself to be the Son of God the title "Son of Man" was Jesus' favorite way of describing Himself. In the book of Matthew He referred to Himself as the Son of God only once but called Himself the Son of Man 30 times. He often used the phrase in the third person singular meaning "I."

He would say things like, The Son of Man has authority for forgive sins (Matthew 9:6), or, The Son of Man is the Lord of the Sabbath (Matthew 12:8), or, The Son of Man is to be delivered up for crucifixion (Matthew 26:2). Sometimes He used the title to refer to the power and authority given to Him by His Father. "Then the arrival of the Son of Man! It will fill the skies - no one will miss it. Unready people all over the world, outsiders to the splendor and power, will raise a huge lament as they watch the Son of Man blazing out of heaven" (Matthew 24:30, Msg). "When he finally arrives, blazing in beauty and all his angels with him, the Son of Man will take his place on his glorious throne" (Matthew 25:31, Msg).

No matter how He uses the title "Son of Man" it draws attention mainly to the Christ's humanity - that He was the offspring of humanity, empowered by His Father with authority and world rulership. It denotes a corresponding special kinship with mankind. He uses it many times in the New Testament to signify the interest He felt in humanity - His peculiar love and concern and friendship for people. No doubt He uses the title to convey His willingness to devote Himself to the best interests of the race. In short, the title "Son of Man" reveals the Christ's brotherhood with mankind while the title "Son of God" denotes a special connection to the Father.

ADOPTED AS SONS AND DAUGHTERS

The Son of Man was conceived in the womb of a virgin and was born the Son of God. We, as sons and daughters of a man and a woman, are adopted into the heavenly family by the heavenly Father through faith in Christ Jesus (Galatians 3:26). The Father gives those that believe in His Son the right to become His children through spiritual adoption (John 1:12). If we are being led by the Father's Spirit we are His sons (Romans 8:14). Indeed, The Father's Spirit tells us that we are His sons (Romans 8:16). "What marvelous love the Father has extended to us! Just look at it - we're called children of God! That's who we really are. But that's also why the world doesn't recognize us or take us seriously, because it has no idea who he is or what he's up to" (1 John 3:1, Msg).

However, not everyone is a son or daughter of the Father. Being born into the world does not make anyone a child of the Father. We are born creatures of God but not sons or daughters of the Father. Not everyone is a member of the Father's family. Adam is our natural father by birth but God is our spiritual Father by adoption. "In other words, it is not the natural children who are God's children, but it is the children of the promise who are regarded as Abraham's offspring" (Romans 9:8, NIV). "Children of the promise" are those in Christ.

SONSHIP AND GRACE

By His grace God endowed Adam with His own moral and rational nature, breathing His Spirit into his nostrils, giving him life and a divine image (Genesis 1:27; 2:7), making him a son (Luke 3:38). Yet, when Adam disobeyed God's command - not to eat from the tree of the knowledge of good and evil (Genesis 2:17) - God punished him (Genesis 3:24), taking away his sonship because he had just become a sinner. Nonetheless, Adam's moral and rational nature made his offspring potentially capable of becoming sons of the Father.

So, by His grace, God raised up Abraham and made him the father of a new race. Abraham received direct communication from God and obeyed God's call to separate himself from an ungodly nation. God graciously planted religious seeds in Abraham's heart from which, through the Christ, the Church of the future sprang.

By His grace God gave us His moral law through Moses. Without the Mosaic law we would not have known sin against God. Neither would we have recognized the spiritual bondage of the law, the condemnation which it imposes. Ironically, without the law, we would not have been aware of the lack of freedom under it. Thus, Moses is a gracious gift from God. In Moses God provided a pedagogue to point the way to the Christ (Galatians 3:24).

Finally, by His grace, God gave us the gift of His Son. In Christ God fulfilled His covenant promise (Jeremiah 31:33), embedding the law in the hearts of the Christ's disciples. In accordance with the conditions of this final covenant, conditions that God established, sonship is obtained by responding, from the heart, to God's grace through faith in the work of the Man Christ Jesus.

Men and women are free to accept or reject God's grace. Because God has given men free will they may oppose God's will (John 5:40). Yet, because of their innate moral and rational nature, all men are potential sons of God. God has graciously given them that option. And He has graciously provided the world His Son to bring them into their heritage as flesh and blood sons of God.

A man's heart determines his spiritual status. His moral condition, his attitude toward God, his acceptance or rejection of God's grace, determine whether he becomes a son of God. If a man's heart is indifferent or hostile toward God there is nothing about his nature that is able to bear the title of son. But to those who choose to follow Christ the Man, God sends forth "the Spirit of His Son into our lives crying out, Papa! Father!" (Galatians 4:6, Msg).

COMMUNICATION BETWEEN DEITY AND HUMANITY

The Christ said, "The Father has given me all these things to do and say. This is a unique Father-Son operation, coming out of Father and Son intimacies and knowledge. No one knows the Son the way the Father does, nor the Father the way the Son does" (Matthew 11:27, Msg). The infinite God was incomprehensible - that is, until He made Himself known in His Son. The Christ's remark also suggests an ongoing communication between Father and Son, Between Deity and humanity, since only the Son knows the Father.

From the beginning of His life - through communication of the two natures He embodied - "the child grew and became strong *in spirit*, filled with wisdom, and the grace (favor and spiritual blessing) of God was upon Him" (Luke 2:40, Amp).

The Christ knew the Father because He came from the Father's bosom, the center of the Father's heart. "This one-of-a-kind God-expression, who exists at the very heart of the Father, has made him [the Father] plain as day" (John 1:18, Msg). When questioned about His ancestry the Christ replied, "Yes, you think you know me and where I'm from, but that's not where I'm from. I didn't set myself up in business. My true origin is in the One who sent [begot] me, and you don't know him at all. I come from him - that's how I know him. He sent me here" (John 7:29, Msg).

When God's Holy Spirit, the Christ's Father, Deity, came upon the virgin Mary (Luke 1:35), the Christ was conceived. The holy offspring was a Manchild with all the fulness of God the Father dwelling in Him (Colossians 2:9). Two natures - all the fulness of Deity as well as all the fulness of humanity - were embodied in one person.

The embodiment of two natures in one person demands communication between the two natures. "All things have been handed over to Me by My Father" (Matthew 11:27, NASB). Indeed, the Father was in constant communication with His Son. Speaking in anticipation of His Son in the Hebrew Scriptures Jehovah said, "Thou art My Son, today I have begotten [sent] Thee" (Psalm 2:7, NASB). Speaking in the New Testament God said, "This is my Son, chosen and marked by my love, delight of my life" (Matthew 3:17, Msg).

The Christ proclaimed, "The one that God sent [begot] speaks God's words. And don't think he rations out the Spirit in bits and pieces. The Father loves the Son extravagantly. He turned everything over to him so he could give it away - a lavish distribution of gifts" (John 3:34, Msg). Regarding the administration of His creation, Deity turned everything over to humanity. The Father delivered all worldly affairs into the hands of His Son - a Man.

(In a literal sense "sent" does not mean "begotten." On the other hand, in a spiritual sense, "sent" and "begotten" mean the same thing. If the Son had not been begotten He could not have been sent. Thus, sent means begotten. Both past participles are dependent upon each other - spiritually speaking.)

What the Father does, the Son does. Jesus told His detractors, "I'm telling you this straight. The Son can't independently do a thing, only what he sees the Father doing. What the Father does [says], the Son does. The Father loves the Son and includes him in everything he is doing" (John 5:19,20, Msg). The Son follows the Father's communication.

Jesus Christ's dual nature demands worship of both natures. "The Father handed all authority to judge over to the Son so that the Son will be honored equally with the Father. Anyone who dishonors the Son, dishonors the Father, for it was the Father's decision to put the Son in the place of honor" (John 5:23, Msg). All worldly authority and judgment is given to the Son.

Jesus is in charge. "Anyone here who believes what I am saying right now and aligns himself with the Father, who has in fact put me in charge, has at this very moment the real, lasting life and is no longer condemned to be an outsider" (John 5:24, Msg). The world is under the Christ's final jurisdiction.

"Just as the Father has life in himself, he has conferred on the Son life in himself. And he has given him the authority, simply because he is the Son of Man, to decide and carry out matters of judgment" (John 5:26,27, Msg). God appointed a Man to carry out His will on earth.

The Christ listens to God's will. "I can't do a solitary thing on my own: I listen, then I decide. You can trust my decision because I'm not out to get my own way but only to carry out orders" (John 5:30, Msg). The Christ is a Man who follows God's orders.

Regarding the sacrifice of His life, speaking as both God and Man, the Christ said, "This is why the Father loves me: because I freely lay down my life. And so I am free to take it up again. No one takes it from me. I lay it down of my own free will. I have the right to lay it down; I also have the right to take it up again" (John 10:18, Msg). Humanity lays down His life and Deity takes it up again.

The Father dwells in the Son. Jesus told Philip,"Don't you believe that I am in the Father and the Father is in me? The words that I speak to you aren't mere words. I don't just make them up on my own. The Father who resides in me crafts each word into a divine act" (John 14:10, Msg). Deity does not dwell in Deity, but the Father dwells in the Son.

To summarize this section, which does not include humanity's prayers to Deity, the Son's prayers to the Father (God does not pray), the reader must keep in mind that communication between Father and Son is communication between two natures - Deity and humanity, not Deity and Deity.

HUMANITY 5

FATHER AND SON

The difference is basic. Father and Son are not two persons of God. Spiritually speaking the term "Father" brings to mind Deity. The title "Son" designates humanity. Deity is eternal - no beginning, no ending. Humanity demands a beginning. The Son died but the Father did not die. The distinction is crucial in understanding the two natures of Jesus Christ.

Except as a designated plan in the Father's heart the Son of Man did not exist before conception in the womb of His mother. The limitations of flesh and blood do not exist in heaven. Before conception the Son was in the Father's mind and heart as the advocate of the Father's plan of redemption. Before being begotten (sent) the Son did not exist as a Man.

Deity did not *become* humanity at the Christ child's birth. God did not become a Man at the incarnation. Deity *never* changes from one form to another. God is invariable and steadfast, "who does not change like shifting shadows" (James 1:17, NIV). What's more, God is Spirit (John 4:24) and Spirit does not pass from one phase to another.

At the incarnation the Son embodied the Father's Holy Spirit. That's what the word "incarnation" means: "Embodiment of Deity *in* earthly, human form" (Webster's Seventh New Collegiate Dictionary, emphasis added). All the fulness of God's Spirit resided *in* the body of Christ the Man (Colossians 2:9). Deity did not take up residence in Deity but resided in the humanity of Jesus Christ. The two natures were separate, distinct, and united. And clearly, there was intimate communication between the two.

The Son of Man was begotten (sent) by God the Father. That is, at the incarnation God assumed (took upon Himself) a body of flesh and blood to bring men back to Himself. He clothed Himself in a human body to fulfill His plan of redemption. He took on our human nature to take over our debts (sins) as His own. As the advocate of His plan of redemption Jesus Christ called Himself the Son of God (Deity) as well as the Son of Man (humanity).

Begotten by the Father means God procreated, fathered, sired His Son. He sent His Son into the world to save us from the consequences of sin, to redeem us from the devil's bondage. Begotten implies a process that includes conception, a period of gestation, and birth. By begetting His Son, God prepared himself a body (Hebrews 10:5) because, besides including Himself, His plan of redemption included roles that only a human being could fulfill.

DIFFERENT ROLES OF HUMANITY - THE SON

"Since the children are made of flesh and blood, it's logical that the Savior took on flesh and blood in order to rescue them by his death...That's why he had to enter into every detail of human life. Then, when he came before God as high priest to get rid of people's sins, he would have already experienced it all himself - all the pain, all the testing - and would be able to help where help was needed" (Hebrews 2:17,18, Msg). Indeed, the work of salvation requires the fulfillment of a number of roles that only a human being could fulfill. Besides the role of high priest - our agent, our Man in heaven acting on our behalf - some of these roles include Sacrifice, Substitute, Kinsman-redeemer, Reconciler, Mediator, Redeemer, Justifier, Advocate, Last Adam, Example, Prophet, Savior, Intercessor.

SACRIFICE

A sacrificial human death in the new covenant was as necessary to secure forgiveness of sin as was animal sacrifice under the old covenant. God did not change His plan of redemption: "...without the shedding of blood there is no forgiveness" (Hebrews 9:22, NIV). The difference is that the Christ's sacrifice ended sin once for all while animal sacrifice provided only temporary forgiveness of sin. "I'll forever wipe the slate clean of their sins. Once sins are taken care of for good, there's no longer any need to offer sacrifices for them" (Hebrews 10:17,18, Msg). Those who believe that the Son of Man's blood sacrifice propitiates sin are guaranteed access to heaven.

SUBSTITUTE

In the Hebrew Scriptures the law stipulated that an animal was to be killed to atone for sin. By way of animal sacrifice the Old Testament Jew acknowledged that *he* deserved to die. Such was the law. But the authority of Old testament law began to weaken when Isaiah prophesied the Messiah would die for sin. "But He was crushed for our iniquities; the chastening for our well-being fell upon him, and by His scourging we are healed" (Isaiah 53:5, NASB).

The Christ, our Substitute, "redeemed us from the curse of the law, having become a curse for us" (Galatians 3:13, NASB). In another place it is written that the Christ tasted death for everyone (Hebrews 2:9). Only a Man, born under the law (Galatians 4:4), a member of the human race, could be our substitute and take our place in God's plan of redemption. Deity could not take our place.

KINSMAN-REDEEMER

Though consciously aware of His divinity the Christ ranked Himself to be our relative. Though all of us are sinners and He was sinless, the Christ was not ashamed to call us brethren (Hebrews 2:11). While preaching to the multitude, when told that His mother and brothers wanted to speak to Him, the Christ pointed to His listeners and said, "These are My mother and brothers"(Matthew 12:49). Indeed, even after His resurrection from the dead, when Mary Magdalene and the other Mary came to look at the grave, Jesus appeared to them and told them, "Do not be afraid; go and take word to My brethren to leave for Galilee, and there they shall see Me" (Matthew 28:10, NASB). Jesus called us His brethren. The Christ suffered, died, and was resurrected as our brother, as our kinsman-redeemer.

Kinsman-Redeemer is an office ordained by Jehovah in the book of Leviticus: "If a fellow Jew becomes so poor he has to sell his property, then his kinsman is to redeem what had to be sold" (Leviticus 25:25, paraphrase). In our poverty, while we were yet sinners, the Christ died for us (Romans 5:8). That is, we were redeemed by our kinsman-redeemer.

RECONCILER

Because of Adam's sin we were made sinners (Romans 5:19), enemies of God. God can have nothing to do with sin so He turned His back on the world. Yet, knowing that Adam would sin, God had a plan of reconciliation which He held in His heart until the proper time, a plan that could only be carried out by a Man. Why? Because it was a man who alienated us from God.

Sin alienates us from God. Thus, sin had to be vanquished to restore communion with God. By God's grace reconciliation took place on the cross of Calvary when God placed our sins on the Son of Man. "God put the wrong on him who never did anything wrong, so we could be put right with God" (2 Corinthians 5:21, Msg). Indeed, " while we were enemies, we were reconciled to God through the death of His Son" (Romans 5:10, NASB). The Father gave us His Son to execute His plan of reconciliation. "Through the Son, then, God decided to bring the whole universe back to himself. God made peace through his Son's sacrificial death on the cross..." (Colossians 1:20, GNNT).

MEDIATOR

A mediator comes between two parties at variance to resolve their differences. He must therefore know and understand both positions. Thus, if the enmity between God and man was to be settled the Mediator had to be both God and Man. As Man He had to be sinless because only a sinless Man can approach a holy God. The Son of God was that sinless Man, a Man with two natures - one human and one divine. Born of a virgin, whose Father was God, the Mediator between God and men was both God and Man.

REDEEMER

Originally, in Greek literature, of which the New Testament writers were familiar, redemption denoted the ransom price paid for a prisoner of war.

When the ransom price was paid the captive was set free. In the New Testament redemption denotes liberation from the bondage of sin and the devil's captivity - deliverance from his lies and deceptions. Because Christ the redeemer paid the ransom price (the price of sin is death) with His life, God, accepting the sacrificial price, set His people free and destroyed the devil's dominion over His people. Thus, the Son is the Redeemer while the Father provides redemption based on the Son's work on the cross.

JUSTIFIER

Justification means that God declares a sinner in Christ to be righteous and worthy of a place in heaven. In Christ a sinner demonstrates the Christ's righteousness before God's throne (Romans 3:25), not his own righteousness (Romans 3:28). Justified by the work of Christ the Man, God sees the sinner surrounded by the Christ's morality.

To be declared righteous by God, that is, to be justified by God, does not mean the sinner is made righteous: he will always carry his sinful nature with him. Being declared righteous means that the sinner in Christ is righteous in God's eyes, that God sees him as being perfected in Christ. Because of his position in Christ the sinner stands before the bar of God justified (Romans 8:1,33,34). The Son is the Justifier and the Father provides justification.

SANCTIFIER

Through the Sanctifier, the Man Christ Jesus, God purifies the sinner in Christ of all sin. Sanctification is an inner cleansing of heart and conscience by God (1 Peter 3:15). It is instantaneous as well as ongoing. When the new believer, once dead in trespasses and sin (Ephesians 2:1), comes to the Christ, God gives him new life. He is immediately sanctified. His soul is instantly set apart to begin the process of becoming Christlike (1 John 3:3) - which takes a lifetime. The Son's work on the cross makes Him the Sanctifier while the Father provides sanctification.

ADVOCATE

Sanctification means that the sinner's sinful nature is in the process of being cleaned up by God. It doesn't mean he is made morally pure but he is in the process of being made Christlike. Because his sinful nature will not go away the sinner will sin even after conversion. Yet, "If any one sins we have an Advocate with the Father, Jesus Christ the righteous one" (1 John 2:1, NASB).

The Christ is our Advocate in heaven because only a sinless man is able to undertake our cause. But because we are convicted sinners the Christ does not manage our cause in the same manner as an advocate in a human court. On the contrary, He confesses our sin and admits our guilt. Then, with the confidence of the resurrection, He boldly approaches God's throne of grace and pleads God's mercy. And what is God's verdict? By His grace and His love for His Son He provides mercy to those who believe the gospel. On the other hand, God's justice is dealt to those who don't believe.

LAST ADAM

The first Adam was made a human being when Jehovah formed him from the soil and breathed His Spirit into his nostrils. The last Adam became a human being (John 6:57) when God's Spirit impregnated the womb of a virgin. The same Spirit that gave life to the first Adam gave life to the last Adam.

That's where the similarity between the first and last Adam ends. All other analogies are of a contrary kind. The first Adam brought sin and death into the world (Genesis 3:24; Romans 5:12). The last Adam took sin out of the world (John 1:29) resulting in life. "For as in Adam all die, so also in Christ shall all be made alive" (1 Corinthians 15:22, NASB). "The First Adam received life, the Last Adam is a life giving Spirit" (1 Corinthians 15:45, Msg). "The First Man was made out of earth, and people since then are earthy; the Second Man was made out of heaven, and people can now be heavenly" (1 Corinthians 15:47, Msg). "Made out of heaven" means that the second Man was divinely conceived in God's heart in heaven before the foundation of the world (1 Peter 1:20) and physically conceived on earth at the fulness of time (Galatians 4:4).

We are born with a sinful nature, inherited from the first Adam. Our born-again nature comes from the last Adam. From the first Adam we get human existence which is easily manipulated by the devil. From the last Adam we get divine guidance and strength to withstand the attacks of the devil. The first Adam stands as head of those who are born and die. The last Adam stands as head of those who are born-again and receive a new spiritual body in heaven (1 Corinthians 15:44).

In short, the first Adam was the source of physical life while the last Adam is the source of eternal life in heaven. Yet, both the first Adam and the last Adam are human.

EXAMPLE

The Christ's resurrection allowed God's anointed penmen to complete the Bible. The completed Word - namely, the final expression of God's heart, mind, and will - was made flesh in Christ (John 1:14). The Son's heart was the manifest heart of the Father (John 1:18); the Son's mind was the manifest mind of the Father (John 6:68; 12:49; 17:8); the Son's will was manifestly surrendered to the Father's will (Romans 12:2; Ephesians 1:9; Colossians 1:9; Hebrews 10:9). For these reasons, because Christ the Man explicitly revealed godlike attributes, He is the example we are to imitate.

PROPHET

A prophet is a man who speaks forth the oracles of God (Acts 7:37,38). That is, a prophet makes clear, by words or actions, the will of God and reveals the promises of God. The Christ's words, ministry, and life illustrate the fulfillment of the prophetic office. Indeed, Moses pointed to the Christ as *the* prophet: "God, your God is Going to raise up a prophet for you. God will raise him up from among your kinsmen, a prophet like me. Listen obediently to him"(Deuteronomy 18:15, Msg).

Some examples of the Christ as prophet follow:

- The Spirit of the Lord was upon the Christ to bring good news to the afflicted, to proclaim release of the captives, (Isaiah chapter 61; Luke 4:18);
- God commanded the Christ's disciples to listen to what He had to say (Matthew 17:5);

- The Christ revealed God's wisdom, righteousness, sanctification, and redemption (1Corinthians 1:30);
- The Christ opened the door to faith and trust (Acts 14:27), as opposed to law and works;
- The Christ exposed the law's deficiency as a system of salvation (Matthew 5:17);
- The Christ revealed God's grace (John 1:17);
- The Christ manifested the Messiah's two natures (1 Timothy 3:16);
- The Christ replaced ritual and ceremony with spiritual worship (John 4:23);
- After the resurrection the Christ sent His Spirit back to earth to work in the hearts of men (Acts chapter 2);
- By His resurrection the Christ proclaimed eternal life (Matthew 25:46; John 10:28) which not was not clear in the Hebrew Scriptures;
- Even after His resurrection the Christ revealed future events to the apostle John (see the book of Revelation).

The Christ was a Man who revealed, by actions and by words, God's truths. As a Man He communicated God's will to His people and disclosed the future to them. He was a Man who had to die because He was a prophet - the final prophet of God. On His way to Jerusalem to be crucified Jesus said, "It is not right for a prophet to be killed anywhere except in Jerusalem" (Luke 13:33, GNNT).

HEAD OF THE CHURCH

The Head of the Church must be a Man - of the same substance as its members. He must be related to its members - flesh and blood. In addition, the Head of the Church must possess within Himself all those things necessary for the life, thinking, purpose, functioning, and activity of its members. That is, He must rally and inspire the Church. In short, the Head of the Church must edify its members which tend to get disheartened by world events.

Jesus Christ is such a Man. Nonetheless, Jesus Christ is Head of the Church according to both natures. Just as the Father - Jesus' divine nature - is Head of the Son, the Son is Head of the Church.

All this energy issues from Christ: God raised him from death and set him on a throne in deep heaven, in charge of running the universe, everything from galaxies to governments, no name and no power exempt from his rule...He is in charge of it all, has the final word on everything. At the center of all this, Christ rules the Church...The Church is Christ's body, in which he speaks and acts, by which he fills everything with his presence (Ephesians 1:22,23, Msg).

The Son of God - Deity and humanity - is the Head of the Church according to both natures. Moreover, the Church is the Son of God's body, meaning that the Church's relation to the Son is the same as our head/body relationship. The relationship forms the entire person - a close and necessary union. The one is not complete without the other and each is dependent on the other.

The two are inseparable - the Son of God in heaven, His body on earth. In reality - in the spiritual realm - distance is no problem. The Head of the Church and His body are not separated but united by His Spirit - His Holy Spirit.

SAVIOR

God - Spirit - is not the Savior. God cannot save men from going to hell. God will not violate mankind's free will. Because a man (Adam) made us sinners, only a Man can undo that wrong, only a Man can save men from the consequences of sin. By His grace God - Spirit - *provides* salvation based upon faith in the work of the Man Christ Jesus. "He is the one whom God exalted to His right hand as a Prince and a Savior, to grant repentance to Israel, and forgiveness of sins" (Acts 5:31, NASB).

Only a Man can save us from eternal death because it was a man who brought death into the world. Salvation was in God's heart from the beginning, "but now has been revealed by the appearing of our Savior Christ Jesus, who abolished death, and brought life and immortality to light through the gospel" (2 Timothy 1:10, NASB); "...for in this way the entrance into the eternal kingdom of our Lord and Savior Jesus Christ will be abundantly supplied to you" (2 Peter 1:11, NASB).

"And we have seen and testify that the Father has sent [begot] his Son to be the Savior of the world" (1 John 4:14, NIV). God did not send (beget) another god to be the Savior of the world, but sent (begot) a Man.

INTERCESSOR

This role is related to the roles of High Priest and Advocate. The petitions, prayers, and praises of the believer are received by God in the name of a Man, Christ Jesus. "I am writing this to you, my children, so that you will not sin; but if anyone does sin, we have someone who pleads with the Father on our behalf - Jesus Christ, the righteous one" (1 John 2:1, GNNT).

CONCLUSION

The roles that the Son fulfilled - High Priest, Sacrifice, Substitute, Kinsman-Redeemer, Justifier, Sanctifier, Advocate, Last Adam, Example, Prophet, Head of the Church, Savior, Intercessor - were set up by the Father before creation as part of His plan of redemption. From the beginning these roles - that only a Man could complete - were in God's heart. He established these roles in the Old and New testaments so that His plan of redemption could be understood by men.

The invisible, incomprehensible Father revealed Himself in His Son. Through the Son the Father made Himself known in a manner that His creation could understand. Thus, by setting up the above roles and begetting (sending) His Son to work them out we are better able to see that there is no difference between Father and Son regarding intention. They - Man and God - are one in purpose. They both have the same thing in mind - man's redemption. God originated the plan of redemption (Romans 8:29-32) and the Son, working together with the Father, put it into effect.`

HUMANITY 6

INTRODUCTION

To deny Jesus Christ's Deity is fatal: "For it was the Father's good pleasure for all the fulness of deity to dwell in Him" (Colossians 1:19, NASB). Denial of His full humanity - even subtly - is equally dangerous: "Many deceivers have gone out over the world, people who do not acknowledge that Jesus Christ came as a human being. Such a person is a deceiver and the enemy of Christ" (2 John 7, GNNT). (To preach "God the Son" - thus limiting the Son to be God only - is to subtly deny the Son's humanity.) Christian faith demands belief in Jesus Christ's full Deity as well as His full humanity. Christian doctrine maintains that Jesus Christ is both God and Man - Father (Spirit) and Son (flesh).

The biblical truth that Jesus Christ was both God and Man might cause the imaginative soul to wonder. If Jesus Christ was the God-Man when He walked the earth, was he really a Man like His brethren? Or was He a Superman who simply went through the motions of manhood? Did He have a real body with soul and spirit like everybody else? Was He affected by temptation? Was He a Man in appearance only? Here are some responses.

A PHANTOM CHRIST?

Could the Christ have been a phantom, a specter that had the appearance of humanity? Did He only seem to be composed of flesh, bones, and blood?

After all, an angel in the appearance of a human body could have carried out the ministry committed to the Messiah; and blood could have been produced as it was generated in Adam. Moreover, that the Christ was humiliated would seem to be unworthy of an all powerful God; that God assumed a true human nature seems fantastically degrading.

Indeed, in Genesis 32:24-30, Daniel 3:25 and 7:13, God manifested Himself to the fathers and prophets of old in angelic appearances. Even in the New Testament there are verses that could lead one to believe that the Christ was merely a specter. For example, Romans 8:3 says God sent His Son in the likeness of sinful flesh. In the likeness Only? Not really? And Philippians 2:6,7 says that He who was equal with God was made in the likeness of men. Again, the question could arise, In likeness only? Moreover, it could have been an apparition that walked on the water (Matthew 14:26). And there are other examples that could cause misunderstanding about the fulness of Jesus Christ's dual nature.

But the Son of Man could not have been a mere phantom of a man. He had to be a true, sinless Man made of real flesh and blood for one simple reason. If the Christ's humanity was a fantasy then God's plan of redemption is only make-believe and we are not really redeemed but still in sin. Neither are we justified but only seemingly so and only a semblance of eternal life is promised. We would always be in doubt. The work of the Christ would be a mockery of our wretched humanity. The whole plan of salvation would be a farce. Would God do such a thing? Would He deceive us that way? Of course He wouldn't.

A HEAVENLY BODY?

Can it be imagined that the Son of Man brought His body with Him from heaven? That is, was His body made of a purified heavenly substance? Was His flesh and blood really like ours? Is it possible that the Christ was only a guest in the virgin Mary's womb, passing through her body in the same manner water passes through a pipe, assuming nothing from the pipe?

Certain passages of Scripture, if interpreted literally, could convey the notion that the Christ's body came from heaven. For example, speaking to Nicodemus Jesus said, "No one has ever gone into heaven except the one who came from heaven - the Son of Man" (John 3:13, NIV). "Son of Man" definitely refers to the Christ's humanity - His flesh and blood. But did flesh and blood exist in heaven? Did flesh and blood descend from heaven? Absolutely not.

Because some of the disciples grumbled when Jesus suggested they drink His blood and eat His flesh, He said ironically, "What would happen if you saw the Son of Man ascending to where He came from?" (John 6:62, Msg). Again, the Christ uses the title "Son of Man," a definite reference to His flesh and blood. But, was His flesh and blood in heaven before the Incarnation? Impossible.

When Jesus says He "came down from heaven" and He would ascend to heaven "where he came from" He is speaking as God, not as Man. He is making reference to His Holy Spirit in heaven coming to earth and assuming a body. Whenever the Christ speaks of Himself being in heaven it is His divine nature speaking through His human nature. On the one hand, Jesus' divine nature, His Spirit, is eternal, having no beginning and no end. The Christ's human nature, on the other hand, his flesh, did not exist before conception and birth except as a plan in the mind of God.

Like other men the Christ's bones, His flesh and blood, were formed in the womb of a woman. God could have fashioned the Christ's physical body out of nothing. Or He could have formed the Christ's flesh and blood out of dust and breathed life into His nostrils. Indeed, He could have made Him from the rib of a woman. But He willed that the Christ's flesh be formed in the womb of a woman and given life like other human beings (Matthew 1:20). Neither did His blood come from heaven but from the virgin Mary whose blood was purified by God's Spirit through Her faith in what God said (Luke 1:38).

Here are Scriptures, from Genesis through Revelation, that stress the Christ's flesh and blood humanity:

- The Messiah will come from the seed of a woman (Genesis 3:15);
- The Christ will be the fruit of the loins of David (Psalm 132:11 and Acts 2:30);
- The Christ will be a rod and a shoot from Jesse (Isaiah 11:1);
- The Christ is the son of David who is the son of Abraham (Matthew 1:1);
- God's Word - the Hebrew Scriptures - became flesh (John 1:14);
- The Christ is the firstborn among many brothers (Romans 8:29);

- God Himself also partook of (assumed) flesh and blood (Hebrews 2:14);
- Jesus Christ is the root and offspring of David (Revelation 22:16). This verse tells of Jesus Christ's two natures: the root of David is God; the offspring of David is the Christ.

HUMANITY AND DEITY OF THE MESSIAH

All the fulness of God was Jesus Christ's Father. All God's majesty came down to earth and impregnated the womb of the virgin Mary (Luke 1:35). After a nine month gestation period she gave birth to a Son. Thus, because the Father was divine and the mother was human the Son of God was both human and divine. "For the full content of divine nature lives in Christ, in his humanity" (Colossians 2:9, GNNT). That is, until humanity died.

How a virgin became pregnant by God's Holy Spirit remains a mystery. Such a thing cannot be fully understood by the finite mind. Equally as mysterious is the phenomenon of the fulness of God's Holy Spirit dwelling in a Man. Yet, "it was by God's own decision that the Son has in himself the full nature of God" (Colossians 1:19, GNNT).

THE DEVIL TESTS THE CHRIST'S HUMANITY

After His baptism in the Jordan river the Christ was tested by the devil. Baptized as the new Head of humanity (Adam was the old head of humanity) God's Spirit led the Christ into the wilderness to be tried as a Man (Matthew 4:1). The devil knew that the Christ was God's Son. But He also knew that the Son of Man was a human being and therefore fair game.

When God's Spirit led the Christ into the wilderness to be tested by the devil He was preparing Christ the Man to be our high priest in heaven. Just as we are being tested in the wilderness of the world to determine our place in eternity, so the Christ was being prepared for His position at the right hand of God.

The Son of Man overcame the devil's temptations, not as God, but as a Man with the Spirit of God's strength available to Him. The Christ frustrated the devil's onslaughts by the sword of God's Spirit, God's Word (Ephesians 6:17). Each time the devil attacked the Christ responded with, "It is written." The first attack was against the Christ's body - His hunger. The devil proposed a solution: "Since you are God's Son, speak the word that will turn these stones into loaves of bread" (Matthew 4:3). The Christ responded, "It takes more than bread to stay alive. It takes a steady stream of words from God's mouth" (Matthew 4:4; Deuteronomy 8:3).

The second attack was against the Christ's soul - His ego. The devil took Him to Jerusalem where a lot of people were watching and wondering. To prove to the people that He was the Messiah the devil proposed that He throw Himself off the highest pinnacle of the temple to show the people that God's angels would take care of Him; thus, drawing attention to self. Again, the Christ picked up the sword of God's Spirit and said, "It is written, 'You shall not put the Lord your God to the test'" (Matthew 4:7; Deuteronomy 6:16).

The third attack went straight to the Christ's human spirit: "Fall down and worship me and all the kingdoms of the world are at your command" (Matthew 4:9). The devil wanted the Christ's adoration. But again the Son of Man manipulated the Word of God as His counter attack, saying, "It is written, you shall worship the Lord your God, and serve Him only" (Matthew 4:10; Deuteronomy 6:13).

Three times the tempter stormed the Christ's humanity - His body, soul, and spirit - and three times the sword of God's Spirit flashed in the Son of Man's hand to rebuff the devil with, "It is written." Three times the Christ's message of victory over the devil was made clear - submission to the Word of God. Because the Word of God, the verbal expression of God's mind and will, the revealed intent of His heart, is alive and full of power (Hebrews 4:12), the devil left his human prey for a season.

THE CHRIST'S HUMAN SOUL, SPIRIT, AND WILL

Because the virgin Mary was a human being, made like us, body, soul, and spirit, she gave birth to her Son's body, soul, and spirit. In the opening phrases of her prayer of praise, while visiting her relative Elizabeth, Mary referred to her human soul and spirit: "My soul exalts the Lord, and my spirit has rejoiced in God my Savior" (Luke 1:46,47, NASB). And during His ministry the Christ spoke of His human soul and spirit:

- The Son of Man came to give His soul as a ransom for many (Matthew 20:28);

- I lay down My soul for the sheep (John 10:15);
- The Christ was aware by His spirit that the Jews were reasoning against Him (Mark 2:8);
- Father, into Your hands I commit My spirit (Luke 23:46).

Though Deity dwelt in the Son of Man's body, God's will did not overwhelm and take the place of the Christ's human will. On the contrary, the Christ voluntarily submitted His will to God's will. And thanks to the Christ's submissive will our spirit is reconciled with God's Spirit. In Christ we are reunited with God:

- Father, not what I will, but what thou wilt (Mark 14:36);
- Father, not My will, but thine be done (Luke 22:42);
- I do not seek My own will, but His who sent (begot) Me (John 5:30).

THE SON, HONORING THE FATHER

The Father (Deity) that resided in the Son (humanity) was Spirit - Spirit spelled with a capital "S." The Son who personified the Father was body, soul, and spirit - spirit spelled with a small "s." Both natures - divine and human - were active and functioning in the Son in the land of Israel 2000 years ago - not independently but separately. That is to say, each nature performed that activity or function which was proper to it.

For example, The Father (Deity) devised the plan of redemption/reconciliation and the Son's (humanity's) job was to carry it out. The Son knew the program. And, like Adam, He had a choice. He could either obey or disobey.

Because of the hierarchical relationship between Father and Son it might be imagined that the Son did not have a choice, that the influence of the Father dominated the Son's capacity to make a free choice. Or, perhaps the Father forced His Son to obey - or else. Not so! The Father does not operate that way. He expects submission but does not demand it.

When the time came - though He could have called 10,000 angels to save Him - the Son submitted to the Father's plan of redemption/reconciliation and died a selfless, obedient death - and the worst kind of death: crucifixion. The Son's obedience was not prompted by intimidation but by His love for the

Father and a longing that His Father receive the praise due Him. Love for the Father was the Son's motive for submission.

"Because of that obedience, God lifted him high and honored him far beyond anyone or anything, ever, so that all created beings in heaven and on earth - even those long ago dead and buried - will bow in worship before this Jesus Christ, and call out in praise that he is the Master of all, to the glorious honor of God the Father" (Philippians 2:9-11, Msg).

FELLOWSHIP WITH GOD THROUGH A MAN

Fellowship with God - who is Spirit and all those incomprehensible things like omnipresent, omnipotent, omniscient, eternal, infinite - would be impracticable were it not for His Son. Worship yes, but fellowship with God would be difficult and unwieldy. Before the Christ only one man was able to understand Him.

Before the Christ only Moses interacted with God (Exodus 24:2). Abraham, Isaac, and Jacob *heard* from God. Enoch (Genesis 5:24) and Noah (Genesis 6:9) and others "walked with God." But before the Christ Moses was the only man to commune with God (Exodus 25:22). Ordinary people were separated from Him.

God gave us His Son so we might fellowship with Him. Because the Son of God is both Man and God, fellowship with the Son *is* fellowship with the Father. "God is faithful, through whom you were called into fellowship with His Son, Jesus Christ our Lord" (1 Corinthians 1:9, NASB). Deity calls us to fellowship with Him through humanity. Thanks to God who gave us Jesus Christ "...our fellowship is with the Father and with his Son" (1 John 1:3, NIV).

Fellowship with God includes prayer in Jesus' name. When God, in Jesus' name is involved in prayer the believer is edified. Jesus, asking us to pray in His name, said, "This is what I want you to do: Ask the Father for whatever is in keeping with the things I've revealed to you. Ask in my name, according to my will, and he'll most certainly give it to you" (John 16:23, Msg).

And we can be sure God hears the prayer that is called out in the name of His Son. Indeed, in the midst of trials and wants, and a sense of weakness and unworthiness, the believer can take consolation in the privilege of coming to God in the name of Jesus. A Man brings us near to God.

THE CHRIST DESIRES OUR FELLOWSHIP

Social intercourse was important to the Christ. He enjoyed fellowship - weddings and talking to people. He participated in religious holidays and never undervalued their significance. That He joined in fellowship with people revealed His true humanity. Fellowship would probably not have been in His agenda were He not human.

In the final hours of His life the Christ intensely wanted to share Passover with His friends and disciples. "You've no idea how much I have looked forward to eating this Passover meal with you before I enter my time of suffering. It's the last one I'll eat until we all eat it together in the kingdom of God" (Luke 22:15, Msg). No doubt the Christ felt that fellowship with His friends would strengthen His human nature against the physical pain He was about to endure.

Fellowship with friends - and intercourse with non-friends - played a significant role in the Christ's ministry. Fellowship and intercourse with people revealed His humanity. Friends and even enemies meant a lot to Him. He did not withdraw from life and its abrasions. He was completely human.

At the Passover meal the Christ instituted the Lord's Supper which entails communion with the Christ's human nature - flesh and blood. "During the meal, Jesus took and blessed the bread, broke it, and gave it to his disciples: Take, eat. This is my body. Taking the cup and thanking God he gave it to them. Drink this, all of you. This is my blood, God's new covenant poured out for many people for the forgiveness of sins" (Matthew 26:26-28, Msg). Thus, for 2000 years, Christians throughout the world have acknowledged the flesh and blood humanity of Christ Jesus.

Even in heaven the Christ desires fellowship with us. "Behold, I stand at the door and knock; if anyone hears My voice and opens the door, I will come into him and will dine with him, and he with Me. He who overcomes, I will grant to him to sit down with Me on My throne, as I also overcame and sat down with My Father on His throne" (Revelation 3:20,21, NASB).

Those who persevere are the overcomers. The door, of course, is the door of your heart. "Dine with you" means the Christ fellowships with the believer by His Holy Spirit or by His Word. Both Jesus' Spirit and God's Word proclaim divine guidance, made possible by Christ the Man's sacrifice.

CONCLUSION

By His grace and love the eternal Father prepared Himself a body (Hebrews 10:5) and called Himself the Son of God. God voluntarily assumed a temporal human nature to save many from eternal damnation (2 Corinthians 5:19). Being born of a woman the humanity He took upon Himself was real. God's Word asserts that His blood was real and His flesh was real (1 Corinthians 11:27), not a supernatural material from outer space.

Nor was the Christ's human nature crushed by His divine nature so there was only a semblance of a human soul, spirit, and will. On the contrary, the Christ's humanity was terrorized to the point of sweating blood (Luke 22:44). At the specter of spending eternity in hell for the sins of the world He flinched but did not fall. His will was completely surrendered to God's will. Indeed, Satan knew He was human. Consequently, He was the object of attack as all humans are.

HUMANITY 7

GOD-MAN

God the Father, by His Holy Spirit, implanted His seed in the womb of the virgin Mary (Luke 1:35). She gave birth to a Son, a Man like all men - except He was sinless. He embodied two natures, one divine and one human. He was named Jesus, meaning Jehovah provides salvation, a reference to His divine nature. He was called the Christ, meaning God's anointed one, or Savior, a reference to His human nature.

As Man He had limited knowledge (Mark 13:32); as God He was omniscient (Matthew 24:36). As Man He received power and authority from His Father (John 17:2); as God He was omnipotent (John 17:2). As Man His ministry was limited to Israel; as God His Spirit was omnipresent. As the God-Man, omniscience, omnipotence, omnipresence were present in a Man; that is, these incomprehensible qualities dwelt in a Man (Colossians 1:19).

How is this possible? How can a Man be God and Man, too? Where can an explanation be found? Human reason cannot be followed. Philosophical ideas and scientific axioms cannot be consulted. Rules of mathematics and measurements of geometry are no help. Jurisprudence and medicine deal only with worldly and physical affairs. Erudite professors and those puffed up with authority express limited points of view. Regarding two diverse natures in one person? Faith is the only refuge.

God's Word said it (Luke 1:35) so it must be true. What, then, is the result of the virgin birth? According to God's Word the Man Christ Jesus embodied "the whole fulness of deity (the Godhead) - giving complete expression of the divine nature" (Colossians 2:9, Amp). God dwelt in a Man.

"The whole fulness of Deity" includes those unfathomable attributes like omniscience, omnipresence, omnipotence, eternal, infinite - things that are impossible to comprehend and a burden to the finite mind. By "the whole fulness of Deity" nothing of God is excluded. The Christ was fully God.

Where, then, should we seek the Godhead if not in Christ the Man? Where would we lay hold of God the Father if not in the flesh of His Son? Where would we expect to find God's Holy Spirit emanating from heaven if not in the Spirit of Jesus Christ? Indeed, Jesus Christ's human nature embodied the Holy Spirit of God. The Man Christ Jesus contained *all* the reality of God.

This is our faith, our doctrine, our comfort, our strength, our life, our salvation. If anyone denies Jesus Christ's dual nature he or she cannot call themselves a Christian. While on earth the body of Christ was the temple, the domicile, the habitation of God. For our well-being, by His grace, mercy, and love, God - Spirit - took up residence in Jesus Christ.

DEITY IN HUMANITY

God and the Christ are two separate Beings. One is human and the other is divine. The relation of the two natures can best be understood by looking at the verb "to dwell" as it is used in strategic verses of the Bible that deal with the two natures of the Christ. Two prominent verses are Colossians 1:19 and Colossians 2:9. Each essentially says, "Deity *dwells* in humanity."

"To dwell" has two senses - one literal and the other spiritual (figurative). Dwelling or living in a house, city, or foreign country is the literal sense. The dwelling (or indwelling) of the Christ in our hearts or the indwelling of sin is the spiritual sense. We are concerned with the spiritual sense.

In a spiritual sense "to dwell" means to take up residence as an activating principle. God took up residence in the Christ. Following are more examples of the spiritual significance of "to dwell."

- And he who swears by the temple, swears both by the temple and by Him who *dwells* therein (Matthew 23:21).
- The God who made the world and all things in it, since He is Lord of heav-

en and earth, does not *dwell* in temples made with hands (Acts 17:24).

- So the Christ may *dwell* in your hearts through faith (Ephesians 3:17).
- But according to His promise we are looking for new heavens and a new earth where righteousness *dwells* (2 Peter 3:13).
- And to the angel of the church in Pergamum write: "I know where Satan's throne is...where Satan *dwells*" (Revelation 2:12,13).

The above verses define sets of relationships. Specifically, the spiritual (God, the Christ's Spirit, the spirit of righteousness, Satan) and the physical (temple, heart, new heavens and earth, Pergamum). In each verse the spiritual dwells in the physical.

Thanks to the virgin birth the whole fulness of God's Spirit took up residence in the Man Christ Jesus. The Bible (specifically the verses that deal with the Christ's dual nature) does not say that Deity dwelt in deity, for that would be absurd. On the contrary, Deity dwelt in humanity. Deity dwelling in a Man is the essence of *all* spiritual truth. That's why the Man Christ Jesus is called God.

By way of explanation the fulness of God's Spirit dwelling in the Christ's humanity can be compared to the soul and spirit abiding in a body - immaterial essences embodied in the flesh of a human being. The soul and spirit are governing forces determining the body's actions. Just as the soul and spirit activate the body, so God's Spirit activated the Christ's soul and spirit. Indeed, the Bible says the Christ lived by every word that proceeded out of the mouth of God (Matthew 4:4). God gave the Christ a job to do and He set his soul and spirit to do it (John 14:31) - even though His soul and spirit wavered (Luke 22:44).

INTEGRITY OF EACH NATURE

When God implanted His seed in the womb of a virgin He assumed a human body. God did not *become* a man for God *never* changes form. He is, was, and always will be Spirit (John 4:24). He took upon Himself a human body as a man puts on a coat. God's Holy Spirit dwelt in a body.

Therefore, because of the virgin birth, God and the Christ were One (John 10:30). The virgin Mary (humanity) produced humanity (the Son of Man) which was generated by the seed of Deity. The Son born to Mary was the Son of God, equal to the Father according to His divine nature but limited according to His human nature. Galatians 4:4 declares that Christ the Man was born *under* (and therefore subject to) God's law. God is *above* His law.

Though one nature was bonded to the other the attributes of each nature were not modified. The substance and properties of each nature remained unimpaired. The Son of God's divine nature was without limitations while the Son of Man's human nature had its limitations. Physical death was the most limiting element of the Christ's human nature.

There was a communion but no mixing of the two natures. There was communication between the two natures but no transfusion of one nature into the other. The human nature did not blend into the divine nature. At the transfiguration Jesus' divine nature was exposed but His humanity did not change.

The inherent character of each nature was not altered either before or after the resurrection. Before the resurrection God dwelt in a human being. At the resurrection a human being was elevated to the right hand of God.

Except for the absence of sin the two natures were not equal. One was flesh and the other Spirit. Indeed, if there was a commingling, a conversion, or an equating of natures, God would not be the fulness of God and the Son of Man would not be completely human - like us - and He could not have taken our place on the cross

COMMUNION OF TWO NATURES

The interchange of the human body and soul provides a good illustration of the communion between the Christ's two natures - Deity and humanity. Just as there was no commingling, conversion, or equating of the human and divine natures of the Christ, there is no mixing, altering, or similarity of body and soul. Body and soul are two separate entities. The body is flesh and blood and the soul does not consist of matter.

The Christ's humanity consisted of body, soul, and spirit. His indwelling divinity was pure Spirit. The Christ's human soul controlled His body's activities and God's Spirit influenced His spirit. Though subjected to temptation He did not sin (Hebrews 4:15) because He allowed His soul and spirit to be governed by God's Spirit.

The human soul communicates its influence to the body, not as a physical part of the body, but through tacit communion with the body, thereby activating it. Without the soul the body is a lifeless instrument. The body receives its potential power from the soul. You get out of bed because your soul tells you to, not because your body says, "get up."

Thus, the soul sees with the eyes of the body. It hears with the ears, smells with the nose, and speaks with the vocal cords. The soul uses the mind for understanding and remembering. The soul of the Christian directs the mind and heart away from things of the world and toward things of God.

Without the soul the eyes cannot see, the ears cannot hear, the mind cannot understand, and the heart cannot respond. Our organs operate not by their own natural power or by some essential condition of their own but by means of the soul which is united to them. When these organs have been injured or destroyed the soul continues to operate but the body's activities are limited. When the soul is separated from the body, the body does not function at all.

The soul is composed of two parts, or divided into two parts - mind and heart. The mind concerns itself with things of the world and of the flesh. The heart regards spiritual and emotional things like God and love.

The soul - mind and heart - controls the organs of the body which have their own characteristics. They are part of the body to assist the soul in carrying out its function. The organs of the body communicate their needs to the soul, not through physical infusion or intermingling, but by communion. The body feels a touch, the eyes see, the ears hear, the mind and heart understand, not with a power of their own, but by the power and strength of the soul united to them. For example, a blind man "sees" through his soul. His soul compensates for his physical blindness; his soul makes up for the lack of sight. He "sees" in a different way through the power of his soul.

It is beyond controversy that communion of the soul with the body, and vice versa, is real. Yet, communion takes place without commingling, conversion, or equating of the essential attributes of body and soul. Body and soul are separate but communicate one with the other. Body is body and soul is soul, two different natures.

The interchange of body and soul illustrates the communion of Jesus Christ's two natures - Deity and humanity. The union of God and Man produced communion; yet, without commingling, conversion, or equating of the two natures. God is God and Man is Man. Though the essence of each nature was completely different - flesh and Spirit - the communication was real.

Thus, the entire plan of God - salvation, redemption, justification, sanctification, restoration, expiation, reconciliation, spiritual liberation - was communicated by God to Christ the Man. The Christ knew what He had to do in order to accomplish God's plan, and He did it.

GENESIS 1:26,27

Because God does not dwell in time He calls things that do not exist as if they already existed (Romans 4:17) and speaks of events that have not yet happened as if they had already happened (Isaiah 9:6). It is not surprising, therefore, that God should speak to His Son even before His Son was born. Peter put it this way: "For He was foreknown before the foundation of the world, but has appeared in these last times for your sake" (1 Peter 1:20, NASB).

God spoke to His Son in the first chapter of the Old Testament. The conversation took place in Genesis 1:26,27. A synopsis goes like this: God, speaking to His Son down through the corridor of time, says, "Let us make man into our likeness"(vs.26). Then, "God creates man in His own image"(vs.27). First, God promises to *make* man into the *likeness* of His Son. Then, acting alone, God *creates* Adam after His own *image*.

Four words, that is, two sets of two words - make/likeness, create/image - are emphasized to highlight a point to be made. First, We'll look at the nouns - likeness and image - and then look at the verbs - make and create. These four words are important in coming to an understanding of the prophecy of Genesis 1:26,27.

Likeness (*demuwth* in Hebrew) is an inner attribute unseen by the eyes but perceived by the senses. Godlikeness is fashioned in a man's inner being through God's Son. When God bypassed time and spoke to His Son as if He already existed He prophetically anticipated the Christ's ministry - being a model for us to follow. It is worthy of note that in the prophecy of Genesis 1:26 the adjective "our' (make man into *our* likeness) refers to God and Man - both Deity and humanity. God gave us His Son to be an example of Godlikeness.

Verse 26 indicates that God and His Son will work together to mold men into Godlikeness/Christlikeness - those inner qualities such as love, grace, mercy, and compassion. In addition, meaning, purpose, inner strength, significance, and confidence are inner qualities that the Father helps His children to appropriate using His Son as a guide and model. So, when God said "our" likeness, He was referring to Himself and His Son.

In Genesis 1:27, turning from His conversation with His Son, God sovereignly creates man "in His own image." Image (*tselem* in Hebrew) is different from likeness. Likeness is an inner condition of the soul. Image, on the other hand, implies an outward similarity, an imitation of external qualities, a tangible and visible representation. Adam was the first visible representation of God's image, created in God's image to take care of His creation (Genesis 1:28). The Christ is the final image of the invisible God (Colossians 1:15), begotten to take care of (save) mankind.

God's image is seen in the things a man makes and creates. The external, visible works of a man represent the image of God, who is always working and creating. Indeed, a man is an incredible machine. Of all God's creatures he's the only one that reasons. He's the only one to create a language to express himself. Only a man is capable of creating (inventing) an object from an abstract concept he visualizes. That's exactly what God did in the beginning. He visualized the complex mechanism of the creation and then in six days He set it in motion.

In Genesis 1:26,27 God employs two verbs to indicate the work He did on the sixth day of creation. The two verbs are make (*asah* in Hebrew) and create (*bara* in Hebrew). Each verb is similar in sound and meaning but each verb describes a different operation. The first operation (make) presents the idea of God making and molding man into God's likeness through the Christ. The second operation (create) gives an account of Adam being instantaneously created and given life by the Spirit of God blown into his nostrils.

The common definition of create is to bring something out of nothing into existence in a heartbeat - or thereabout. The common definition of make is to take existing material and fashion it into something more desirable over a period of time, as a potter takes a clump of clay and molds it into a vase. Both Isaiah and Jeremiah, using the figure of potter and clay, tell about making the house of Israel into the likeness of God by the works of His hands (Isaiah 64:8; Jeremiah 18:4-6).

God chooses His words carefully. He *creates* Adam in His own *image*. Then, knowing Adam would fall, He outlines His plan to *make* Adam's descendants into His *likeness* through His Son. These two pairs of words -

create/image, make/likeness - prophetically reveal, in the first chapter of the Bible, God's intent for His people: created in His image and, through His Son, made into His likeness.

BEFORE THE INCARNATION

At the incarnation God came down to earth and dwelt in a Man (Colossians 2:9). God, an invisible Spirit, assumed a body of flesh, blood, and bones. The miracle of the virgin birth produced the God-Man. In Jesus Christ all the fulness of Deity and all the fulness of humanity were united. Father (Deity) and Son (humanity) were embodied in one person. Jesus said, "I and the Father are one" (John 10:30). "I" refers to humanity and "Father" refers to Deity. The Father is seen in the Son (John 14:9).

However, the body of flesh and bones that the Father assumed *at* the incarnation did not exist *before* the incarnation. The Christ's human nature took its beginning in the belly of Mary when the time was ripe (Galatians 4:4). Jesus' divine nature has nothing to do with time and is eternal. It was Jesus' Spirit, His divine nature, Deity that came to earth and took on a body of flesh. God did not have a human soul before the incarnation, nor a body, nor blood. The Son did not exist before the Father begot Him - except as a plan in the Father's heart.

At the incarnation Deity dwelt in humanity. Before the incarnation, however, the roles were reversed. *The idea of humanity* dwelt in Deity, in God's heart and mind, from the beginning. "It is true He was chosen and foreordained (destined and foreknown) before the foundation of the world, but He was brought out to public view (made manifest) in these last days - at the end of the times - for the sake of you" (1 Peter 1:20, Amp).

That is, in His heart and mind God foreordained and predetermined that the Man Christ Jesus should be the great atoning sacrifice for sin. The plan of salvation was formed, and the arrangements made for the atonement, before God created the world - from eternity. God devised His plan before the material universe was brought into being. He held it in His heart until the proper time. It was a plan that God arranged before man was created, when only God knew that Adam would fall. To fulfill that plan He begot His Son.

In short, except as a plan of salvation/reconciliation in God's heart (John

16:28), the Christ's humanity did not exist before the incarnation. The Christ's humanity had a beginning in the womb of a virgin. On the other hand, Jesus' divine nature, God, dwells in heaven eternally. Jesus' Holy Spirit - God the Father - continues to be God before, during, and after the incarnation. The Son's resurrected humanity now sits at the right hand of God. The Father's plan of salvation/reconciliation existed as a solution of the sin problem in the mind of God from eternity and was fulfilled by the Son in these last times for our benefit.

BEFORE THE INCARNATION (CONTINUED)

Before the incarnation the Son of God inhabited heaven as God. (Jesus' divine nature *is* God.) The Son of Man was still a vision in the mind and heart of God. He did not substantively exist since there is no flesh and blood in heaven. The apostle John uses a number of "came forth" verses to describe the manner in which the Son of Man came from "out of" God

- Speaking to the Jews, Jesus said, If God was your Father, you would love me, for I came from God and arrived here. I didn't come on my own. He sent [begot] me (John 8:42, Msg).
- Jesus, knowing that the Father had given all things into His hands, and that He had come forth from God, and was going back to God, rose from supper..." (John 13:3, NASB).
- I came forth from the Father, and I have come into the world (John 16:28, NASB).
- Now we know that You know all things, and have no need for anyone to question You; by this we believe that You came from God (John 16:30, NASB).
- For the uttered words that You gave Me I have given them. And they have received *and* accepted [them], and have come to know positively *and* in reality - to believe with absolute assurance - that I came forth from Your presence. And they have believed *and* are convinced that You did send [beget] Me (John 17:8, Amp).

Notice that these "came forth" verses say that the Son of Man came from God. They do not say He *is* God. The Son of Man is not God, but God dwelt in Him.

In the above verses the Christ declares, and His disciples recognize, that He came forth from out of God. According to the dictionary of Strong's Concordance "came forth" means, both figuratively and literally, "issuing from, coming forth out of, departing from, proceeding forth from out of." In Greek grammatical construction "came forth" (*exerchomai*) is composed of a preposition and a past participle: "ex" denoting origin - the point from which the action proceeds - and "came." God, of course, has no point of origin and did not "come forth" from anything. Hence, "ex" denotes humanity coming from out of Deity.

Webster's Seventh New Collegiate Dictionary provides further clarification of the meaning of "out of." The two words are used as a function word to indicate a change in quality, state, or form. That is, the Christ changed from a plan in God's heart to a human being by way of the virgin birth. God did not change from Spirit to flesh.

Since humanity does not exist in heaven how else would the Christ exist before the incarnation except as a plan in God's heart to save the world from sin. God's plan to save the world embodied itself in the Christ. The vessel that brought Him into the world was the virgin Mary.

Before the incarnation the Christ was the Word that existed in the mind of God prior to being expressed. That is, the Word was with God - enclosed in His Being. Indeed, the Word was God because it originated in Him (John 1:1).

"Word" (*Logos* in Greek) denotes reason, motive, thought, or plan within the mind (Strong's Concordance). Just before the beginning the Word was not yet expressed. Then God uttered the Word ("God said") and the creation came into being. Then time began at Adam's fall and God wrote His Word, the Old Testament. At the fulness of time (Galatians 4:4) God implanted the seed of His Word in the womb of a virgin and the Word became flesh (John 1:14).

Scripture (Colossians 2:9) indicates that God *dwelt* in a Man. It is improper to say that God *became* a Man because God does not change. The verb "become" implies change. But it is absolutely proper to say that the Word *became* flesh because the word "Word" (*Logos*) represents God's heart and mind.

Though the Christ's human body did not exist before the incarnation, the Christ's human nature existed as reality in God's plan of redemption. In a real sense, because it existed in the mind and heart of God, the Christ's human nature existed in glory from the infinite annals of timeless eternity (1 Peter

1:20) to come into Being at the fulness of time (Galatians 4:4).

As a Man, in His final intercessory prayer, the Christ asks the Father to restore that glory. "I glorified you on earth by completing down to the last detail what you assigned me to do. And now, Father, glorify me with your very own splendor, the very splendor I had in your presence before there was a world" (John 17:5, Msg).

Because the Son is about to be crucified to fulfill the Father's plan of redemption, because He is about to make atonement for sin, because He is about to open the way to save a race of rebels from eternal death, the Christ prays that both He (humanity) and the Father (Deity) be glorified through what is about to take place.

The idea of the Son was in the Father's heart from the beginning. From the beginning, knowing that Adam would fall, the Father formed a plan to save Adam's descendants. The Son was the visible, tangible, working expression of that plan. Thus, there was never a time that the Son, the Man, the Savior, was not in the Father's heart and mind.

Humanity 8

BODY AND BLOOD

Eucharist, meaning gratitude, is a Christian rite instituted by Jesus on the eve of His crucifixion. The elements of the Eucharist are bread and wine which symbolize the body and blood of the Christ. Whenever the rite is performed a prayer is said over the elements and they are presented to the Lord as symbols of His body and blood. They are then consumed by the participants as tokens of gratitude for the sacrifice of the Christ's life. The rite is also called communion - communion of the Christ's humanity with ours. In addition, the rite is called the Lord's Supper because it was instituted at the Lord's last meal on earth.

Clearly, the Son of Man placed the emphasis of this rite on His humanity, on His body and blood. Blood, of course, occupies a prominent role in salvation. In Egypt, prior to the Exodus, an animal's blood on the doorposts of a Jewish family's house saved them from death (Exodus 12:13). And at the altar of the temple in Jerusalem, the sacrificial blood of an innocent animal eased the conscience of an Old Testament Jew. Indeed, there is no remission of sin without shedding of blood (Hebrews 9:22).

The Christ said His body is the bread of life, comparing it to manna from heaven that Jews ate in the wilderness: "I am the living bread that came down out of heaven; if anyone eats of this bread, he shall live forever; and the bread also which I shall give for the life of the world is My flesh" (John 6:51, NASB). When the Jews began to murmur about this statement the Christ responded,

"Unless you eat the flesh of The Son of Man and drink His blood, you have no life in yourselves" (John 6:53, NASB).

It is absurd to suppose the Son of Man meant we should literally eat and drink His flesh and blood. It is equally absurd to suppose the disciples literally consumed His body and blood at the Supper. By describing bread and wine as body and blood the Christ meant that they *represent* His body and blood: "Is not the cup of blessing, which we bless, a sharing in the blood of Christ? Is not the bread which we break a sharing in the body of Christ?"(1 Corinthians 10:16, NASB).

Bread and wine, representatives of the Christ's body and blood, draw attention to the fact that He was a human being. Body and blood focus on His humanity. Indeed, in the expiation of sin, the Christ's humanity was of primary importance. The sacrifice of His body and blood opened the way for God to provide forgiveness of sin. As a result of the Christ's sacrifice for sin God was able to extend salvation and reconciliation and all the other blessings made possible by the Christ's labor of love.

The Christ knew the consequences of bearing "our sins in His body on the cross" (1 Peter 2:24): Death, condemnation to hell (Romans 6:23); that is, separation from God. Before going to the cross the Christ sweat water and blood (Luke 22:44) not because He was going to die but because He expected to be eternally separated from God; He was made a curse for us (Galatians 3:13).

Indeed, just before death, before giving up His spirit (Matthew 27:50), God's indwelling Spirit withdrew from Him (Matthew 27:46). But, because the Christ was sinless, He did not have to die. Thus, God was justified in raising Him from the dead.

Because the Christ knew He was going to bear the sins of the world in His body (Luke 22:19) He set up the Eucharist as a reminder of His manhood. In the book of 1 Corinthians Paul relates that He received the revelation of the establishment of the rite directly from the Lord.

> For I received from the Lord the teaching that I passed on to you: that the Lord Jesus, on the night he was betrayed, took a piece of bread, gave thanks to God, broke it, and said, "This is my body, which is for you. Do this in memory of me." In the same way, after the supper he

took the cup of wine and said, "This cup is God's new covenant, sealed with my blood. Whenever you drink it, do so in memory of me" (1 Corinthians 11:24,25, GNNT).

"In memory of me" is in remembrance of His humanity, not His Deity. The word "remembrance" is made up of the Greek prefix *ana* meaning up, or again and *mimnesko* meaning to be mindful of. The Christ uses this word as a gentle command to be continually mindful of His work on the cross as a Man.

According to Vine's Expository Dictionary of New Testament Words "remembrance" does not mean a memorial or in memory of. It signifies "to be mindful of." The Christ uses the rite of the Eucharist as an affectionate command to call to mind the person of Christ Himself, His body and blood, the fact that He was a human being, an innocent Man who gave His life for the sins of the world. In other words, the consumption of bread and wine is a tender appeal to the senses to celebrate the Christ as a human being even though He was also God.

GLORIFIED FLESH AND BLOOD

Flesh and blood (Adam) brought sin and death into the world. The Savior's flesh and blood sacrifice allowed God to take sin and death out of the world (Romans 8:3). Freed from the stain of sin and its consequence - death - God joins our flesh and blood to the Christ's in observance of Communion so we may be strengthened in our earthly walk by His resurrection and glorification. Our flesh and blood spiritually united to the Christ's builds up the spirit-man in each of us.

Since the children are made of flesh and blood, it's logical that the Savior took on flesh and blood in order to rescue them by his death. By embracing death, taking it into himself, he destroyed the Devil's hold on death and freed all who cower through life, scared to death of death (Hebrews 2:14, Msg).

It is encouraging to know that our glorification is *in* Christ - in the glorified body and blood of the Christ. His human nature, resurrected and seated at the right hand of the Father (Matthew 26:64), tugs on God's arm and pleads our cause (Hebrews 7:25). Our lowly, earthly body is made stronger by the Eucharist - by being joined to His glorified body in heaven (Philippians 3:21).

Just as the Son's human nature is joined to the Father's divine nature so our human nature is spiritually united to God's divine nature by the rite of the Eucharist. God will not lay aside the human nature He assumed. The union of the human and divine natures in Jesus Christ remains in perpetual unity. That is to say, through the association by communion of the Christ's human nature with ours we too are joined to God forever.

GOD SPEAKING IN HIS SON

God provides spiritual direction through His Word. The Christ is God's Word made flesh (John 1:14). God communicates His divine will through the Christ's humanity. Indeed, our fragile human nature could not endure the direct and blinding light of God's nature, "for our God is a consuming fire" (Hebrews 12:29, NASB). For this reason the Father provided the gift of His Son, the Man Christ Jesus, to make a way of communion and fellowship with God.

Had God dealt with us directly, by sheer Deity, we would all be fried; pure Deity would cook us all. Instead, by His grace, He chose to speak to us in His Son (Hebrews 1:2). It is comforting to know that God's Son, God Himself manifested in flesh (1 Timothy 3:16), a Man like us, should join Himself to us in, with, and through a human nature of the same substance as ours - body and blood.

COMFORT OF EUCHARIST

The Church struggles under the burden of the cross. With the weakness of the flesh, and the overwhelming temptations and tribulations of the world, and its multitude of stumbling blocks, and the frightful snares of the devil, the Church reels. In these end times the devil is working overtime because he knows he doesn't have much time left. Yet, in the midst of the battle we can take comfort because the Christ, our brother, willed to be present with His family on earth.

For this reason He instituted His Supper. In a heavenly and supernatural manner He is with His Church to give strength and encouragement whenever the elements of His body and blood are consumed. Though the Christ is not in the world according to the ordinary nature of things the comforting hope of His Spirit is palpably present in the mystical union of Eucharist.

PLEDGE OF EUCHARIST

The Son of Man unites Himself to us through the mystical rite of Eucharist. God's Spirit through the Christ restores our spirits. The Christ's humanity is the link in our union with Deity. For example, before going to the cross the Christ prayed for His disciples: "Even as Thou, Father, art in Me, and I in Thee, that they also may be in Us" (John 17:21, NASB). The pronoun "Us" embraces both Deity and humanity.

Bread and wine, typifying the Christ's body and blood, serve as elements of God's pledge to man. First, a pledge of salvation from the power, effects, and guilt of sin - that is, reconciliation. Second, a pledge of glorification promised by the Christ's resurrection. In instituting the rite of Eucharist the Christ intended that we keep in mind the confirmation of God's pledge, a pledge made on account of the sacrifice of the Christ's body and the shedding of His blood.

The Christ's birth, life, death, and resurrection are guarantees of God's provision of salvation and glorification. Needless to say, the pledge of salvation and glorification would be weakened had the Christ not instituted the rite of Eucharist; if the elements of the Christ's human nature were removed from Christian ritual, our salvation and glorification would be dimmed, for His absolute humanity might be overlooked. Yet, the last act the Christ performed before dying was the institution of Eucharist. Because it was His final act before dying it is significant. Therefore, when the Christ says the bread and wine we receive with our mouth symbolize His body and blood we best believe it with our heart.

DISCERNMENT IN THE SUPPER

It is unnatural to think that the Christ's physical body is present at the celebration of His Supper. Because we are subject to the laws of nature the presence of the Christ in His Supper is spiritually discerned. Indeed, the non-spiritual man rejects the things of God's Spirit. Unless the mind and heart are enlightened by God's Spirit religious revelation is foolishness to the natural man.

But the natural, nonspiritual man does not accept *or* welcome *or* admit into his heart the gifts *and* teachings *and* revelations of the Spirit of God, for they are folly (meaningless nonsense) to him; and he is incapable of knowing them - of progressively recognizing, understanding and becoming better acquainted with them - because they are spiritually discerned *and* estimated *and* appreciated (1 Corinthians 2:14, Amp).

How, then, is the spiritually enlightened man to discern the meaning of bread and wine as flesh and blood? Surely it is not in accordance with Roman doctrine which prescribes that the wafer literally changes into the body of the Christ in the stomach - for the Christ is one body, not many. The presence of the Christ in His Supper is not by some kind of supernatural multiplication.

Neither can it be said that only the divine nature of Jesus is represented in Communion since the Christ specifically states that the bread and wine represent His body and blood which are unmistakably elements of His human nature alone. God is Spirit without flesh and bones. Discernment in the Supper, then, is to make a distinction between the Christ's humanity and His Deity. Specifically, in the rite of Communion, the Christ's relation to us as human beings is emphasized - His humanity, not His Deity.

DISCERNMENT IN THE RITE OF THE LORD'S SUPPER

Participation in the Lord's Supper proclaims the Lord's humanity (death) till He returns (1 Corinthians 11:26). For 2000 years, in Christian churches all over the world, bread and wine have been set forth, exhibited, and consumed as emblems of the Christ's body and blood. The purpose of the rite is to publically express that He died as a Man (God cannot die) to rid the world of sin.

Had the Christ not instituted the sacrament of His Supper doubt might have arisen regarding the presence of His humanity in the Church. There is no doubt, however, about the presence of His Spirit, His Deity, His spiritual influence. It is seen in changed lives. But the presence of the Christ's humanity in the Church is a different matter. Humanity - if not seen and heard - is easily dismissed.

After His death the Christ's humanity might have been overlooked had He not set up the rite of Eucharist. After His departure from the world uncertainty might have crept into the Church respecting His humanity. The reality of His manhood might have diminished. Indeed, the Christ's humanity could have become obsolete were we not reminded of it each time we participate in His Supper.

Discernment in the rite of the Lord's Supper connotes the capacity to distinguish Jesus Christ's two natures. Discernment highlights the ability to recognize and worship both natures. In the institution of His Last Supper the Christ emphasizes His humanity and His humanity reminds us of His death for sin.

Discernment in the rite of the Lord's Supper signifies that the Christ was a Man. Though His Holy Spirit - His spiritual influence - dominates worship service it must not be forgotten He was a Man who sacrificed His life for our well-being. That we pray to God in Jesus' name means that we come to God through a Man.

CLARIFICATIONS

The Christ was both God and Man. When He walked the earth all the fulness of Deity dwelt in humanity (Colossians 2:9). The following clarifications regard the relationship of Deity and humanity *after* the Christ's death; that is, they look at the Christ's humanity *after* His ascension:

- At the Christ's death Deity left humanity (Matthew 27:46);
- The Christ's lifeless body was placed in a tomb and after three days Deity raised Him from the dead (Acts 10:40);
- The Christ's glorified body will not appear on earth until the millennium (Revelation 19:11ff);
- The glorified humanity of the Christ now sits at the right hand of God (Ephesians 1:20-23), "the first fruits of those who are asleep" (1 Corinthians 15:20), interceding for His people (Romans 8:34);
- Humanity's intercession in heaven (as on earth - see John chapter 17) implies continual intercourse with Deity;
- Because the glorified Christ sits at the right hand of Deity it cannot be imagined that the Messiah has become all knowing, all powerful, and expanded in some supernatural way to make Him coextensive with Deity who is everywhere present. In heaven the Christ's human nature sits at the right hand of God - a glorified Man. His divine nature *is* God.

- In heaven -as on earth - there is no real difference in the relationship of Deity and humanity. The only noticeable difference is that on earth all the fulness of Deity dwelt in humanity while in heaven glorified humanity dwells in Deity. On earth as in heaven the Christ's human spirit is united with God's divine Spirit;
- In heaven as on earth the two natures of Jesus Christ remain unimpaired: Deity remains Deity and humanity remains humanity. Neither Deity nor humanity change. In heaven as on earth the two natures are embodied in one person, but separate (John 10:30).

Deity raised humanity from the dead because He was sinless and didn't have to die but willingly gave His life for us. While on earth God was *in* the Man Christ Jesus reconciling the world to Himself (2 Corinthians 5:19). Now the glorified Christ resides in heaven interceding on behalf of His disciples. At the proper time He will come back in righteousness, with all the power and authority of God at His disposal, to rule and judge the world.

In heaven the Christ is still a Man as He was on earth. Though a glorified Man He is not omnipresent. The essential relationship between His human nature and His divine nature continues unchanged in heaven. God remains God and Man remains Man.

HUMANITY 9

THE CHRIST AND THE LOGOS

In the prologue to the fourth Gospel the apostle John employs the Greek word *Logos* to describe the Christ. Most Bible versions translate *Logos* as "Word" - the Word of God. The Spanish Bible translates *Logos* as the "Verb" - or word of action - of God. As "verb" the imagery portrays God as noun with the Christ carrying out God's plan of salvation.

"In the beginning was the Word, and the Word was with God, and the Word was God" (John 1:1, NASB). That is, the Word was the mind and heart of God manifested in the flesh (1 Timothy 3:16). "And the Word became flesh and dwelt among us..." (John 1:14). God didn't become flesh but His Word became flesh; just as His Word, in the beginning, put the creation into action: "Then God said...".

No doubt John borrowed *Logos* from either Greek literature or Hebrew Scripture where the Word of God is the divine agent in creation. (God uttered the Word and it happened - Genesis 1:1-31.) In either case, whether *Logos* comes from Greek literature or Hebrew Scripture, the translation is appropriate because "Word" represents the expressed will of God. His thought, reason, grace, and plan are realized in His Word. His Word tells us everything we have to know. All else we learn by doing.

Every word is preceded by a thought. Thought denotes the faculty of reason - or the thought inwardly conceived. Word implies the thought is outwardly expressed.

Can it be imagined that God was ever without a thought? Or without expression? Or without a plan for the universe He created? Of course not. Hence thought, plan, expression, Word are as eternal as Deity. Indeed, the Son of Man was foreknown, a thought in God's mind, before the foundation of the world (1 Peter 1:20). At the incarnation God expressed *Himself* in a Man - not another self, not another person of God.

Thought, reason, plan, Word (*Logos*) are activities of the mind and heart. Because God's plan to save the world originated in His mind and heart its outward expression was an absolute certain future event. God designed the plan of salvation. The implementation of that design is found in His Word. His Word became flesh and dwelt among us.

Word, reason, thought, plan are blended together and intimately connected in the Greek word *Logos*. They are abstract concepts in God's mind and heart until expressed and made specific. The purpose of this chapter is to briefly track the evolution of the term *Logos* from classical Greek through Hebrew Scripture to its final revelation in the fourth Gospel. And, by this tracking, to reveal why the apostle John was prompted to employ the term *Logos* - the Christ - as the embodiment of God's Word.

GREEK ORIGINS

Of course, the ancient Greeks didn't know God. But the classical Greek mind was searching for God. The most prominent seekers that come to us through Greek literature are Heraclitus, Anaxagoras, Plato, Aristotle, and the Stoics. (Stoicism was a school of philosophy holding that a wise man should show indifference to pleasure or pain.) The following summaries touch on the Greek definition of *Logos*.

HERACLITUS

Heraclitus (5th century B.C.) sought to account for the order that existed in a world of continual transformation. He saw everything in a condition of change; everything was forever passing into something else. Things came into being and passed away. Children were born, got old, and died. To Heraclitus fire became the symbol of this perpetual *becoming*. Fire was the symbol that represented his world view. It was restless, all consuming, and yet all transforming - darting upwards as a flame, dying as an ember, vanishing as smoke. This was how Heraclitus saw life.

But to Heraclitus fire was no arbitrary or lawless element. Everything was changing; yet, he observed change did not mean chaos. All change seemed to take place according to a governing plan, an established law. This plan or law Heraclitus called *Logos*. *Logos*, however, according to Heraclitus, was not in the heavens or in the past or future. It was part of the world system. Its energy sustained and harmonized the endless variety of flux in the world.

ANAXAGORAS

Anaxagoras (5th century B.C.) expanded Heraclitus' thought. He introduced the idea of a supreme intellectual principle which was independent of the world, and at the same time governed it. Anaxagoras took Heraclitus' *Logos* out of the world and suggested the principle of a supreme intelligence apart from the world which created and managed it. He changed the name of this principle from *Logos* to *Nous* (Mind).

PLATO

Plato (4th century B.C.) developed the principle of divine intelligence. Translators of Plato call this principle "reason," a category of *Logos* and Mind. The concept of reason or *Logos* was elevated by Plato. He made a distinction between the world of senses (sight, hearing, smell, taste, touch) and the world of thought. Deity - something outside ourselves - belonged to the realm of thought while mankind belonged to the world of senses. According to Plato true reality and absolute being consisted of ideas or thoughts residing in the reason (*Logos*) of the divine mind. Compared to the realm of ideas the world of the senses was a world of shadows.

ARISTOTLE

Aristotle (4th century B.C.) agreed with Plato, that there was a divine mind as well as a human mind. But Aristotle brought Plato's ideas down from heaven. He brought the dualism of the divine mind and the human mind down to earth. He wrote that the mysteries that baffled the world were capable of being known by human rationality if human rationality participated in the rationality of the divine mind. Aristotle's thinking - the idea of a human mind and a divine mind working together - set the Greek stage for Paul and the entrance of Christianity. Moreover, Aristotle's writings prepared the Greek mind - and the western world - for monotheism. Aristotle taught that the divine mind, ultimate reality, was pure thought existing apart from the world in eternal blessedness. He made the point that there was only *one* divine mind.

STOICS

It was the system of Stoic thought (founded by Zeno in 300 B.C.) that gave the doctrine of the *Logos* its greatest extension in Greek philosophy. According to the Stoics the *Logos* was a principle, a comprehensive and fundamental law, the primary source of opinion, belief, and practice and therefore the root of all activity. It was identified to be divine. *Logos* and *supreme* reasoning meant the same thing to the Stoics.

Logos was an unseen productive power. Indeed, as divine productive power the Stoics coined a phrase to describe the doctrine of the *Logos*. They called it *Logos Spermatikos*, "Seminal Logos." That is, *Logos* was the seed of reason, the generative principle of the world. Stoicism spoke of the *Logos* as unseen germinal power that manifested itself in the consciousness of mankind.

To the Stoics the *Logos* was a never-ending, always-persistent, all-pervading, ever-creating, all-consuming force that made the world go round. And because the *Logos* was grounded in reason it provided a universal basis for moral life and ethical conduct. Thus, 300 years before the incarnation, Stoic thought opened the door for the Christ's entry into the world. Most likely this was God's doing.

HEBREW ROOTS OF THE WORD

According to the development of Greek thought the *Logos* was conceived to be a rational principle or impersonal energy by means of which the world was fashioned and ordered. To the Hebrew mind, on the other hand, the Word of course was Jehovah, still impersonal, yet Jehovah. The Greeks considered the *Logos* to be abstract reason. To the Jews the Word was God expressing Himself in the Hebrew Scriptures.

Greek thinking was rationalistic and speculative. To the contrary, speculative thinking was not an issue for the Hebrew mind. Jehovah revealed Himself to Abraham, Isaac, and Jacob and spoke through His prophets for over a thousand years. The voice of the living God called His people out of Egypt to faithfulness in a covenant relation in exchange for divine blessing. And God planted His chosen people in the land of Israel. To the Hebrew mind there was nothing speculative or rationalistic about God.

The Hebrew Scriptures convey God's power in His Word. "By the word of the Lord were the heavens made, their starry host by the breath of His mouth" (Psalm 33:6, NIV). His Word is continually effective. "So will the words that come out of my mouth not come back empty-handed. They'll do the work I sent them to do, they'll complete the assignment I gave them" (Isaiah 55:11, Msg). His wisdom is poetically personified in His Word (see Proverbs chapter 8).

The Word was a common concept in the Hebrew Scriptures. Psalm 119 is a representative illustration. In its 22 stanzas (176 verses) of meditations and prayers it displays a love for the beauty and power and succor of God's Word. The term "Word" is used 38 times, at least once in each stanza. Some of the more prominent examples follow:

- How can a young man keep his way pure? By keeping it according to Thy word, v. 9;
- Thy word I have treasured in my heart, that I may not sin against Thee, v. 11;
- My soul weeps because of grief; strengthen me according to Thy word, v. 28;
- May Thy lovingkindness come to me, O Lord, Thy salvation according to Thy word, v. 41;
- Thy word is a lamp to my feet, and a light to my path, v.105;
- Thou art my hiding place and my shield; I wait for Thy word, v. 114;
- The unfolding of Thy word gives light; it gives understanding to the simple, v. 130.

If literally translated from the Hebrew the "ten commandments" would be the "ten words" (Exodus 34:28). Indeed, most of the legislation from the Pentateuch is represented as coming to Moses from the mouth of God (Exodus 20:1; Leviticus 4:1).

The Word is presented as an instrument of judgment in the Old Testament.

"I have slain them by the words of My mouth"(Hosea 6:5, NASB). It is present-ed even as an agent of healing. "He spoke the word that healed you, that pulled you back from the brink of death"(Psalm 107:20, Msg). Jehovah tells His people to listen to His words. "Why do you spend your money on junk food, your hard-earned cash on cotton candy? Listen to me, listen well: Eat only the best..."(Isaiah 55:2, Msg). Jehovah speaks only to His people. "He speaks the same way to Jacob, speaks words that work to Israel. He never did this to the other nations; they never heard such commands. Hallelujah!"(Psalm 147:15, Msg).

The concept of the Word as the voice of God has deep roots in the Hebrew Scriptures. God makes His will known by spoken utterances. He progres-sively unfolds His nature by His Word. In Greek philosophy the *Logos* was substantially a doctrine of (abstract, inner) Reason while in the Hebrew Scriptures the Word deals with the (factual, outward) expression of God. The Christ is God's ultimate expression.

THE WORD IN JOHN'S GOSPEL

This section begins with a premise. (A premise is a proposition that sets the ground-work for discussion.) The premise is this: The Word (*Logos*) in the prologue to the apostle John's gospel (John 1:1-18) means just that: Word. What is a word? As outlined in the preceding sections a word is a thought which is expressed. In John's prologue the Word is the thought *and* the thought expressed. In the Old Testament, in the beginning, before creation it was an impersonal concept. Then it took on life. In verse one of John's gospel, in the beginning, the Word was a thought and in verse 14 the thought was expressed:

In the beginning was the Word, and the Word was with God, and the Word was God (John 1:1);

And the Word became flesh (John 1:14).

God did not become flesh but His Word became flesh. In the beginning, before the world was made, when there was as yet nothing, neither rocks nor hills nor man nor beast, the Word existed in God's mind - a non-substantial existence. Because the Word existed in God's mind and heart before creation it was not a creature or begotten being. It was simply an idea in God's mind and heart. The Word was not yet a Man but what would become a Man. In the beginning the Man Christ Jesus was not yet *with* God except in the sense that He was a projection in God's mind and heart to save the world from sin. Only the thought and subsequent Word was in God's mind. The Man Christ Jesus was begotten, "became flesh," at a point in time.

So what was the idea, the thought behind the expression of the Word? Before being expressed the Word was a plan fomenting in God's mind, a plan prompted by God's heart of compassion for lost souls. It was God's plan of salvation. In the beginning the plan He had in mind was still a plan - not yet spoken or expressed. In heaven the Word was with God before He spoke it into existence on earth. "In the past God spoke to our ancestors many times and in many ways through the prophets, but in these last days he has spoken to us through his Son" (Hebrews 1:1,2, GNNT).

The significance of "Word" in John's prologue includes *both* the idea (plan of salvation) in the mind of God *and* its expression in the Man Christ Jesus - the embodiment of that plan. In the beginning the Word was not yet a tangible object. It was in God's heart as a solution to the sin problem. Then, at the proper time (Galatians 4:4), God's Word became flesh. God expressed and embodied His heart in the Man Christ Jesus.

Word, as John employs it, signifies both the inward thought and its outward manifestation. The notion of the Word in John's prologue takes us from an inner abstract conception to an outer factual form. That is, John 1:1 includes the thought - the plan of salvation. John 1:14 reveals the perpetrator of that plan - the Christ. Both the idea of plan and perpetrator are included in John's use of the word "Word." Contained in God's Word , contained in the Man Christ Jesus are all God's thoughts regarding His plan of salvation.

In John 1:14 ("The Word became flesh") the Greek verb *ginomai* is correctly translated "became." Or, as the KJV puts it, "was made." *Ginomai* means, according to the dictionary of Strong's Concordance, to come into existence, to come into being, to be generated.

To become or to be made implies change or development from one state to another. At the Incarnation the Word changed from a thought in God's mind to flesh in the womb of the virgin Mary. The Word that became flesh refers to the manifest expression of God Himself since God does not change or develop. God's Word *is* God, just as there is no differentiation between a man and his word.

Moreover, God IS (Hebrews 11:6). He does not become other than what He is (Psalm 102:27; Malachi 3:6; James 1:17). God's Word is the seed that became the flesh and blood of the Christ by the agency of His mother.

Webster's Seventh New Collegiate Dictionary provides a religious definition for "Word." It defines "Word" as the "expressed or manifested mind and will of God." In a nutshell this is precisely the premise of this section - that the expression of God's mind and will is seen in His plan of salvation, that that plan was given life in the birth, death, and resurrection of the Lord Jesus Christ.

Not that Christ the Man existed before the Incarnation, but the plan (Word) of redemption *through* the Christ was in the mind and will of God from eternity past - knowing, by foreknowledge, that Adam would fall. Indeed, Scripture declares that the Christ was prophetically "foreordained before the foundation of the world, but was manifest in the last times for you" (1 Peter 1:20, KJV). Here Peter points to the Christ's humanity - not His Deity. Before there was anybody on earth the Christ was foreknown. Then He was manifested in the flesh at the Incarnation. God's mind and heart were made known in a Man. His will for mankind was made known in His Son.

MOSES AND JOHN

Both Moses and John open their contribution to the unfolding revelation of God with the expression, "In the beginning." Moses writes, "In the beginning God created...". John writes, "In the beginning was the Word...". In both cases the frame of reference is eternity, before creation. As far as we know there was nothing. "Earth was a soup of nothingness, a bottomless emptiness, an inky blackness" (Genesis 1:2, Msg).

Then God began to speak. His Word became the agent by which He began to reveal Himself. By His Word he created the universe and all that is therein. God said it and it came into being (Genesis 1:3, 6, 9, 11, 14, 20, 24, 26). Light, land, stars, seasons, vegetation, fish, birds, animals, and Adam sprang into existence simply by the utterance of God's Word, the breath of His Spirit.

"For since the creation of the world God's invisible qualities - his eternal power and divine nature - have been clearly seen, being understood from what has been made" (Romans 1:20, NIV). In the Old Testament God was known by what He made. All things in the universe that are observed and touched were brought into being by the power of God's Word. God said it and for that reason it happened.

The revelation of God in the book of Genesis unveils the observable creative power of God's Word - the creation, the material world. On the other hand, the Word in the apostle John's gospel reveals the unobservable aspects of God's nature. Namely, His love, grace, compassion, and mercy. God reveals His heart through the manifestation in the flesh of His Word. The Man Christ Jesus of course is God's heart that became flesh. Those things about God's heart that were unclear in the Hebrew Scriptures were made clear in the Lord Jesus Christ. Everything intended by the word "heart" is contained in God's Word made manifest in Jesus.

"WITH GOD" AND "WAS GOD"

"In the beginning...the Word was with God, and the Word was God" (John 1:1). As has been established the Word is God's thought or God's plan of salvation - in His Son - that He conceived when He created the universe knowing Adam would fall. It is in this sense that the Word was with God from the beginning, before creation. The Word was in God's heart of compassion waiting to be expressed. "With" does not mean that in the beginning there was friendship and intimacy between two separate entities. The Christ (the Word) had not yet been made flesh, had not yet been born (expressed). Moreover, God is One (Deuteronomy 6:4) and sovereign. He does not discuss His plans with anyone.

John's use of the preposition "with" signifies that the Word was an integral *part of* God, *in God*, not separate from Him. Thus, in the beginning the Word was with God and at the same time was God. Then, when time had matured (Galatians 4:4), at the Incarnation, God dispatched His Word just as He dispatched His Word to bring the universe into being.

Since it cannot be said that God is *with* himself, it follows that the Word is in some sense distinct from God. But that distinction does not mean the Man Christ Jesus existed in heaven from the beginning. On the contrary, the

Christ had a beginning in the belly of a woman. The distinction lies, for example, in the difference between a man and his word. In reality there is no difference. A man and his word are the same thing. Consequently, because Christ the Man was not with God from the beginning, He was not the Word until it, God's Word, became flesh. The Word did not become flesh until God expressed himself.

When John writes that the Word was with God and the Word was God he brings to the reader's attention that God's Word is always with Him. Indeed, His Word is probably creating different cosmoses throughout the galaxies right now. His Word is part of His creative Being. In our world the Word is undeniably the Christ, God manifested in the flesh.

John does not write that God's Word is separate or detached from Him. Neither does he imply that God's Word is another divine being with Him in heaven. God's Word relates, i.e., tells the story of God's concern for fallen humanity. That is, God's Word expresses all those things God is - including love. Jesus Christ is the expression of God's love. What's more, "No eye has seen, nor ear heard, no mind has conceived what God has prepared for those who love him" (1 Corinthians 2:9, NIV).

EXISTENCE?

Existence is not a good word to apply to God. Existence comes from two Latin words: "from out of" and "to stand"; *ex + sistere.* In other words, existence means to stand or come into being from out of something else. Hence, because God is, was, and always will be the same He does not exist, or come out of, but IS (Hebrews 11:6). By contrast, the idea of existence can and should be applied to humanity. Humanity came from out of God.

At the same time the idea of pre-existence holds a more fuzzy meaning. If existence applies solely to humanity, does the idea of pre-existence apply to humanity too? That is, did the Christ's humanity pre-exist the Incarnation? The answer of course is a resounding no. Bones, flesh, and blood do not inhabit the spiritual realm.

The Holy Spirit of Jesus is God Himself because God's Spirit conceived Him (Luke 1:35). The humanity of the Christ, however, did not pre-exist the Incarnation except as a plan in the mind of God. Therefore, it cannot be said the Son of Man pre-existed the Incarnation.

PRE-EXISTENCE?

When the Son of God speaks of Himself, in the first person singular, He speaks as either God or Man - Deity or humanity. Clearly, in the "I AM" verses he speaks as God. Unless you believe that I AM, Jesus said, you shall die in your sins (John 8:24). In another place He said that before Abraham was born, I AM (John 8:58). (I AM is a reference to Exodus 3:14 where Jehovah tells Moses His name.) Jesus also refers to Himself as God the Father (Jehovah or I AM) when He tells the disciples He will not leave them fatherless (John 14:18).

On the other hand, in the "sent" (or begotten) verses, the Christ refers to Himself as a Man. That is, He declares He was sent (begotten) to do a job as a Man - not as God. Deity sent humanity.

In a number of passages the Christ states that His Father sent Him into the world. (Remember, God sent His Son into the world by begetting Him in the womb of a virgin.) Here are some examples. "Anyone who accepts what I do accepts my Father, who sent me. Accepting a messenger of God is as good as being God's messenger" (Matthew 10:40, Msg). "For God did not send his Son into the world to condemn the world, but to save the world through him" (John 3:17, NIV). "For the works which the Father has given Me to accomplish, the very works that I do, bear witness of Me, that the Father has sent Me" (John 5:36, NASB). "I did not come on my own authority but he [God] sent me" (John 8:42, GNNT). "Just as You [Father] sent Me into the world, I also have sent them into the world" (John 17:18, Amp). These are just a few random examples of God sending (begetting) his Son into the world. There are more - maybe twenty-five more.

"God sent his Son, born of a woman" (Galatians 4:4, NIV). "Born of a woman" means that the Son was a Man - humanity. Deity was not born of a woman. Mary was not the mother of God. The Son she bore was a Man with all the fulness of Deity dwelling in Him (Colossians 2:9) because His Father was God. The Father revealed Himself in the Son.

Born of a woman signifies that the Christ came out from the Father's heart. The virgin birth was no accident. God planned it that way. "I came out from the Father," the Christ said, "and have come into the world" (John 16:28, Amp). God appointed the Son for a special purpose. In His heart God formed a plan, put flesh on that plan, and then the Son, under orders from the

Father, put that plan in operation - on earth. In short, the "sending" verses emphasize the humanity of the Son and the specific purpose for which the Son was given life. When the Christ, speaking as a Man, says that He is sent from God, it has nothing to do with pre-existence, for humanity does not exist in heaven.

HUMANITY 10

IMITATING THE CHRIST'S HUMILITY

In the presentation of Jesus Christ's two natures the apostle Paul employs words that are puzzling - at least the words translated from the Greek are puzzling. When translating from another language the idea is not always rendered clearly - especially in a technical discourse. As a result some ideas give rise to discussion. Perhaps even the words were not clear in the original language.

Philippians 2:6,7 is a good example of obscurity. Paul speaks of Jesus Christ as God and Man; God who assumed the body of a Man. But the language is cloudy. The essence of the two verses is that, though He was God, Christ the Man humbled Himself and became a servant.

Here are a couple of translations of Philippians 2:6,7, one from the KJV and one from the NIV.

- 6)Who, being in the form of God, thought it not robbery to be equal with God;7) But made himself of no reputation, and took upon him the form of a servant, and was made in the likeness of men (KJV).
- 6)Who, being in very nature God, did not consider equality with God something to be grasped, 7)but made himself nothing, taking the very nature of a servant, being made in human likeness (NIV).

In verse 6 Paul says Jesus is God for God has no equal. "To whom then will you liken Me that I should be his equal? says the Holy One" (Isaiah

40:25, NASB). "To whom will you compare me or count me equal?" (Isaiah 46:5, NIV). "For I am God, and there is no other; I am God, and there is no one like Me" (Isaiah 46:9, NASB)). Jesus embodied the full nature of God. "Equality with God" means the Son of God's divine nature was the very nature of God the Father.

Though He was fully divine Jesus "thought it not robbery to be equal with God" nor did He "regard equality with God a thing to be grasped." "Robbery" or "grasped" mean to take hold for oneself. Jesus as Man did not take hold of being God but humbled Himself and emptied Himself of divine privileges. That is, He laid aside His divine prerogatives.

In contrast to verse 6, verse 7 emphasizes the Christ's humanity, indicating the limitations He placed upon Himself. That the Christ "made himself of no reputation" and "made himself nothing" means He voluntarily surrendered His glory and dignity as God. It does not mean He surrendered His nature as God for that would be impossible. He did not discard His inherent divine nature but hid His divinity in humanity. His divine attributes were available to Him, yet He chose not to use them. Instead of acting in His rightful role as King of kings He humbled Himself and became a ministering servant to mankind

The phrases "form of God" (KJV) and "being in very nature God" (NIV) in verse 6, contrasted with the phrases "form of a servant"(KJV) and "taking the very nature of a servant" (NIV) in verse 7 clearly speak of Jesus Christ's two natures - God and Man, the God-Man. As Man He is our Savior. As God He provides salvation - gives us new life.

RICH AND POOR

Another verse that expresses Jesus Christ's two natures is 2 Corinthians 8:9. In this verse Paul deals with the notions of rich and poor. It goes without saying that Jesus, as God, was rich, proprietor of all things. On the other hand, the Christ, as Man, chose a life of poverty. By His grace, for our well-being, He "took upon himself the form of a servant" (Philippians 2:7, KJV), a ministering servant.

You know the grace of our Lord Jesus Christ; rich as he was, he made himself poor for your sake, in order to make you rich by means of his poverty (2 Corinthians 8:9, GNNT).

As a Man the Christ made Himself poor (in material things) so we might be made rich (in spiritual things). Not that material poverty means spiritual wealth or material wealth means spiritual poverty. The Christ's message of poverty is that material wealth is not to be pursued, that there are more important goals in life than the pursuit of money. The Christ's example of poverty stands before the whole world as a memorial that men need more than wealth to fill the heart's vacuum. Money is not evil but the love of money is the root of all evil (1 Timothy 6:10).

In addition, Paul probably uses the word "poverty" to include more than the idea of want of property. More than likely poverty means all the circumstances surrounding the Christ's low estate and humble condition, His sufferings and woes to procure for us a role in the kingdom of heaven. By poverty Paul undoubtedly means a lifelong ministry of suffering as part of the work of atonement - ending in death.

The point is, He *chose* poverty. As God, "rich as he was, he made himself poor." He didn't have to be poor. And He didn't have to die. He was a sinless Man.

FIRST AND LAST ADAM

Adam is a Hebrew word meaning "man." "The first man, Adam, became a living soul. The last Adam became a life-giving spirit" (1 Corinthians 15:45, NASB). Here Paul speaks expressly of the Christ's humanity. He compares the Christ with Adam, the first man.

God formed the first Adam from the dust of the ground. He became a man when God blew the breath of His Spirit into Adam's nostrils (Genesis 2:7). On the other hand, by His Spirit, God generated the last Adam in the womb of a virgin (Luke 1:35). The first Adam came from the earth; the last Adam came from a woman. Yet both men derived their being from God's Holy Spirit.

In comparing the Christ with Adam there is also a distinction by contrast between the two. From the first Adam we take our vital or animal existence while from the last Adam we take our heavenly existence. Our dying bodies come from the first Adam and our undying bodies come from the last Adam. Our eternal destinies were adversely affected by the first Adam and beneficially affected by the last Adam. Both men sustain a peculiar relation to the race of human beings and in this respect they were the first and the last.

In the beginning, in the garden of Eden, God's Spirit was in direct communion with Adam's human spirit. But when Adam sinned God withdrew His Holy Spirit; He turned His back on Adam. He expelled Adam from Eden to cultivate the ground from which he was formed (Genesis 3:23). Adam - and all of Adam's seed - were separated from God by sin. Consequently, everyone is a sinner (Romans 3:23). And the wages of sin is death (Romans 6:23).

The last Adam, however, did not sin. God's Holy Spirit was in direct communion with the Christ's human spirit throughout His life. That is, until His death. At His death He assumed our sins - at which time God had to forsake Him for God cannot fellowship with sin. When the last Adam assumed our sins, however, God canceled the consequences of sin - death - for those who believe. Then, at His resurrection, the last Adam became a life-giving spirit; i.e., bestowing new life from heaven.

Indeed, the Christ said as much about Himself *before* sacrificing His life. "For just as the Father raises the dead and gives them life, even so the Son also gives life to whom He wishes" (John 5:21, NASB). Just as the Father raised the Son from the dead even so the Son renews the heart and gives new spiritual life to those who believe in Him.

In another verse John says something similar. "Just as the Father is himself the source of life, in the same way he made his Son to be the source of life" (John 5:26, GNNT). The Father is the source of *all* life. The Father has made the Son to be the source of new spiritual life for those who consider themselves dead in sin.

When Paul compares the two Adams he compares the ministries of two men. The first brought death and condemnation. The last, by His resurrection from the dead guaranteed immortal life. "For just as all people die because of their union with Adam, in the same way all will be raised to life because of their union with Christ" (1 Corinthians 15:22, GNNT). "So then, as the one sin condemned all mankind, in the same way the one righteous act sets all mankind free and gives them life" (Romans 5:18, GNNT).

By His resurrected human nature, by His human spirit in heaven, the Christ provides new spiritual life to His followers on earth. And God will resurrect them on the last day. Just as we now bear the image and likeness of the earthly Adam, we shall also bear the image and likeness of the heavenly Adam. "Just as we wear the likeness of the man made of earth, so we will wear the likeness of the Man in heaven" (1 Corinthians 15:49, GNNT).

That is, like the first Adam we are frail, decaying, and dying. Yet, by faith in the last Adam we are given new life on earth and eternal life in heaven. Faith is the key. In God's eyes the spiritual bond formed by faith in the last Adam is as personal as the physical bond with the first Adam.

"I CAME DOWN FROM HEAVEN"

Christ the Man did not pre-exist His birth. His humanity was not eternal. He was begotten. God, knowing the men and women He created would need a Savior, graciously provided one. In the beginning He conceived the plan of salvation in His heart. Then, at the proper time (Galatians 4:4) the Father, through the virgin birth, "sent" His Son into the world to do a job only a sinless Man could do. "I came down from heaven," the Christ said, "not to follow my own whim but to accomplish the will of the One who sent me" (John 6:38, Msg).

Here the Messiah speaks of Himself as a Man who came down from heaven, sent to accomplish the will of God. What He said must be understood in an exceptional sense because men do not exist in heaven. At least not as human beings. That is, the Christ derived His humanity from God just as Adam derived his humanity from God. Both took on life by God's Spirit. God was each one's Father: See Genesis 2:7 and Luke 1:35. Deity was the source of each one's manhood. In this sense the Christ came down from heaven.

What the Messiah does not mean is that He pre-existed as a Man in heaven before He was born. His human existence began 2000 years ago. Adam's existence began a few thousand years before that. Adam's mother was mother earth. The Messiah's mother was the virgin Mary, a descendant of Adam.

"TO ACCOMPLISH THE WILL OF THE ONE WHO SENT ME"

What did the Son accomplish? What was the will of the One who sent the Son on His commission? The answer to both questions is this: The annihilation of sin; the removal of the sin barrier between God and man. By the sacrificial death of the Christ the relationship between God and man changed. In a word God and man were reconciled. Thus, the door for God to provide salvation to sinners was opened.

Had not sinless humanity paid the penalty for sin there would have been no way Deity could have extended salvation to mankind.

In addition to the annihilation of sin the Christ states another purpose for which the Father sent the Son, another reason Deity begot humanity. "This is what my Father wants: that anyone who sees the Son and trusts who he is and what he does and then aligns with him will enter real life, eternal life. My part is to put them on their feet alive and whole at the completion of time" (John 6:40, Msg).

This verse is a good example of Deity and humanity working together to save mankind. It reveals that it was Deity's will that the world's people look to humanity's sacrificial death (God cannot die) as propitiation for their sins. As a result the Father extended His gracious provision of salvation to those who trust and align themselves with His Son's work on the cross. The Christ's "part [in preparing them for salvation] is to put them on their feet alive and whole at the completion of time." God's part is to raise them to eternal life in heaven.

MEDIATION

Reconciliation was made possible by God's mediation. Two thousand years ago He intervened on our behalf to settle the sin problem. He sent (begot) a Mediator. He graciously fathered a Son to express His love and to show His readiness to forgive our sins. He impregnated the womb of the virgin Mary to reconcile us to Himself. He sent His Son into the world to die for our sins. "Now all these things are from God, who reconciled us to Himself through Christ..." (2 Corinthians 5:18, NASB). Thanks to God's mediation the Christ "has now reconciled you in His fleshly body through death, in order to present you before Him [God] holy and blameless and beyond reproach..." (Colossians 1:22, NASB).

God, Deity, acting alone, could not have reconciled us to Himself. Indeed, in a moral sense, God's righteousness can have nothing to do with sinful, rebellious, and unrighteous men and women, much less provide reconciliation. Moreover, until the debt of sin was paid God was in no position to negotiate reconciliation. In other words He could not indiscriminately reach down and deliver men from sin to settle the sin problem. A sinless Man was needed to settle the account.

A man sold us to the devil so a Man had to buy us back. A Man had to pay the penalty for sin – which is death. He also had to be a sinless Man. A sinner could not pay the debt. God would not accept the payment. He had to be a sinless Man, able to approach the throne of God's purity. He had to be capable of standing before God's holiness as our representative. Thanks to God's mediation He provided the Man - born of a virgin (Luke 1:35). By His mediation, by sending His Son, God provided a solution for the sin problem. At the same time He reconciled us to Himself.

MEDIATOR

God's mediation - the virgin birth - produced the Man, the Mediator. The word mediator means, properly, one who intervenes between two parties at variance as intercessor or reconciler. Of course he must be intimate with the needs and claims of both parties. Spelled with a capital "M" the word Mediator applies to the great Mediator between God and men, the God-Man, the Lord Jesus Christ.

Mediation between God and men requires that the Mediator should Himself possess the nature and attributes of the One toward whom He acts, and should likewise participate in the nature of those for whom He acts - and be sinless. In addition, only by being both God and Man could he comprehend the love, grace, mercy, and justice of God, and at the same time understand the needs of men. Further, only the God-Man would have known that He would have to offer Himself as an expiatory sacrifice on behalf of His brothers and sisters.

In other words, as Mediator He would have to know the exigencies of both sides: How to placate God's hatred of sin and how to bring men back to God. Not knowing the needs and claims of each side He could only represent one side. Not being both a sinless Man and God He would not qualify as Mediator.

PARTAKERS OF THE DIVINE NATURE

Christ the Man provides access to God's heart because He came from God's heart. The Christ's human nature is the believer's guide to God's divine nature. The Christ's human nature makes it possible for the believer to share in God's divine nature. Through humanity believers find their way to Deity. Indeed, the Christ said, "I am the way" (John 14:6), meaning there is no other way to God. He also said, "I am the door" (John 10:9), meaning there is no other access to God. Humanity's flesh opens the door and makes the way to Deity's Spirit.

The human nature of the Christ reveals the divine nature of God. The Christ's human nature manifests the exact representation of God's divine nature. "God, after He spoke long ago to the fathers...in these last days has spoken to us in His Son...and He is the radiance of His glory and the exact representation of His nature..." (Hebrews 1:1-3, NASB). Through the Son, through the human nature of the Christ, believers become partakers of the divine nature of God. Through the promises of the Christ we "escape from the destructive lust that is in the world, and...come to share the divine nature" (2 Peter 1:4, GNNT).

What is meant by partaking of the divine nature? It's a reference to participating in the *moral* nature of God. The meaning is that those who are renewed by the Christ's work on the cross become participants in the *moral* nature of God. That is, they come to take on the same views, feelings, thoughts, purposes, principles of action. By nature they are born sinful, prone to evil. Born again they begin to become Godlike. Through the Christ they are made like God. In this sense they are partakers of the divine nature.

Right and wrong, good and evil are no longer fuzzy words, abstractions, but concrete realities. In the mind of believers character counts. Because believers are made righteous they become righteous. In Christ believers become moral agents.

It should be noted that of all creatures on earth, only man is capable of rising to this condition. The nature of all other orders of creatures is incapable of such transformation. If such transformation among men takes place on earth can you imagine the change in heaven outside of these incarcerated bodies? To actually partake of the divine nature! To be able to look upon the immense works of God directly. Indeed, "What we see now is like a dim image..." (1 Corinthians 13:12, GNNT). "Eye hath not seen, nor ear heard, neither have entered into the heart of man, the things which God hath prepared for them that love him" (1 Corinthians 2:9, KJV). (I'm a vagabond at heart and look forward to visiting all the other worlds God has created.)

"IN THE FLESH" AND "ACCORDING TO THE FLESH"

"In the flesh" and "according to the flesh," are New Testament expressions that apply to the Christ in a special way. However, they are used in a peculiar manner. Within the context of the verse in which they appear they don't make much sense. That is, it's hard to understand why they are added to the context. They seem to form a redundancy within the verse. Are they really necessary to make the meaning clear? Here are some examples from the NASB.

- ...concerning His Son, who was born of a descendent of David according to the flesh...(Romans 1:3).
- ...whose are the fathers, and from whom is the Christ according to the flesh...(Romans 9:5).
- For Christ also died for sins...having been put to death in the flesh...(1 Peter 3:18).
- ...every spirit that confesses that Jesus Christ has come in the flesh is from God...(1 John 4:2).
- For many deceivers have gone out into the world, those who do not acknowledge Jesus Christ as coming in the flesh (2 John 7).

Clearly, these expressions identify the Christ's human nature. But their uncommon use implies that He had another nature, a nature that was *not* according to the flesh. These expressions imply that there was a sense in which Jesus was not descended from David and a sense that there was a nature that did not die.

If these expressions were applied to a mere man it might be asked, "How else could he be born other than in the flesh?" or "How else is a man put to death other than in the flesh?" Indeed, in all of Scripture it is not said of any prophet or apostle, Moses or king, or any man in any capacity that he came "in the flesh" or that he was descended from certain ancestors "according to the flesh." In short, these are New Testament expressions used to emphasize the distinction between Jesus Christ's human nature and His Deity - His dual nature.

CONCLUSION

The union of God and Man in the womb of a virgin took place for a specific purpose: To provide a Mediator between God and men. That God, who is Spirit, assumed a body emphasizes the fact that the Mediator had to be both God and Man. By assuming a body of flesh and blood God decreed that two roles - humanity and Deity - were necessary to mediate between heaven and earth. Both roles were needed in one person to represent both positions.

God's plan of salvation was accomplished by the Mediator. Joined in tandem and working together, Deity and humanity were vital in completing Deity's plan of reconciliation. Deity alone could not have saved mankind from the consequences of sin. The Savior had to be a Man, a sinless Man. Moreover, neither could a sinless Man alone have accomplished salvation. Only Deity is in a position to extend forgiveness of sin to mankind. The bottom line is this: Deity formulated the plan of salvation and sinless humanity executed it.

> Therefore I'll reward him extravagantly, the best of everything, the highest honors, because he looked death in the face and didn't flinch, because he embraced the company of the lowest. He took on his shoulders the sin of many, he took up the cause of the black sheep (Isaiah 53:11,12, Msg).

For God to pardon the guilty sinner it was necessary that the Mediator suffer and die. The penalty for sin, which is death, had to be paid. In the Old Testament it was prophesied that the Mediator would endure pain, distress, and death. The two most striking passages that describe the Mediator's suffering and death are Psalm 22 and Isaiah chapter 53. These Old Testament Scriptures, combined with Isaiah 7:14 and Isaiah 9:6, indicate that the Mediator would be Man as well as God.

God assumed a body of flesh and blood so His adopted children might experience new life on earth. God manifested Himself in the flesh of the Mediator (1 Timothy 3:16) so believers might spend eternity in heaven with Him. However, apart from these blessings is the additional fact that the Mediator rendered "powerless him who had the power of death, that is, the devil" (Hebrews 2:14, NASB). The Mediator defeated the devil but did not kill him. God has let him "prowl about like a roaring lion, seeking someone to devour" (1 Peter 5:8, NASB). Eventually, God the Father, because of the work of His Son, will destroy the devil and his deceivers. Humanity cannot destroy what God created.

Lucifer is God's creation. He is superhuman but not divine. He exists and has his being by divine will. Therefore, he will be destroyed by divine will. No man can do it. The Son of Man's victory over Satan defeated his empire but God has allowed him to continue to operate in the world for the time being. However, by humanity's work on the cross the devil has been (legally) set aside for Deity's final judgment when the affairs of this world are finished.

Thus, to fulfill the plan of salvation and to defeat the plan of the devil each nature of Jesus Christ's two natures performed that function which was proper to it. Humanity made a way for Deity to provide salvation and do away with the works of the devil. Christ the Savior (humanity) paid the ransom price. God (Deity) accepted the payment. Hence, we who believe are saved from the consequences of sin and endowed to recognize the lies of the devil.

Part 2

DEITY 1

GOD IS SPIRIT, NOT FLESH

The expressions Spirit, Spirit of God, Holy Spirit, Holy Spirit of God - all four mean the same - are found in the Hebrew Scriptures as well as the New Testament. In the Old Testament the Hebrew word for Spirit is *ruwach* meaning breath. God gave life to Adam by breathing His Spirit into Adam's nostrils (Genesis 2:7). In the New Testament the Greek word for Spirit is *pneuma*, coming from the verb *pneo*, to breathe. Holy Spirit is *pneuma hagion.*

In the New Testament we also find the expressions, Spirit of the Father, Spirit of Jesus, Spirit of the Lord, Spirit of the Christ. In each case Spirit refers to God: The Father is God or Spirit; the Spirit of Jesus is God; The Spirit of the Lord is God; the Spirit of the Christ is God. In short, God is Spirit - and His Spirit is Holy. Each New Testament expression refers to the one God of Israel as announced in the Old Testament: "Hear, O Israel! The LORD is our God, the LORD is one!" (Deuteronomy 6:4, NASB).

The Bible declares that God is Spirit (John 4:24), meaning that there is no distinction between God and Spirit, between God and *Holy* Spirit. His Spirit is part of His Being. It goes out from Him and will not return to Him void (Isaiah 55:11). God's Spirit is not a separate personality or function of God but *is* God. Indeed, without His Spirit (breath) God is dead.

Breath (Spirit), then, is a figurative expression of God's Being, signifying that, though without a body, He is alive. That God is Spirit means He is without a body. Without a body simply means God is not material, nor is He composed of parts or persons. There is only one person of God and that is the person of Jesus Christ.

The most important aspect of the fact that God is Spirit is that the Spirit that dwelt in the Man Christ Jesus was all the fulness of God. Thus, the God-Man's two natures. Because He was born of a woman, as any other person is born, i.e., with a body, soul, spirit, He was a human being. Yet, because His Father was God, Jesus was also Spirit. Inherent in the Man were all the divine characteristics of God. When the Christ walked the earth the Spirit that dwelt in Him was all the fulness of God. All the fulness of God was incarnate in the body of the redeemer. Spirit took on a body and appeared to the world in human form.

This is the great and central doctrine of the New Testament that is to be maintained about the Christ. Every system which denies or changes or adds to this teaching is subject to suspicion. Indeed, almost all heresy is begun by some form of denial of this great and central truth: That Jesus Christ was fully God and fully Man, Spirit (God) as well as body, soul, and spirit.

Paul was a minister of God. He was not a minister of the law but of the Spirit. Under God's direction Paul was a servant "of a new covenant, not of the letter [law], but of the Spirit; for the letter kills, but the Spirit gives life" (2 Corinthians 3:6, NASB). Here the notion of God (Spirit) points to one person: "Now the Lord is the Spirit" (2 Corinthians 3:17, NASB). According to the context of 2 Corinthians 3:17 the word "Lord" clearly refers to Jesus. The Christ is the Spirit. That is, He is the sum and substance of Old Testament law.

The two terms, God and Spirit, are synonymous. They both mean the same thing and refer to the same person, Jesus Christ. Holy is an adjective describing God.

When God is present by His Spirit the law is recognized as obsolete, valid but obsolete. God, Jesus Christ, by His Spirit, sets us free from the burden of the law. Because He poured His Spirit onto the world at Pentecost there is nothing that separates us from God. The dispensation of His Spirit did away with the authority of the law. Through the eyes of Jesus we are able to look God squarely in the face without being condemned by the law.

Before God dispensed His Spirit at Pentecost, the Holy Spirit of Jesus Christ, God was a dim specter in the hearts of His people the Jews. They could not go directly to God. Now, after Pentecost, separated from the oppression of the law, we go directly to God, without shame or guilt, and "...our faces shining with the brightness of his face. And so we are transfigured much like the Messiah, our lives gradually becoming brighter and more beautiful as God [by His Spirit] enters our lives and we become like him" (2 Corinthians 3:18, Msg).

John the Baptist, introducing the New Testament, speaking to those he baptized with water, prophesied that Jesus, as God, would soon baptize them with the Spirit of God, the divine nature that dwelt in the human nature of the Christ. John prophesied that when the believer asks Jesus into his heart Jesus immerses him into His Spirit and he becomes a new person, born again by the Spirit of Jesus and all things take on new life and a new perspective. Precisely, then, the Spirit that dwelt in Jesus was the Holy Spirit of God, the activating influence that regenerates the soul.

The Christ, speaking of His death, told the disciples He would come back, that He would not leave them as orphans. "I will not leave you orphaned. I'm coming back. In just a little while the world will no longer see me, but you're going to see me because I am alive and you're about to come alive. At that moment you will know absolutely that I'm in my Father..." (John 14:18,19, Msg).

How would the disciples see Him? How would He come back? How would He make them come alive? He would come back at Pentecost, by His Spirit, the Spirit of the Father that indwelt Him. Though absent in body, yet He would be present with them by His Spirit. And they would see His Spirit by the eye of faith.

By His Spirit we become like Jesus. We don't become like Jesus as God, but like Christ the Man, the image of God. By His Spirit we become Christlike. We are gifted with the qualities of God because Jesus is God. His divine nature, His Spirit is God. His human nature as well as His divine nature is embodied in the title "Son of God."

However, the title "God the Son" is unscriptural and misleading. Because this title is not found in the Old or New Testaments its use as a reference to Jesus' divine nature is false. The title "Son" refers *strictly* to the Christ's humanity, the male offspring of the virgin Mary, and not to God who dwelt in the Son. God's Spirit was not born and God's Spirit did not die.

The title "God the Son" is misleading because it is a contradiction in terms. "God" refers to God. "Son" refers to humanity. The Son is not God.

God *dwelt* in the Son (Colossians 2:9). On the other hand, the "Son of God" is a valid title because it refers to both natures.

In the Hebrew Scriptures and in the gospels the Spirit stays in the background until Pentecost. Why? Because "Jesus had not yet been glorified" (John 7:39, NIV). It wasn't until the death of the human nature that the fulness of the divine nature could be dispensed. The Spirit that operates in conversion and sanctification could not fully function because the Christ had not yet ascended to heaven, to the honor and glory that awaited Him. While alive, because His death was the procuring cause of the blessing of His Spirit, He could not yet ask His Father to pour out His Spirit. Thus, the Christ says that His Spirit cannot come until He, Christ the Man, goes away (John 16:7).

DEITY 2

GOD'S NAME

God's name in the Hebrew Scriptures is YHWH, pronounced Jehovah, meaning, "I AM." When Moses asked Jehovah, "What shall I say when the sons of Israel ask, 'Who sent me?'", Jehovah replied and told Moses to say, "I AM has sent me to you" (Exodus 3:14). God's name, I AM, implies the past without beginning and the future without end. It connotes continued and unchanging being without respect to time.

Jesus took His Father's name, Jehovah. Speaking as God, Jesus said, "*I am who I am* long before Abraham was anything" (John 8:58, Msg). His listeners knew He was calling Himself Jehovah, God, and plotted to kill Him for blasphemy.

JESUS IS JEHOVAH

Following, in chart form, is scriptural evidence that Jesus is Jehovah. The left column lists an attribute of Jehovah. The two columns on the right indicate where the attribute is ascribed to Jehovah in the Old Testament and where it is ascribed to Jesus in the New Testament.

Attribute	Jehovah	Jesus
Advocate	Jeremiah 50:34	1 John 2:1
Almighty	Genesis 17:1	Revelation 1:8
Comforter	Isaiah 51:12	John 14:16
Coming with His saints	Zechariah 14:5	Jude 14
Creator	Isaiah 45:8	Colossians 1:16
Every knee shall bow	Isaiah 45:23	Philippians 2:10
Exalted alone	Isaiah 2:11	Acts 5:31
Father	Isaiah 63:16	John 10:38
First and last	Isaiah 44:6	Revelation 1:17
Forgiver	Isaiah 43:25	Mark 2:7
Fountain of living water	Jeremiah 17:13	Revelation 7:17
Gives rest	Exodus 33:14	Matthew 11:28
Governor	Psalm 22:28	Matthew 2:6
Healer	Exodus 15:26	1 Peter 2:24
Holy One	Isaiah 43:15	Acts 3:14
Horn of salvation	Psalm 18:2	Luke 1:69
Husband	Hosea 2:16	Ephesians 5:22-32
I AM	Exodus 3:14	John 8:58
Judge	Isaiah 33:22	Acts 10:42
Judge of the nations	Isaiah 2:4	Matthew 25:32
King (Lord) of glory	Psalm 24:10	1 Corinthians 2:8
King of Israel	Zephaniah 3:15	John 1:49
Lawgiver	Isaiah 33:22	Hebrews 9:15
Life	Deuteronomy 30:20	John 11:25
Light	Psalm 27:1	John 8:12
Lord of lords	Deuteronomy 10:17	Revelation 19:16
Mighty God	Jeremiah 32:18	Luke 9:43
Only just God	Isaiah 45:21	Acts 7:52
Only Savior	Isaiah 60:16	Titus 2:13
Opens blind eyes	Psalm 146:8	Matthew 11:25
Redeemer	Isaiah 44:6	Galatians 3:13
Reigns forever	Exodus 15:18	Luke 1:33
Righteousness	Jeremiah 23:6	1 Corinthians 1:30
Rock	Psalm 18:2	1 Corinthians 10:4

Attribute	Jehovah	Jesus
Salvation in His name	Joel 2:32	Acts 4:12
Shepherd	Psalm 23:1	1 Peter 5:4
Treads winepress	Isaiah 63:1-6	Revelation 19:15
Way prepared before Him	Isaiah 40:1-3	Matthew 3:1-3
Whom they pierced	Zechariah 12:10	John 19:34

MORE ON JEHOVAH

Isaiah, speaking of Jehovah, says His arm shall rule for Him (Isaiah 40:10). In another place Isaiah says Jehovah's arm shall bring salvation (Isaiah 59:16). Then Isaiah identifies the Messiah as Jehovah's arm (see Isaiah chapter 53).

Zechariah (11:13) prophesies that Jehovah will be valued at thirty pieces of silver. Matthew (26:15) says that the chief priests paid Judas Iscariot thirty pieces of silver to betray Jesus. Thus Jesus is Jehovah.

Zechariah (12:8) prophesies that on the last day Jehovah will defeat the enemies that come against Jerusalem. On that great day Zechariah says Jehovah will stand on the Mount of Olives and with all the saints battle against many nations (Zechariah 14:3-5). The New Testament states Jesus is the one coming back to the Mount of Olives as King of kings and Lord of lords to war against the nations (Acts 1:11,12; 1 Timothy 6:14-16; Revelation 19:11-16).

Paul, an Old Testament Jew, knew God by His Old Testament name, Jehovah. When he was stricken on the road to Damascus by a blinding light he didn't know what happened. When he realized he had been hit by a divine visitation he asked, "Who are you, LORD?" As a devout Jew Paul knew it was God. In other words, Paul asked, "Who are you, *Jehovah*?" The LORD answered and said, "I AM Jesus" (Acts 9:5).

It was Jehovah who dealt with Moses: Jehovah came to Moses at the burning bush. He told him what to say to Pharaoh; He helped him lead the sons of Israel out of Egypt; and He gave him the ten commandments. But the New Testament says Moses led the Jews out of Egypt - by faith - because he "feared the reproach of the Messiah, looking toward his reward in heaven" (Hebrews 11:26, NASB). In reality Moses dealt with the Spirit of Jesus Christ the Messiah, that is, Jehovah.

David describes a scene in heaven when Jehovah will free those held captive by Satan (Psalm 68:18). Paul applies this prophecy to Jesus (Ephesians 4:7-10).

Isaiah prophesies that Jehovah's glory will be revealed to all flesh, not just to the Jews (Isaiah 40:5). It was the Spirit of Jesus that revealed the Lord of glory to all flesh (1 Corinthians 2:8-10).

That Jesus is Jehovah, the God of the Jews, the God of natural and spiritual Israel, should be clear. But, because the gospel of Jesus Christ has gone out to the whole world, the Hebrew name of God has lost its distinctness. Each language has its own name for God. The name of God, Jehovah, in the English New Testament, is Jesus.

DESCRIPTIVE TITLES OF JEHOVAH APPLIED TO JESUS

Old Testament writers added descriptive nouns to the name Jehovah. The following table presents a few examples. The left column lists the hyphenated name (and translation). The center column indicates where the name is located in the Old Testament. The right column shows where the name is applied to Jesus in the New Testament.

Name	Old Testament	New Testament
Jehovah-elyon (Most High)	Psalm 7:17	Luke 1:32
Jehovah-tsidkenu (Righteous One)	Jeremiah 23:6	1 Corinthians 1:30
Jehovah-kanna (Righteous Zeal)	Isaiah 9:7	John 2:14-17
Jehovah-sabaoth (Lord of Hosts)	Isaiah 1:9	James 5:4-7
Jehovah-jireh (Provider of Salvation)	Genesis 22:14	Hebrews 10:10-12
Jehovah-nissi (Banner or victory)	Exodus 17:15	1 Corinthians 15:57
Jehovah-shalom (Peace)	Judges 6:24	John 14:27

Jehovah-shammah (Ever Present One)	Ezekiel 48:35	Matthew 28:20
Jehovah-kadhash (Sanctifier)	Isaiah 48:17	Titus 2:14
Jehovah - rapha (Healer)	Deuteronomy 32:39	James 5:14, 15
Jehovah - raah (Shepherd)	Psalm 23:1	John 10:11
Jehovah - asah (Our maker)	Psalm 95:6	Philippians 3:21

"I AM" IN THE BOOK OF JOHN

Jesus refers to Himself as "I AM" no less than 23 times in the book of John: 4:26; 6:20, 35, 41, 48, 51; 8:12, 18, 24, 28, 58; 10:7, 9, 11, 14; 11:25; 13:19; 14:6; 15:1, 5; 18:5, 6, 8. From 13 of these 23 references seven categories emerge:

1. I AM the Bread of Life (6:35, 41, 48, 51);
2. I AM the Light of the World (8:12);
3. I AM the Door of the Sheep (10:7, 9);
4. I AM the Good Shepherd (10:11, 14);
5. I AM the Resurrection and the Life (11:25);
6. I AM the Way, the Truth, the Life (14:6);
7. I AM the True Vine (15:1, 5).

The above list covers 13 of the 23 verses in the book of John that refer to Jesus as Jehovah, the great "I AM." The remaining ten verses reveal Jesus as Jehovah when He addresses His listeners:

- When talking to the woman at Jacob's well, Jesus says, "I AM the Messiah" (4:26);
- When the disciples row across the sea of Galilee and a storm begins, Jesus appears walking on the water and says, "I AM, don't be afraid" (6:20 - literal translation from the Greek - Westcott and Hort);

- In His discussion with the Pharisees Jesus says, "I AM and I bear witness of Myself" (8:18 - literal translation from the Greek - Westcott and Hort);
- In another discussion with the Pharisees, Jesus says, "Unless you believe that I AM you shall die in your sins" (8:24, NASB);
- Speaking to the Pharisees about His death and resurrection Jesus says, "When you lift up the Son of Man you will know that I AM" (8:28, NASB);
- Jesus tells the Jews, "Before Abraham was born, I AM" (8:58, NASB);
- Jesus tells the disciples, "Believe that I AM who I say I AM" (13:19, NASB).
- Three times, to identify Himself, Jesus tells the Roman soldiers who He is: "I AM" (18:5,6,8).

The expression "I AM," though in the present tense, is clearly designed to express a past and a future. The words "I AM," by which we express the eternal now, are used by God to denote His continual and unchanging being. Thus in Psalm 90:2 (NASB) we read, "Even from everlasting to everlasting, thou art God." Even from eternity to eternity God is God. "I AM" denotes continued life without respect to time. Hence, Jehovah assumed "I AM" as His name.

While arguing with the Jews, Jesus tells them, "I most solemnly tell you, before Abraham was born, I AM" (John 8:58, Amp). As a Man Jesus was not yet 50 years old (John 8:57) and therefore could not have seen Abraham. Hence, here Jesus refers to another nature, not His human nature but His divine nature. But the Jews didn't recognize what He was saying for they took up stones to kill Him for equating Himself with God.

DEITY 3

FATHER

The notion of God as Father had its origin in the Hebrew scriptures. The concept of God as progenitor is revealed in the creation of the nation of Israel. The covenant relation of God with the nation of Israel took the form of fatherhood (Jehovah) and sonship (Israel).

- Jehovah commanded Moses to go to Pharaoh: "Then shall you say to Pharaoh, 'Thus says the LORD, Israel is My son, My first-born'" (Exodus 4:22, NASB).
- "But you're our living Father, our Redeemer, famous from eternity (Isaiah 63:16, Msg).
- "Yet, O Lord, You are our Father; we are the clay, and You our potter, and we all are the work of Your hand" (Isaiah 64:8, Amp).
- "For I am a Father to Israel..." (Jeremiah 31:9, NASB).
- "I called out, 'My son!' - called him out of Egypt" (Hosea 11:1, Msg).

Though Abraham was the natural, physical father of the nation of Israel, Jehovah made a covenant with Israel and assumed the office of their spiritual Father. Paul points this out in the New Testament. "It wasn't Abraham's sperm that gave identity here, but God's *promise*. Remember how it was put: 'Your family will be defined by Isaac'? That means that Israelite identity was never racially determined by sexual transmission, but it was *God*-determined by promise" (Romans 9:4, Msg).

But Israel proved to be a rebellious nation. Indeed, a large part of the Hebrew Scriptures reveals the difficulty Jehovah had in dealing with His sons and daughters. Much of the Old Testament dwells on Jehovah as Father disciplining His children. Through Isaiah Jehovah said, "Sons I have reared and brought up but they have revolted against Me...They have abandoned the LORD" (Isaiah 1:2,4, NASB). Many times Jehovah upbraids His offspring and reprimands them, saying, "You walked out on the Rock who gave you life, forgot the birth-God who brought you into the world" (Deuteronomy 32:18, Msg).

Yet Jehovah had pity on His children. "For I am a Father to Israel...I will surely have mercy on him" (Jeremiah 31:9,20, NASB). The nation of Israel's rebelliousness did not diminish the Father's love. Jehovah observed His children's rebellious ways, but said, "If they return, I will heal them" (Isaiah 57:18, NASB). "I will heal their apostasy, I will love them freely, for My anger has turned away from them" (Hosea 14:4, NASB). The prophet Micah said, "Who is a Father like thee, who pardons iniquity and passes over the rebellious act of the remnant of his inheritance? He does not retain His anger forever, because He delights in lovingkindness" (Micah 7:18, NASB).

Thus, in the Hebrew Scriptures, Jehovah establishes the idea of spiritual sonship - the relation of son to father - by bringing the nation of Israel into existence - governed by His Spirit from heaven. His purpose was to make the nation of Israel His representative on earth. Jehovah chose the nation of Israel to be His chosen people - His Son.

Jehovah, speaking to Moses, said, "Thus you are to be holy to Me, for I the LORD am holy; and I have set you apart from the [other] peoples to be Mine" (Leviticus 20:26, NASB). "...[Y]ou are a people set apart as holy to God, your God. God, your God, chose you out of all the people on Earth for himself as a cherished, personal, treasure" (Deuteronomy 7:6, Msg). Contrasting His people with other people Jehovah said, "You will become My spokesman in the world. They for their part may turn to you, but as for you, you must not turn to them" (Jeremiah 15:19, NASB).

In the Hebrew Scriptures Jehovah, as Father, invested His chosen children with an elevated rank of spiritual responsibility. The odds were against them, however, and they failed their mission.

FATHER IS SPIRIT

God is Spirit (John 4:24);
The Father is God;
Therefore, the Father is Spirit.

The above syllogism says it all. It reckons the Father is Spirit. That is, God (Spirit) is the Father of His Son, the Man Christ Jesus (Luke 1:35), just as God was the Father of His sons and daughters - the nation of Israel - in the Old Testament.

"FATHER" - NOT A NAME

It is important to keep in mind that the term "Father" is not a name of Deity. "Father" encompasses an aspect of God's nature but it is not His name. This title serves to describe a facet in the make-up of God's infinite character.

The phrase "God the Father" is analogous to the phrase "Jesus the carpenter." "Father" describes an inherent characteristic of God just as "carpenter" identifies the Christ's work as a young man. Thus, the term "Father" is a title, like "king." It provides a descriptive explanation of one of God's distinguishing traits - Creator, for example. The name of God in the Hebrew Scriptures is Jehovah. The name of God in the New Testament is Jesus.

"Name," when used in a spiritual sense, is a term that expresses the *entire* spiritual nature or essence of God. Thus the phrase, "praise His holy name." The name "Jesus" fully identifies God the Father. Jesus revealed God's character, His law, His will, His plan for men, His mercy.

In His final prayer (as a Man) to the Father, the Christ explained, "I spelled out your character in detail to the men and women you gave me" (John 17:6, Msg). He added, "I have made your very being known to them - who you are and what you do..." (John 17:26, Msg).

In other words, Jesus is the only name that makes God known to the world. The name Jesus embraces not only the title "Father" but all that God is. "Father" is a title that limits the definition of God.

Christians are persecuted both emotionally and physically for believing in Jesus. No one is harassed for believing in God or Father or Spirit unless the name Jesus is attached to these titles. Before going to the cross Jesus told His disciples, "And you will be hated by all on account of My name..."(Matthew 10:22, NASB). In another place the Christ said hatred and persecution can be expected from the pagan world: "They will treat you this way because of my name..."(John 15:21, NIV).

Scripture says, "Let every detail in your lives - word, actions, whatever - be done in the name of the Master Jesus..."(Colossians 3:17, Msg). Doing all in the name of Jesus, in word or deed, includes baptism (Acts 19:5), anointing with oil (James 5:14), calling upon His Name (Romans 10:13), bowing the knee (Philippians 2:10), giving thanks (Hebrews 13:15), trusting (Matthew 12:21), praying (John 14:13), experiencing new life (John 20:31) practicing faith (Acts 3:16), suffering shame (Acts 5:41), preaching (Acts 9:28). Doing these things in the "name" of the Father would be inappropriate because the name of God the Father is Jesus.

JESUS AS GOD IS THE FATHER

God is God the Father;
Jesus is God;
Therefore, Jesus is God the Father

The above syllogism determines that Jesus is the Father. If there is only one God and He is the Father, and if Jesus is God, it follows that Jesus is the Father. The prophet Isaiah declared that the Messiah will be called "Eternal Father"(Isaiah 9:6). Colossians 2:9 proclaims that all the fulness of God dwelt in the Man Christ Jesus. Since all the fulness of God includes the role of Father, the Father dwelt in the Son.

Jesus Himself taught that He was the Father. When asked by the Pharisees, "Where is this so-called Father of yours?" Jesus answered, "You're looking right at me and you don't see me. How do you expect to see the Father? If you knew me, you would at the same time know the Father"(John 8:19, Msg). When asked again, "Just who are you any way?" Jesus answered, "What I've said from the start" (John 8:25, Msg). However, "They still didn't get it, didn't realize that he was referring to the Father" (John 8:27, Msg).

Jesus said, "I and the Father are One" (John 10:30). The Pharisees under-stood Him as affirming He was God for they took up stones to kill Him for blasphemy (v.33). The Jews did not grasp the meaning of the Christ's dual nature, that He was the Son in His humanity and the Father in His Deity.

- Jesus prophesied He would resurrect His own body from the dead (John 2:19). Yet Peter preached that God the Father "...untied the death ropes and raised him up" (Acts 2:24, Msg).
- Jesus said the Father would send the Helper (John 14:26). But, in anoth-er place He said He Himself would send the Helper (John 16:7).
- In one place Jesus said the Father "draws people to me" (John 6:44). On another occasion He said, "And I, as I am lifted up from the earth, will attract everyone to me and gather them around me" (John 12:32, Msg).
- Jesus declared, "...I Myself will raise him up..." (John 6:40, NASB). He was referring to the resurrection of the believer. Paul, on the other hand, wrote that God the Father "... honored the Master's body by raising it from the dead. He'll treat yours with the same resurrection power" (1 Corinthians 6:14, Msg).
- Regarding prayer Jesus said, "From now on, whatever you request...I'll do it" (John 14:14, Msg). Yet, in another place He said, "ask the Father for whatever is in keeping with the things I've revealed to you. Ask in my name, according to my will, and he'll most certainly give it to you" (John 16:23, Msg).

The above scriptural comparisons show that Jesus, in His Deity, is the Father. Jesus and the Father say the same thing and perform the same func-tion. Both terms, Jesus and Father, relate to God.

Here there is need for discrimination, however. The apparent incongruity of Jesus being the Father (as well as the Son and the Spirit) is discerned if it is understood that Jesus is a name while Father, Son, and Holy Spirit are titles or descriptive designations of dignity, honor, distinction or preeminence. A name, in biblical terminology, constitutes every distinctive designation of God. That is, the name Jesus portrays all that God is. A title, on the other hand, serves to explain a particular aspect of God's nature. God has only one name (Jesus in English, Jehovah in Hebrew) yet He has an infinite number of titles.

FATHER (DEITY) AND SON (HUMANITY)

Both Father and Son are titles that refer to Jesus Christ. One title (Father) expresses Jesus' Deity and the other title (Son) expresses the Christ's humanity. The two titles do not relate to the same Being. Father never alludes to humanity and Son never alludes to Deity. (The title *Son of God*, however, is sometimes used to refer to Jesus Christ's dual nature; however, "God the Son" is a misnomer and nowhere found in Scripture and should never be used to describe Deity.)

While Jesus Christ is both Father and Son it cannot be said the Father *is* the Son. Correct terminology would describe the Father *dwelling* in the Son (Colossians 2:9). When the Christ, speaking as Man, says, "I and the Father are One" (John 10:30, NIV) He expresses a union of humanity and Deity.

Scripture reveals the relationship of Father and Son. The Christ's own words describe His kinship with God. Speaking as Man the Messiah says, "The Son [humanity] can't independently do a thing, only what he sees the Father [Deity] doing" (John 5:19, Msg; see also John 5:30 and 8:28). To this He adds "...the Father is greater and mightier than I am" (John 14:28, Amp). In speaking of His second coming, the Christ says, "But the exact day and hour? No one knows that, not even heaven's angels, not even the Son. Only the Father" (Mark 13:32, Msg). Paul states that God the Father is head of Christ the Man (1 Corinthians 11:3).

When the New Testament speaks of the Father "sending" the Son into the world it is an allegorical statement meaning that it has a hidden spiritual meaning that transcends the literal sense of the text. "Sending" connotes a symbolic representation of God the Father entering time and space. Deity does not send humanity from heaven for humanity (flesh and blood) does not exist in heaven. On the contrary, God Himself came to earth and clothed Himself in a body, the body of His Son, to manifest His love and to fulfill His plan to save the world from sin.

Why did the Father "send" the Son? To be the Savior of the world - which only a sinless Man could do. God came to earth and dwelt in His Son to manifest His glory and to reveal His grace and to show His love for His creation: "God didn't go to all the trouble of sending His Son merely to point an accusing finger, telling the world how bad it was. He came to help, to put the world right again" (John 3:17, Msg).

The plan of salvation did not originate with the Son (humanity) but with the Father (Deity). In John 6:38 (Msg), Jesus, speaking as both God and Man, says, "I [God] came down from heaven not to follow my [humanity's] own whim but to accomplish the will of the One who sent me." The Son did not come into the world of His own will, humanity's will, but He came to earth from the heart of the Father through the virgin birth; i.e., God inseminated the womb of a virgin woman and dwelt in the Son that was produced. Additional verses revealing the Son being sent from the heart of the Father are John 7:28; 8:42; 16:28.

Jesus, speaking as Man, says, "What I teach comes from the One who sent [begot] me" (John 7:16, Msg). Christ the Man does not speak for Himself but for God.

Provoked by the crowd, the Christ says, "Yes, you think you know me and where I'm from [the son of Mary]. [But] I didn't set myself up in business. My true origin is in the One who sent [begot] me..." (John 7:29, Msg). The Son's origin was in heaven in the sense that He came from the Father's heart to be the sinless, human Savior of the world.

In John 8:50 and 7:14 the Son does not seek His own glory but the glory of the Father. In John 12:49, 50 and 15:10 the Christ says His commandments do not come from Himself but from His Father.

Viewing the above verses as distinguishing between the divinity of Jesus (Father) and the Christ's humanity (Son) provides an insight into His two natures. Understanding Jesus Christ's two natures also makes clear the reason the Son is subordinate to the Father. By definition God the Father is omnipotent, omniscient, eternal, and omnipresent. The Son was limited by His humanity and death. The reason the Father assumed a body of flesh and blood (1 Timothy 3:16) was to unveil His heart of grace and mercy in Jesus Christ.

DEITY IS THE HOLY SPIRIT OF JESUS

It is Jesus' Holy Spirit (God) emanating from heaven that moves the sinner to faith, the faith which accepts what has been done for him by the Christ. That is, God, Jesus Christ's divine nature, justifies, sanctifies, and saves by faith. Faith can only come as the result of Jesus' Holy Spirit working on the sinner's heart. Had the Christ not suffered and given His life on the cross God would not have poured out His Holy Spirit. Had the Christ not sacrificed His life the world would not have known the active presence of His divine nature.

God is purely a spiritual Being. And He is Holy. The Holy Spirit is another title for God - like God the Father. Indeed, all three terms, Holy Spirit, God, and God the Father refer to the Son of God's divine nature. God is Holy (1 Peter 1:16) and God is Spirit (John 4:24). And because there is one God, His Spirit is Holy (1 Corinthians 12:11; Ephesians 4:4). Consequently, Holy Spirit is another term to describe God, the one Father in heaven whose Son's resurrected soul sits at His right hand interceding on our behalf.

FATHER AS PROGENITOR

The notion of father implies generation or bringing children into existence. Without the idea of bringing someone into being the word father has no meaning. It signifies nothing. Without a son or daughter the concept of father is voided. Without offspring a man is not a father.

So, when the prophets of the Hebrew Scriptures divinely conceived the title "Father" and applied it to Jehovah it meant God *had* to have children. Jehovah first assumed the role of Father in the Old Testament, in the second book of the Old Testament, the book of Exodus. Speaking to Moses, Jehovah said, "Then you are to tell Pharaoh, 'God's Message: Israel is my son, my first-born!'" (Exodus 4:22, Msg).

By creating the nation of Israel, Jehovah (re)entered the world's atmosphere and began to influence the affairs of men. He gave Moses His law.

However, Jehovah knew His law would not fulfill His will with respect to human conduct. Though the law included all the divine commands necessary to regulate a man's moral behavior - and it revealed sin - it made no provision to reconcile the sinner to Himself. Reconciliation to God was not included in the law.

But when the time arrived that was set by God the Father, God sent his Son, born among us of a woman, born under the conditions of the law so that he might redeem those of us who have been kidnapped by the law. Thus we have been set free to experience our rightful heritage. You can tell for sure that you are now fully adopted as his own children because God sent the [Holy] Spirit of his Son into our lives...And if you are a child, you're also an heir, with complete access to the inheritance (Galatians 4:4-7, Msg).

In other words, God Himself, through the graceful provision of the virgin birth, came to earth to fulfill His plan of reconciliation (redemption), personifying Himself in His Son, the Man Christ Jesus.

In the New Testament the notion of "Father" as religious progenitor has two variations - one physical and one spiritual. The physical variation regards God as the literal Father of the Son (Luke 1:35). The spiritual variation relates to the kinship of God and new-born believers who become, by adoption, sons and daughters of God. By faith in His Son, God sovereignly brings new believers into His spiritual fold.

The physical variation of the Father as progenitor involves the actual, natural act of reproduction (the virgin birth) while the spiritual variation includes a process of supernatural reproduction (the born-again experience). Yet, both variations are significant to those seeking to know God. Moreover, the same thing applies to God's chosen people in the New Testament as it did in the Old Testament. That is, God invests His offspring with a new rank of responsibility.

DEITY 4

JEHOVAH: GOD -SPIRIT -FATHER

Of these four terms only Jehovah is a name. The other three are not names. Yet, all four refer to one Being.

"God" is a popular, easy to understand term used by Christians, non-Christians, and atheists alike to describe their concept of divinity. "Spirit" is accepted by Christians as a title to describe divinity as an animating or vital principle held to give new-life strictly to human beings; that is, "Spirit" implies an activating influence to bring about change or conversion from worldliness to godliness. The term "Father," in Christian parlance, implies an actual spiritual begetting (adoption) by God of the one converted. All three terms describe one Being, God the Father who is Spirit, whose name is Jehovah.

"Father," as a personal reference to Jehovah, was not widely used in the Old Testament. Isaiah gave us the most prominent example when he prophesied of the coming Messiah. "For a child has been born - for us! The gift of a son - for us!" ...and He shall be called, "Eternal Father" (Isaiah 9:6, Msg).

"Spirit," or God's breath, also, was not widely used in the Hebrew scriptures because it had not yet been poured out. The prophet Joel gave us the most prominent example. "I will pour out my Spirit on every kind of people" (Joel 2:28, Msg). (Here, Jehovah promises to pour out His breath - translated as Spirit - indicating that Jehovah's breath comes from Himself and is not apart from Himself.)

There are other verses in the Hebrew Scriptures calling attention to the reality that Jehovah will, in the future, pour out His breath upon His people and revitalize them just as His breath gave life to Adam.

- King Solomon, in the first Proverb, wrote, "Behold, I will pour out my spirit on you" (Proverbs 1:23, NASB). Spirit, here, is the spirit of God's wisdom.
- Quoting Jehovah, Isaiah wrote, "I will pour my Spirit into your descendants, and my blessing on your children" (Isaiah 44:3, Msg).

Zechariah prophesies of the outpouring of Jehovah's breath on the house of David on the day that Jehovah destroys "...all the nations that come against Jerusalem" (Zechariah 12:9, NASB). The time frame is the culmination of the present age - the final judgment. After all is said and done Jehovah comes once again to earth to wrap things up, to complete His grand purposes for and through Israel.

And I will pour out on the house of David and on the inhabitants of Jerusalem, the [My] Spirit of grace and of supplication, so that they will look upon Me whom they have pierced; and they will mourn for Him, as one mourns for an only son, and they will weep bitterly over Him, like the bitter weeping over a first-born (Zechariah 12:10, NASB).

This prophecy deserves more attention. We know from John 19:37 that "Me whom they have pierced" refers to the Christ. Yet, note the two pronouns "Me" and "Him." The use of the two pronouns is appropriate. Both pronouns apply to the Son of God who was both Man and Jehovah. The pronoun "Him" means that Jehovah Himself was "pierced" when His Son was crucified. (See Revelation 1:7.)

RUACH

Ruach is a Hebrew word meaning "breath." In the Hebrew Scriptures it literally means the breath of Jehovah. Idiomatically *ruach* is related to "will" and "feeling" - from which comes the translation "spirit." Sometimes it can also mean "thought" or "purpose." (Cf Job 4:9, 9:18; Psalm 18:15, 146:4; Ezekiel 37:5-10).

Speaking to Job, Elihu said, "The Spirit of God made me what I am, the breath of God Almighty gave me life" (Job 33:4, Msg). Both "Spirit" and "breath" are translated from the Hebrew *ruach*. No doubt Elihu had the creation of Adam in mind: "God formed man out of dirt from the ground and blew into his nostrils the breath of life. The man came alive - a living soul" (Genesis 2:7, Msg). Jehovah's breath, emanating from Himself, gave life to Adam.

That Jehovah's breath is Jehovah's Spirit, unseparated from His Being, is made evident when Jehovah sets Ezekiel down in the middle of the Valley of Dry Bones and taught him a lesson.

God grabbed me. God's Spirit took me up and set me down in the middle of an open plain strewn with bones. He led me around and among them - a lot of bones! There were bones all over the plain - dry bones, bleached by the sun.

He said to me, "Son of man, can these bones live?"

I said, "Master God, only you know that."

He said to me, "Prophesy over these bones: 'Dry bones, listen to the Message of God!'"

God, the Master, told the dry bones, "Watch this: I'm bringing the breath of life to you and you'll come to life. I'll attach sinews to you, put meat on your bones, cover you with skin, and breathe life into you. You'll come alive and you'll realize that I am God!"

I prophesied just as I'd been commanded. As I prophesied, there was a sound and, oh, rustling! The bones moved and came together, bone to bone. I kept watching. Sinews formed, then muscles on the bones, then skin stretched over them. But they had no breath in them.

He said to me, "Prophesy to the breath. Prophesy, son of man. Tell the breath, 'God, the Master, says, Come from the four winds. Come, breath. Breathe on these slain bodies. Breathe life!'"

So I prophesied, just as he commanded me. The breath entered them and they came alive! They stood up on their feet, a huge army (Ezekiel 37:1-10, Msg).

Here, God's breath created a grand army, just as at the creation He produced life from a clod of dirt. Indeed, just as He poured out His breath at Pentecost and created an army of believers.

GOD AND SPIRIT

In this section "Spirit" is understood to mean "Holy Spirit." There is no qualifying difference between the two terms. (God's) Spirit is Holy.

God is omnipresent. Because He is Spirit He is present in all places at all times. When God's Spirit impregnated the womb of the virgin Mary and all the fulness of God took up residence in the child that was born - who then grew up to be the Man Christ Jesus - God's omnipresence was not negated. All the fulness of God's Spirit dwelt in Christ Jesus as well as in heaven. Because He is omnipresent God is able to be God on earth as well as in heaven - simultaneously. The magnitude of God's omnipresence by His Spirit is important to recognize. It cannot be limited by human experience.

The titles "God" and "Spirit" refer to one Being. His name is Jehovah in the Old Testament and Jesus in the New Testament. Peter knew this. When those who believed were of one heart and soul and donated all their possessions as communal property and Ananias sold a piece of property but held back some of the price for himself Peter confronted him and said, "Ananias, how did Satan get you to lie to the Holy Spirit...?" (Acts 5:3, Msg). Then Peter continued to challenge Ananias, saying, "You didn't lie to men but to God" (Acts 5:4, Msg). In verse three Peter said Ananias lied to the Holy Spirit and in verse four he said Ananias lied to God. Yet, both verses refer to one person of God, not two persons of God.

"You realize, don't you, that you are the temple of God, and God himself is present in you?" (1 Corinthians 3:16, Msg). "Or didn't you realize that your body is a sacred place, a place of the Holy Spirit?" (1 Corinthians 6:19, Msg). Again, these two references to God and Holy Spirit apply to the same Being, not two persons of God.

Peter said the prophets of the Old Testament spoke from *God* and were moved by His *Holy Spirit* (2 Peter 1:21, emphasis added). This verse does not refer to two deities.

In reality, when God refers to His (Holy) Spirit, He refers to Himself. His

Spirit reflects His mode of action, His arm of expression. His Spirit manifests His power. God said, "Not by might, nor by power, but by my Spirit" (Zechariah 4:6, Amp), meaning that God gets things done by His Spirit. That's how He operates. His Spirit asserts His style of dealing with things, situations, and people. In short, "Spirit" is another word to describe the one God of Israel (Deuteronomy 6:4).

- "The Spirit of God was hovering over the waters" (Genesis 1:2, NIV). There were not two gods hovering over the waters.
- Speaking of the corruption of men, Jehovah said, "My Spirit will not contend with man forever..." (Genesis 6:3, NIV). By this Jehovah meant that He Himself would not contend with man forever.
- David, asking Jehovah for forgiveness for his sin with Bathsheba, prayed, "Do not take Thy Holy Spirit from me" (Psalm 51:11, NASB). Actually, David prayed that Jehovah Himself not leave him because of his sin.
- Prophesying of Pentecost, Jehovah said, regarding His people, "I'll put my Spirit in you..." (Ezekiel 36:27). By this Jehovah meant that He Himself would come to live in the hearts of His people.

Why did God choose to represent Himself to us as "Spirit"? Why does He describe Himself as "Spirit"? From the beginning He had a plan - that our spirits should be in contact with and devoted to His Spirit.

It's who you are and the way you live that count before God. Your worship must engage your spirit in the pursuit of truth. That's the kind of people the Father is out looking for: those who are simply and honestly *themselves* before him in their worship. God is sheer being itself - Spirit. Those who worship him must do it out of their very being, their spirits, their true selves, in adoration (John 4:23,24, Msg).

Spirit to spirit is God's plan for His people - our spirit in touch with His Spirit, meaning He does not look favorably on rites and ceremonies and pomp of external worship. Our worship, in God's plan, must come from the soul - the mind and heart. Entrance into God's heart comes to us from the simple offering of gratitude, prayer, and supplication with a desire to glorify Him - not through the external forms of religion but from a contrite spirit.

The word "Spirit" implies that God works invisibly in the hearts of men. Spirit describes God's subtle work in action. Spirit renders the idea of the ubiquitous workings of Deity.

God and Spirit are two terms - not names - that figuratively represent the same Being. God is a perfect Being, all powerful, all knowing, and full of never ending goodness and grace whom men worship as Creator and Ruler of the universe. Spirit is an aspect of an infinite God who is an omnipresent, immaterial, animating, vital principle operating in the world, giving life to dying men.

FATHER AND SPIRIT

In this section "Father" is understood to mean "Spirit." The only qualifying difference between the two terms lies in the meaning the two attributes convey. "Father" conveys the idea of Creator. "Spirit" conveys the idea of Operator (Operations Manager). (These are only two of God's infinite number of roles.) In the final analysis, however, God (the Father) is Spirit.

Jesus told Nicodemus, "This is how much God loved the world: He gave his Son, His one and only Son" (John 3:16, Msg). Besides the beauty contained in this verse it holds a practical message as well - God is the Father of His Son.

Yet, other verses of Scripture say the Holy Spirit conceived the Son of God. Matthew says Mary was pregnant by the Holy Spirit (Matthew 1:18). Luke, quoting the angel Gabriel, says, the Holy Spirit will come upon Mary (Luke 1:35).

Is there an apparent contradiction? Was the Son fathered by two persons of god? No. That would be preposterous. Both titles refer to one Being - God the Father who is Spirit.

"Father" and "Spirit" are two descriptive titles that God assigns Himself to make Deity understood to the finite mind. The two terms refer to the same Being but each lays stress on a different aspect (role or function) that God possesses. Each term provides a one word description of how God manifests Himself to help men understand His nature. The following scriptural comparisons reveal that there is no distinction in kind or quality between the terms, that "Father" and "Spirit" constitute two components of one Being who has an infinite number of components.

- Who raised the Man Christ Jesus from the dead? If one imagines "Father" and "Spirit" being two persons (rather than two manifestations) one would be disoriented. Galatians 1:1 says the Father raised the Christ while Romans 8:11 says the Spirit of God raised Him.
- Compare John 5:21 with John 6:63. Jesus is speaking in both verses. In one verse He says the Father raises the dead while in the other verse He says the Spirit gives life.
- We are adopted into God's family by the Spirit (Romans 8:15,16), which makes the Spirit our Father.
- In John 14:17 Jesus says the Spirit abides in believers. Yet in the same chapter He says the Son as well as the Father will make their abode in the believer (John 14:23). Indeed, the Spirit of the Father and the Spirit of the Son ("Spirit" spelled with a capital "S") are the same Spirit dwelling in the believer. ("Spirit of the Son" is a reference to Jesus' divine nature.)
- We are sanctified by the Father and by the Spirit. (1 Peter 1:2 with Jude 1.) This does not mean we are sanctified twice by two persons. We are sanctified once by God the Father who is Spirit.
- Times of persecution, both mental and physical persecution, will come upon believers. Who will speak for us when we are afflicted? Jesus says, "...the Spirit of your Father will supply the words" (Matthew 10:20, Msg). This verse indicates that there is no way that "Spirit" and "Father" can be divided into two persons.

Spiritually speaking there is no distinction between the terms "Father" and "Spirit." That is, in heaven there is no distinction. On earth, in His Word, God assumes different distinguishing characteristics so we can know Him.

On earth, to make Himself understood, God has revealed Himself in a number of identifications. He made Himself known as "Father" and all that the word Father implies - Creator, Begetter, Counselor, etc. He made Himself known as "Spirit" and all it implies - Invisible, Immaterial, Omnipresent, Activating, etc. In addition there are an endless number of titles and attributes that characterize God - expressions such as Rock, Steadfast, High Tower, Eternal, Infinite, Shepherd, All-powerful, Good, Preeminent, Love, etc., etc., etc.

If all the words describing God, if "Father," "Spirit," and all the other roles and functions and actions of God "...were all written down, each of them, one by one, I can't imagine a world big enough to hold such a library of books" (John 21:25, Msg). His Word is inexhaustible. The only Word - or Person - that adequately brings all the manifest details of God together is Jesus.

JESUS AND SPIRIT

In this section "Jesus" is understood to mean "Spirit" - keeping in mind "Spirit" is understood to mean "Holy Spirit." That is, "Spirit" spelled with a capital "S" signifies Jesus' divine nature. "Spirit" identifies Jesus as God - who is Spirit (John 4:24), whose Spirit is Holy.

While imprisoned Paul called upon the Spirit that dwelt in the Christ to enable him to bear his trials. Writing to the saints in Philippi, Paul said, "Through your faithful prayers and the generous response of the Spirit of Jesus Christ, everything he wants to do in and through me will be done" (Philippians 1:19, Msg). "The Spirit of Jesus Christ" is God.

In another place Paul wrote, "The Lord is the Spirit, and where the Spirit of the Lord is, there is liberty" (2 Corinthians 3:17, NASB). Jesus is the Lord whose Spirit (God) sets us free from condemnation.

"You can tell for sure that you are now fully adopted as his own children because God sent the Spirit of his Son into our lives..." (Galatians 4:6, Msg). The Spirit of God's Son - The Spirit that dwelt in the Christ - is the Holy Spirit of God Himself.

Peter wrote that the Spirit of the Christ inspired the Old Testament prophets: "They sought to find out to whom or when this [salvation] was to come which the Spirit of Christ working within them indicated when He predicted the sufferings of Christ and the glories that should follow" (1 Peter 1:11, Amp). Here, Peter indicates that the prophets themselves did not understand the full implication of the amazing words which the Spirit of the Christ (God) had dictated.

Yet, in another verse, Peter said the Holy Spirit inspired the prophets of the Old Testament. "For prophecy never had its origin in the will of man, but spoke from God as they were carried along by the Holy Spirit" (2 Peter 1:21, NIV). Thus, according to 1 Peter 1:11 and 2 Peter 1:21, the Spirit of the Christ is the Holy Spirit.

> The prophets who told us this [salvation] was coming asked a lot of questions about this gift of life God was preparing. The Messiah's Spirit let them in on some of it - that the Messiah would experience suffering, followed by glory. They clamored to know who and when. All they were told was that they were serving you, you who by orders from heaven have now heard for yourselves - through the Holy Spirit - the Message of those prophecies fulfilled. Do you realize how fortunate you are? Angels would have given anything to be in on this!" (1 Peter 1:10-12, Msg).

In these verses Peter reveals there is no difference between the "Messiah's Spirit" and the "Holy Spirit." One Spirit inspired and prompted the prophecies of the Hebrew Scriptures to serve us, and, in the New Testament, the same Spirit revealed these truths to God's people. There was not one Spirit operating in the Old Testament and another Spirit operating in the New Testament.

Jesus said, "...everyone who beholds the Son and believes in Him, may have eternal life; and I Myself will raise him up on the last day" (John 6:40, NASB). Jesus, speaking as God, made it clear He would resurrect the believer. Yet, Paul said the Spirit raises the dead. "And if the Spirit of him who raised Jesus from the dead is living in you, he who raised Christ from the dead will also give life to your mortal bodies" (Romans 8:11, NIV).

Because Scripture is infallible there is no contradiction between John 6:40 and Romans 8:11. Both verses are correct. The Spirit of the Christ and the Holy Spirit are two different expressions describing the same Spirit.

Moreover, Paul equates the (Holy) Spirit of God with the (Holy) Spirit of the Christ in another verse. "You, however, are controlled not by the sinful nature but by the Spirit, if the *Spirit of God* lives in you. And if anyone does not have the *Spirit of Christ*, he does not belong to Christ" (Romans 8:9, NIV, emphasis added).

Jesus told His disciples, "I will not leave you orphaned. I'm coming back" (John 14:18, Msg). (He came back in the form of His Holy Spirit.)

Then, a few verses later, He said, "I'm telling you these things while I'm still living with you. The Friend, the Holy Spirit whom the Father will send at my request, will make everything plain to you" (John 14:26, Msg). At Pentecost God sent His Spirit, The Spirit of His Son, the Christ's divine nature, back to comfort the disciples.

Indeed, Jesus *did* come back. But not in the flesh. His Holy Spirit (God) came back at Pentecost. The resurrected Son (humanity) asked the Father (Deity) to send back His Spirit. And the Father did it.

After His resurrection and before His ascension Jesus promised his disciples, "I'll be with you...right up to the end of the age" (Matthew 28:20, Msg). Of course, Jesus was referring to His Spirit being with the disciples.

"Christ is in you" (Colossians 1:27). Yet, Scripture abounds with verses declaring the believer to be filled with the Holy Spirit. Thus, it can be adduced that the Holy Spirit of the Christ is the Holy Spirit in you.

Here are some appropriate scriptural comparisons to support the fact that the Spirit of Jesus is the Holy Spirit of God.

- Paul prays that the church in Ephesus might be strengthened in the inner man by the (Holy) Spirit; and, may the Christ through your faith make His permanent home in your hearts (Ephesians 3:16 with Ephesians 3:17).
- The Christ sanctifies His church and His Spirit sanctifies His church (Ephesians 5:26 with 1 Peter 1:2).
- The promised *paracletos* is the Holy Spirit of Jesus Christ (John 14:26 with 1 John 2:1).
- There is one intercessor, the Spirit of Jesus (Romans 8:26 with Hebrews 7:25).
- In times of persecution the Holy Spirit of Jesus tells us what to say (Mark 13:11 with Luke 21:15).
- The Holy Spirit of Jesus prevents Paul from presenting the gospel in certain parts of Asia (Acts 16:6,7).

In short, Jesus Christ's divine nature is the Holy Spirit of God. That's why He is called God. But He was also born a Man.

The Christ told His disciples He had to go away (John 14:28). That is, as a Man He had to go away. If not, His Holy Spirit, God, could not come to them. "However, I am telling you nothing but the truth when I say, it is profitable...for you that I go away. Because if I do not go away, the Comforter (Counselor, Helper, Advocate, Intercessor, Strengthener, Standby) will not come to you...But if [when] I go away, I will send Him to you..."(John 16:7, Amp).

"Him" signifies His own Spirit, God, the Spirit that resided in Christ the Man. Because the dual nature of Jesus Christ means He is both Man (humanity) and God (Spirit) there is no other Spirit than Jesus' Spirit to send back. Indeed, it is unclear reasoning to conclude that Jesus (as God who is Spirit) might send back another Spirit.

Why couldn't Jesus send back His Spirit to minister to His disciples until He had departed? Because as long as the Christ was with the disciples - in the flesh - He could not be present with them by His Spirit. Jesus embodied the Holy Spirit of God. He could not guide them by His Spirit. Instead He guided them by His words and miracles. While on earth the Christ kept His all-powerful Spirit temporarily inactive.

While on earth God - Jesus' indwelling Spirit - governed everything the Christ did. God's Spirit governed the Christ alone - not the disciples. The disciples were still governed by the law. All the power of God's Spirit was at the Christ's disposal when He walked the earth but He kept it in abeyance - in accordance with God's instructions - to fulfill - as a Man - God's plan of redemption and reconciliation. But when He departed He was free to send back His Spirit to lead all His disciples to heaven.

DEITY 5

DIVINE COVENANTS

In the Hebrew Scriptures Jehovah dealt directly with His people by covenants. Jehovah's first covenant was with Noah. Because of rampant sin Jehovah told Noah, "Behold, I, even I am bringing the flood of water upon the earth, to destroy all flesh in which is the breath of life, from under heaven; everything that is on the earth shall perish. But I will establish My covenant with you; and you shall enter the ark - you and your sons and your wife and your sons' wives with you" (Genesis 6:17,18, NASB). Then Jehovah did what He said He was going to do.

Jehovah next covenanted with Abram. He promised to give Abram's descendants all of the Holy land, "...from the Nile River in Egypt to the River Euphrates in Assyria..."(Genesis 15:18, Msg).

Then, to confirm His covenant with Abram (who had now become Abraham, Genesis 17:5), Jehovah promised him a son. "...Sarah your wife shall bear you a son, and you shall call his name Isaac; and I will establish My covenant with him for an everlasting covenant for his descendants after him"(Genesis 17:19, NASB).

To further confirm His covenant with Abraham and Isaac, Jehovah covenanted with Jacob, Isaac's son, saying:

I am the LORD, the God of your father Abraham and the God of Isaac; the land on which you lie, I will give it to you and to your descendants.

Your descendants shall also be like the dust of the earth, and you shall spread out to the west and to the east and to the north and to the south; and in you and in your descendants shall all the families of the earth be blessed (Genesis 28:13,14, NASB).

These were verbal covenants Jehovah made with His people. The first blood covenant in the Hebrew Scriptures was made with Abraham. Abraham's own blood had to be shed. Jehovah ordained him to be circumcised, a form of blood ceremony, as a token of the covenant between him and Jehovah (Genesis 17:11).

The second blood covenant was made through Moses. In the Mosaic covenant the blood of an animal had to be shed. In the Mosaic sacrificial system, according to the command of Jehovah, the function of Moses' intercession was to establish the covenant relation between Israel and Jehovah - in blood (Exodus 24:8). Animal (blood) sacrifice represented the life of the worshiper to Jehovah.

Finally, through the prophet Nathan and with reference to all Jews, natural as well as spiritual, Jehovah made a non-blood covenant with David, a prophetic and everlasting covenant based on the blood of Jesus Christ.

And it shall come about when your days are fulfilled that you must go *to be* with your fathers, that I will set up *one* of your descendants after you, who shall be of your sons; and I will establish his kingdom. He shall build for Me a house, and I will establish his throne forever. I will be his father, and he shall be my son; and I will not take My lovingkindness away from him...But I will settle him in My house and in My kingdom forever, and his throne shall be established forever. According to these words and according to this vision, so Nathan spoke to David (1 Chronicles 17:11-15, NASB).

Moreover, confirmation of Nathan's prophecy, a new and final spiritual covenant based on faith, is found in the prophecies of Jeremiah and Ezekiel.

Behold the days are coming, declares the LORD, when I will make a new covenant with the house of Israel and with the house of Judah, not like the covenant which I made with their fathers in the day I took them by the hand to bring them out of the land of Egypt, My covenant which they broke, although I was a husband to them, declares the LORD. But this is the covenant which I will make with the house of Israel after those days, declares the LORD: I will put My law within them, and on their heart I will write it; and I will be their God, and they shall be My people (Jeremiah 31:31-33, NASB; see also Jeremiah 32:40 and Ezekiel 37:26).

"The house of Israel" includes both natural Jews and spiritual Jews (Christians) of the Messianic age. In the new covenant God places His law on the heart of His people by the influences of His Spirit, made possible by "the blood of His cross" (Colossians 1:20).

In the Hebrew Scriptures Jehovah dealt directly with His people through covenants. Rarely in the Old Testament did He work among His people by His Spirit. When His Spirit was dispensed it was upon a particular individual; it was transient; and, it was for a special purpose.

For example, Jehovah's Spirit descended on war heroes such as Othniel, Gideon, Jephthah, Samson, Saul, David, etc., (Judges 3:10; 6:34; 11:29; 13:25; 1 Samuel 10:6; 16:13). His Spirit flowed through prophets with incredible divine revelations (Numbers 24:2; 2 Chronicles 15:1; 24:20; Isaiah 48:16; Ezekiel 37:1). And gifted artisans like Bezalel and Aholiab were anointed by Jehovah's Spirit to perform their work (Exodus 31:2-10). But that is the extent to which Jehovah worked in His people in the Old Testament by the influences of His Spirit.

JEHOVAH'S SPIRIT BEGINS TO MOVE

King David was an exception. He experienced the influence of Jehovah's Spirit working in His heart and recorded His experience in the book of Psalms. When the prophet Nathan reminded him of his sin with Bathsheba and his virtual murder of her husband, Jehovah's Spirit convicted David and he repented from his heart. He acknowledged that he had sinned against Jehovah.

Two Psalms are associated with David's double crime against Jehovah. Psalm 51 tells of his confession and Psalm 32 praises Jehovah for forgiveness.

Confession, of course, implies a spiritual change - repentance. Penitence alone (remorse or regret) does not indicate a spiritual change. David repented and he was forgiven.

In Psalm 51 David begins by recognizing that his transgressions will *ever* be before him (v.3). Then comes a guilty plea in which he invokes Jehovah: "Do not cast me away from thy presence, and do not take thy Holy Spirit from me"(v.11, NASB). Here, David makes no distinction between Jehovah and His Spirit. In David's mind Jehovah's Spirit is Jehovah Himself working in his heart.

David closes Psalm 51 with the biblical truth that Jehovah "...does not delight in [animal] sacrifice, otherwise I would give it; Thou art not pleased with burnt offering. The sacrifices of God are a broken spirit; a broken and contrite heart, O God, Thou wilt not despise" (vss.16,17, NASB). Psalm 51 makes clear that David's repentance came from the prompts of Jehovah's Spirit and not from a sense of duty, i.e., animal sacrifice.

The Spirit that prompted David to pour out his heart and confess his sin against Jehovah is expressed in the opening words of Psalm 32. In this psalm David voiced the liberating experience of confession and being forgiven through confession. By the influence of Jehovah's Spirit David recognized that sin cannot be hidden. Secret sin on earth is open scandal in heaven.

> How blessed is he whose transgression is forgiven, whose sin is covered. How blessed is the man to whom the LORD does not impute iniquity, and in whose spirit there is no deceit. When I kept silent about my sin, my body wasted away through my groaning all day long. For day and night Thy hand was heavy upon me [the image of a hand portrays Jehovah's Spirit]; my vitality was drained away as with the fever heat of summer. I acknowledged my sin to Thee, and my iniquity I did not hide; I said, 'I will confess my transgressions to the LORD'; and Thou didst forgive the guilt of my sin (vss. 1-5, NASB).

Only the Spirit of God can effectively convict the human soul of sin. The sin problem belongs to the spiritual sphere. Without the Spirit of God in the world men are subject only to the fancies of their conscience. And conscience is easily compromised. Animal sacrifice, remorse, or penitence calms the conscience only temporarily. The Spirit of God is the sweet, still, small voice of God Himself convicting the sinner of sin (see 1 Kings 19:11-13).

With King David Jehovah's Spirit began to be recognized as an influence that moves in the heart. The transition from a covenant making God to a gracious God working through the subtle authority of His Spirit began with King David, one thousand years before God's Son was born. With King David Jehovah began to operate as a spiritual influence rather than by direct command of a covenant.

Indeed, when God's Spirit began to move during David's reign it was a turning point in the nation of Israel's history. Following David's kingship the prophets of Israel began to prophesy of Jehovah operating in individual hearts by His Spirit rather than dealing with the nation of Israel as a body. Joel (850 B.C.) was the first prophet after David to predict what will happen in the future regarding the operation of Jehovah's Spirit.

Joel's prophecy, according to Peter's words in Acts 2:16, was a clear pronouncement of Jehovah's plan. "And it will come about after this that I will pour out My Spirit on all mankind" (Joel 2:28, NASB). "On all mankind" means Jehovah will pour out His Spirit on the entire world to fulfill His plan of redemption *by the influence of His omnipresent Spirit.* In the Old Testament Jehovah's Spirit had not yet been poured out. Jehovah was still dealing with Israel through mandated covenants, the law for instance.

Isaiah (750 B.C.) also predicted the coming of Jehovah's Spirit to a desolate world. "Yes, weep and grieve until the Spirit is poured down on us from above..."(Isaiah 32:15, Msg). Here, Isaiah prophesied of the Messianic age - after the Christ's death and resurrection.

Through the prophet Haggai (520 B.C.) Jehovah said, "In a little while I will once more shake the heavens and the earth..." (Haggai 2:6, NIV). This refers to the second "shaking" of the world - the outpouring of Jehovah Himself - the Messiah. The first shaking occurred on Mount Sinai when Jehovah gave (poured out) His commandments to Moses.

The context of Haggai's message was the rebuilding of the temple in Jerusalem by the exiles that returned from Babylon. Haggai encouraged the builders and prophesied that the temple should be made ready for the Messiah's advent. "This Temple is going to end up far better than it started out, a glorious beginning but an even more glorious finish: a place in which I will hand out wholeness and holiness" (Haggai 2:9, Msg). Here, Haggai prophesied that God's Spirit will build His Church on the foundation of Jesus Christ and its glory will surpass the glory of the temple in Jerusalem. (See Hebrews 12:26.)

Zechariah, contemporary with Haggai, also prophesied and preached to the returning exiles from Babylon. His message was the same as Haggai's: Encouragement to the builders of the temple with its broader application of building the Messiah's Church by Jehovah's Spirit. Zechariah prophesied that Jehovah's Church will be built by divine animation and given spiritual life, "Not by might nor by power, but by my Spirit, says the LORD Almighty" (Zechariah 4:6, NIV).

With David Jehovah's Spirit began to move. The reign of David marks the beginning of the change from Jehovah working through covenants to the refined persuasion of Jehovah's Spirit. Joel, after David, prophesied of the dissemination of Jehovah's Spirit. Later, Isaiah foretold of Jehovah's Spirit made manifest to a forsaken world. Then Haggai predicted the shaking of the heavens and the earth by Jehovah's Spirit. Zechariah declared Jehovah's Church would be built by Jehovah's Spirit. The point is, Jehovah started the movement of His Spirit through David, one thousand years before the Christ.

POUR OUT

Solomon, Isaiah, Joel, Zechariah and others employ the verb "pour out" to describe the manner in which Jehovah will bestow His Spirit on the world. In addition, in the last book of the Old Testament, Malachi (410 B.C.) makes a similar illustration. " I will open the windows of heaven for you and pour out a blessing..."(Malachi 3:10, Amp). Ezekiel (580 B.C.), speaking for Jehovah, paints a parallel picture. "And I will cause showers to come down in their season; they will be showers of blessing" (Ezekiel 34:26, NASB).

These, and other writers of the Hebrew Scriptures, also use the idea of "pour out" to portray the outpouring of Jehovah's wrath, anger, and fury.

"Pour out" means to gush forth abundantly from a container. Jehovah is the container and Spirit is that which was contained in God's heart - before Pentecost.

An extended meaning of "pour out" includes the idea of communicating in a big way. On the day of Pentecost, the day that fulfilled Old Testament prophecy, God began to work among His people in a big way, in a new measure - by the authority of His Spirit poured out from heaven. Pentecost defined the beginning of the age of God's Spirit. Pentecost announced the beginning of the reign of God's spiritual influence as opposed to the Old Testament rule of law.

Clearly, the inspired reality of Jehovah pouring out His Spirit was conceived in the Hebrew Scriptures. Then it was born at Pentecost, after the Christ's ascension.

King Solomon, speaking for Jehovah wrote, "If you had responded to my rebuke, I would have poured out my heart [Spirit] to you and made my thoughts known to you" (Proverbs 1:23, NIV). Jehovah, speaking to the children of Israel through the prophet Isaiah, said, "I will pour my Spirit into your descendants and my blessing on your children"(Isaiah 44:3, Msg). Similarly, speaking for Jehovah, Zechariah prophesied, "I will pour out on the house of David and on the inhabitants of Jerusalem, the Spirit of grace and supplication..." (Zechariah 12: 10, NASB).

The most significant prophecy from the Hebrew Scriptures declaring that Jehovah will pour out His Spirit in the New Testament comes from the book of Joel as quoted by Peter in Acts 2:17,18.

"In the Last days," God says,
"I will pour out my Spirit
on every kind of people:
Your sons will prophesy,
also your daughters; Your young men will see visions,
Your old men dream dreams.
When the time comes,
I'll pour out my Spirit
On those who serve me, men and women both,
and they'll prophesy" (Msg).

The outpouring of God's Spirit took place on the day of Pentecost in Jerusalem. From there its influence spread throughout the world. Now, the invisible Holy Spirit of God is made visible and perceptible by His Church.

The day Jehovah poured out His Spirit some 2000 years ago is significant because it establishes the dividing line between the Christ's ministry in the flesh on earth and the ministry of His Spirit from heaven. As a Man the Christ freed the world from the guilt and bondage of sin. He destroyed the sin problem by assuming all sin (Matthew 8:17). As God in heaven His Spirit spreads this message.

THE PREPONDERANCE OF SIN

God (Deity) was enabled to pour out His Spirit because of the Christ's (humanity's) work of reconciliation. The Messiah's sacrifice removed sin from the world, reconciled us to God, and opened the way for God to pour out His Spirit. Prior to the Christ's work on the cross, however, God was unable to share the purity of His Spirit with sinful men and women: God can have nothing to do with sin. But the elimination of sin prepared the way for God to graciously bestow His Spirit on a world sick and dying of sin. To put a handle on this notion let's go back to the fall, or more precisely, to the consequences of the fall.

After the fall God expelled Adam and Eve from the garden of Eden (Genesis 3:24), and, in a sense, turned His back on them. God cannot fellowship with sin. Because of disobedience Adam and Eve were full of irreconcilable sin. They had no Savior.

Before the Christ's work on the cross everyone was alienated from God (Isaiah 59:2; Ephesians 4:18). As a result of sin everyone was subjected to the influences of the devil and held captive by him (2 Timothy 2:26). Sin brought punishment from God - shame, guilt, fear, doubt, death (Genesis 3:10-19) - things that are not of God but of the devil.

Clearly, after the fall, because of sin, God withdrew His Spirit from His creation.(Spirit meaning that animating and vital principle that gives real, free, and abundant life to humanity - the same Spirit that gave life to Adam.) God *had* to withdraw His Spirit. Spirit is pure and cannot associate with the impurity of sin, just as light cannot dwell with darkness.

Yet, God never completely abandoned us. He didn't leave us entirely without the inspiration of His Spirit. Because we were created in the image of God and given life by the breath (Spirit) of God (Genesis 2:7) we were endowed with a sense of God consciousness (Romans 1:20); that is, with a permanent consciousness of divine law which is called our conscience

(Romans 2:14,15). And, by His Spirit, God gave us an inborn sense of continuity and eternity in our hearts (Ecclesiastes 3:11). Thus, because He gave us life by His Spirit, God, to an extent, curbs the ravages of a sinful nature. (God simply created animals and things. He didn't give them life by His breath - Spirit.)

Despite a remnant of God's Spirit in his soul, the natural man, separated from God, lacks spiritual strength to withstand the attacks of the devil. He is easily led astray when trials and testings come. Human nature is no match for the lies and deceptions of the devil. The natural man, alienated from God, is weak and shrinks from trials.

God was aware of the problem and began to move in a direction to resolve it. By direct intervention Jehovah chose the Jews to be His people. He gave them the law and animal sacrifice, providing temporary, transitory relief from God's wrath. By the sacrifice of animals, according to God's graceful provision, the Jew felt Jehovah was being appeased. And rightly so. Jehovah was satisfied and the Jews' heart was pacified. But the Jew was only partially redeemed. And he knew it. Every year he returned to the altar for forgiveness.

It is true that Jehovah intervened directly in the affairs of men by establishing a covenant with the Jews. But He could not send the influences of His Spirit. Neither the Jew nor the Gentile was ready. There was still sin in the world. And because God cannot associate with sin He was unable to pour out the purity of His Spirit.

ATONEMENT

The process of atonement originated in heaven (John 3:16) and was accomplished on earth when God gave us His Son. Atonement is the covering over of sin (*Kaphar* in Hebrew) or reconciliation (*Katallage* in Greek). Atonement, or reconciliation, was designed by Jehovah in heaven and carried out by a Man on earth. Because the Christ died for all mankind, all the sins of the world are covered - in God's eyes - for those who believe. Thus, all sin, which was created by the law, has been cancelled - legally.

Sin has been cancelled legally because in God's economy sin is a legal matter, i.e., transgression of God's written law. In past ages, before Jehovah gave His law to Moses, Jehovah overlooked those times of ignorance (Acts

17:30). "In the generations before us, God let all the nations go their own way" (Acts 14:16, Msg), meaning that, since there was no written law, Jehovah allowed people to conduct themselves without the restraints and instructions of law. Before God's written law the only law was the law of conscience.

Sin became evident when Jehovah gave Moses His written law, "...for through the Law *comes* the knowledge of sin" (Romans 3:20, NASB). Indeed, "...where there is no Law, neither is their violation" (Romans 4:15, NASB). Moreover, "...sin is not imputed where there is no Law" (Romans 5:13, NASB). And, "Apart from the Law sin is dead" (Romans 7:8, NASB).

Actually, sin is still in the world because God's written law is still valid. The law is not abrogated by the atonement. The blood of the Christ covers sin but God's written law is still in effect. The atonement simply blotted out sin. The atonement cancelled sin and through the Christ we are reconciled to God - made sinless - but God did not nullify His law.

By the atonement the believer is freed from the curse of the law (Romans 7:6). Yes, though from God, the written law is a curse (Galatians 3:13) because it condemns but does not forgive; it convicts of sin but does not pardon. Under the law everyone is guilty and without hope of forgiveness. To make matters worse the wages of sin is death (Romans 6:23), or eternal separation from God.

But, thank God, the law was not the final authority in God's economy. The influence of the written law was only temporary. It lasted 1500 years - from Moses to the Christ.

Jehovah planned it that way. He gave the law to Moses to point the way to the Christ (Galatians 3:24). The law convicted of sin and the Christ delivered from sin. According to Galatians 5:18 the Christ's Spirit replaces the law. Different versions of the Bible present Galatians 5:18 in different ways. The Message Bible proposes a question: "Why don"t you choose to be led by the Spirit [of the Christ] and so escape the erratic compulsions of a law-dominated existence?" The NASB puts it another way: "But if you are led by the Spirit [of the Christ] you are not under the Law." The point is, Jesus' Spirit takes us out from under the burden of the Mosaic law.

Indeed, Paul says a new law is in operation: "For the Law of the Spirit of life has set you free in Christ Jesus from the Law of sin and death" (Romans

8:2, NASB). Paul uses the phrase "Law of the Spirit of life" to mean the rule or influence which the Christ's Spirit - the Spirit of life - produces. This new law, this new Spirit of life coming from the Christ's Spirit, gives peace, inner joy, and security - in opposition to the Mosaic law which gives rise to fear, condemnation, and separation from God.

According to Romans 10:4 the law is completed (fulfilled) in the Christ. The Amplified Bible puts it dramatically: "For Christ is the end of the Law - the limit at which it ceases to be, for the Law leads up to Him Who is the fulfillment of its types, and in Him the purpose which it was designed to accomplish is fulfilled - that is, the purpose of the Law is fulfilled in Him."

Not only did the Christ fulfill the Mosaic law but He also fulfilled everything that was written about Him in the Hebrew Scriptures. (Broadly speaking the term "law" is sometimes used to include the entire Old Testament.)

After the Christ was raised from the dead He spent 40 days with His disciples. He said, "Everything I told you while I was with you comes to this: All things written about me in the Law of Moses, in the Prophets, and in the Psalms have to be fulfilled" (Luke 24:44, Msg). Then He went on to open the disciples' understanding of the Word of God, saying, "You can see now how it is written that the Messiah suffers, rises from the dead on the third day, and then a total life-change through the forgiveness of sins..." (Luke 24:46,47, Msg). He finished by promising to send His Spirit back to them after His ascension into heaven - ten days later (Luke 24:49).

The three divisions - the Law of Moses, the Prophets, and the Psalms - comprehend the entire Old Testament. The first division, the Law of Moses, embraces the five books of Moses - Genesis, Exodus, Leviticus, Numbers, Deuteronomy. The Prophets, the second and largest division of the Hebrew Scriptures, includes the books of Joshua, Judges, 1 and 2 Samuel, 1 and 2 Kings. These were called the former prophets by the Jews. Isaiah, Jeremiah, Ezekiel, and the twelve smaller books from Hosea to Malachi were called the latter prophets. By the "Psalms" is meant the Psalms, Proverbs, Job, Song of Solomon, Ruth, Lamentations, Ecclesiastes, Esther, Daniel, Ezra, Nehemiah, and the two books of Chronicles. The resurrected Christ meant to say that in each of these divisions there were prophecies respecting Himself that had to be fulfilled. That they were fulfilled cannot be disputed.

SUMMARY

Sin came through the law, for sin is transgression of the law (1 John 3:4). Without the law there was no transgression. However, though the Christ fulfilled the law, thus cancelling sin, God bequeathed His law to the world as a guide to show the way to the Christ. The law is holy (Romans 7:12) and the law is still in effect. But, in Christ, its power to condemn is broken.

In short, through His Son, God removed the curse of the law but left His law intact. Moreover, the Christ, by removing the curse of the law, by exposing the Law's shortcoming, atoned for (did away with, expiated) sin which was created by the law. Through fulfillment of the law the negative consequences of the law, which included sin and what follows sin - shame, guilt, fear, doubt, death - were cancelled.

The world, cleansed of sin, allowed God to pour out the purity of His Spirit. The law being fulfilled, sin being eliminated, opened the windows of heaven. The work of humanity permitted the dispensation of Deity's Spirit.

DEITY 6

"SPIRIT" IN THE HEBREW SCRIPTURES

In the Hebrew Scriptures the Hebrew word for Spirit is *Ruach*, meaning "to breathe." No doubt the notion of breathing to represent the effluence of Jehovah's divine nature came to the Hebrew writers directly from Jehovah because it renders the idea of life itself. Breathing gives evidence of life.

Indeed, "living God" is a common expression in the Old Testament. Joshua says, "This is how you'll know that God is alive among you" (Joshua 3:10, Msg). A psalm of the sons of Korah says, "My soul thirsts for the living God" (Psalm 42:2, NASB). Jeremiah says, "He is the living God and the everlasting King" (Jeremiah 10:10, NASB). Of course, what is meant by the living God is the Spirit (breath) that emanates from the living God. Without Spirit (breath) there is no life.

The descriptive adjectives "living" and "breathing" were given by Jehovah to the Hebrew writers by divine inspiration to distinguish Him from dead and lifeless idols. Because God is God, and because He is a living/breathing God, He *provides* life and breath. The animation of Adam is a good example of Jehovah as the source of life. Jehovah's Spirit, His breath, gave Adam life. He made Adam a living soul by breathing into his nostrils (Genesis 2:7). God's breath (Spirit) activated the body He created.

Jehovah inspired the writers of the Hebrew Scriptures to use the vital verb "to breathe" to describe the operation of His Spirit. Spirit renders the idea of Jehovah in action. Spirit represents the vitality, the life, and the energy of

Jehovah. Indeed, by His Spirit (breath, Word) He created the universe.

There was no distinction between Jehovah and His Spirit in the Old Testament. There was clear identification of Jehovah with His Spirit. After all, just as a man's breath emanates from his human nature, so Jehovah's Spirit emanates from His divine nature.

David wrote in Psalm 139:7-12 (Msg), that Jehovah is everywhere:

I look behind me and you're there,
then up ahead and you're there, too -
your reassuring presence, coming and going.
This is too much, too wonderful -
I can't take it all in!
Is there anyplace I can go to avoid your Spirit?
to be out of your sight?
If I climb to the sky, you're there!
If I go underground, you're there!
If I flew on morning's wings
to the far western horizon,
You'd find me in a minute -
you're already there waiting!

In Isaiah 63:10 (Msg), Jehovah's Spirit was grieved, meaning Jehovah Himself - not another person of Jehovah - was grieved: "But they turned on him; they grieved his Holy Spirit."

In Jeremiah 31:33 (NASB), Jehovah said He would put His law in the heart of His people, meaning He would put His Spirit (the Spirit of the law) in His people: "But this is the covenant which I will make with the house of Israel after those days," declares the Lord, "I will put My law within them, and on their heart I will write it; and I will be their God and they shall be My people." Jehovah's Spirit in the heart of His people means Jehovah Himself is there.

Similarly, speaking of New Testament times, Jehovah said, " And I will put my Spirit within you and cause you to walk in My statutes, and you will be careful to observe My ordinances" (Ezekiel 36:27, NASB). Here, Ezekiel prophesies the coming of Jehovah by His Spirit at Pentecost. At Pentecost He removed the law from tablets of stone and placed it in the hearts of His people.

The Hebrew mind did not separate Jehovah from His Spirit. Jehovah did not create the universe while His Spirit watched. Neither did His Spirit brood "like a bird over the watery abyss" (Genesis 1:2) while Jehovah watched.

On the contrary, in six days Jehovah created everything by the operation of His Spirit. His Word, a function of His breath, created everything. Jehovah said it and it was so (Genesis 1:3-31). Jehovah conceived the creation in His heart and by His Spirit (breath) He spoke it into existence.

Haggai, speaking for Jehovah, wrote, "My Spirit is abiding in your midst, do not fear" (Haggai 2:5, NASB), meaning Jehovah Himself was abiding with the children of Israel.

Zechariah prophesied (Zechariah 4:6) that it was not by fleshly strength that Jehovah would build His church but by His Spirit. Jehovah does not operate independently and neither does His Spirit operate by itself. In other words, Jehovah and His Spirit are not two persons in the Hebrew Scriptures.

Hezekiah, king of Israel, a godly man, defied the Assyrian king Sennacherib saying to the Jews, "The One with us is greater than the one with him. With him is only an arm of flesh, but with us is the LORD our God to help us and to fight our battles" (2 Chronicles 32:7,8, NASB). When Hezekiah said the LORD our God is with us he was referring to the *Spirit* of the LORD our God.

Just as Jehovah formed the first Adam and gave him life by His Spirit, by breathing into his nostrils (Genesis 2:7), so He brought the second Adam into the world by His Spirit (Luke 1:35). One person of God, by His Spirit, was responsible for both events.

Old Testament writers never entertained the idea of a secondary or even tertiary cause of creation. The idea that there were two or three different personalities performing different functions in the creation of the universe was foreign to Old Testament biblical writers. And because God is the same forever He did not change in the New Testament.

By divine inspiration Old Testament biblical writers regarded the creation of the universe and all that is therein to be the result of the actions of the One God of Israel, by His Spirit. They received inspiration from Jehovah alone who had no component parts. Indeed, the oneness of God (Deuteronomy 6:4) saved the Jews from the polytheism and pantheism of their neighbors.

When the earth was formless and void, when the Spirit of Jehovah hovered over the surface of the waters (Genesis 1:2), it was Jehovah Himself in the process of bringing order out of primeval chaos.

When Jehovah sent forth His Spirit to "renew the face of the ground" (Psalm 104:30, NASB), it was Jehovah Himself who gave form to His physical creation.

When Job said, "By His breath the heavens are made beautiful" (Job 26:13, NASB), he meant that Jehovah Himself cleansed the cosmos by His Spirit (breath).

When Jehovah pours out His Spirit the wilderness will become a fruitful field (Isaiah 32:15). In the Hebrew Scriptures Jehovah's Spirit is considered to be God Himself, not another person of God. His Self *is* Spirit (John 4:24).

In the Old Testament Jehovah had not yet poured His Spirit on mankind. Jehovah's Spirit did not influence all classes of men in the Hebrew Scriptures. He created the universe by His Spirit and He anointed prophets, certain judges and warriors and artisans, but He had not yet freely dispensed His Spirit. He was holding His breath, so to speak, in anticipation of Pentecost. At Pentecost God poured out His Spirit on *all* mankind (Joel 2:28).

Pentecost was a flamboyant day of division (Acts 2:3). It divided The Old Testament from the New Testament. Pentecost marked the transition from Old Testament times to New Testament times - from the rule of God's law to the influence of His Spirit.

The time of the law was finished and the time of the Spirit began. Pentecost did not cancel the Old Testament but brought it to a close. And, with the closure of the Old Testament, the end times began. With Pentecost the emphasis on judgment began and pointed to the culmination of God's plan for mankind (2 Peter 3:10).

But most important, Pentecost instituted the Messiah's reign on earth by His Spirit, by His divine nature, after He had defeated God's enemies by His sinless human nature.

"SPIRIT" IN THE NEW TESTAMENT

The role of God's Spirit in the New Testament can be told in a few words. The prerequisite to keep in mind is that Jesus Christ is both Man and God, fully Man and fully God, fully human and fully Spirit.

Actually, the Spirit has two roles in the New Testament age. First the Spirit (God) was embodied and personified in the Christ when He walked the earth. That is, the ministry of the Lord Jesus Christ is a ministry that God assumed in His Son. The second role of the Spirit in the New Testament age is this: Jesus as God sends back His Spirit at Pentecost (John 16:7).

The first role began when Jehovah poured out the fulness of His Spirit into the womb of the virgin Mary (Luke 1:35) and the Son (humanity) that was born was called the Son of God because the fulness of God (Deity) dwelt in His bodily form (2 Corinthians 5:19; Colossians 1:19; 2:9). That is, all the fulness of Deity dwelt in the Son until the Son's bodily form died.

The second role of the Spirit in the New Testament began at Pentecost, fifty days after the Son's resurrection, when the Spirit that dwelt in the Son returned and manifested itself throughout the world.

(In His farewell discourse, to comfort His disciples, Jesus promised, "I'll come back" (John 14:3). "I'll come back" means Jesus would return by the appearance of His Spirit, not in bodily form.)

In short, the function of the Spirit, Jesus' Spirit, is to provide Christians with the teaching and comfort which would be given by the personal presence of Jesus Himself (John 16:14). Moreover, Jesus' Spirit is omnipresent and applies the work of the Christ to the hearts of all men - whether they receive it or not. Though absent in body Jesus is present in the world today by His Holy Spirit.

"GHOST" IN THE NEW TESTAMENT

"Ghost" is a word, peculiar to the King James version of the Bible, used to portray the image of either life or death. It's an archaic English form of Old High German *geist* meaning spirit. Why the KJV translators used "ghost" to present the idea of life or death is an "unhappy" mystery to most commentators. Nonetheless, its strange use in the seventeenth century merits a comment.

In old English as well as modern English "ghost" signifies the disembodied soul of a dead person, i.e., what remains of his or her heart and spirit. That is, the word ghost applies to somebody, not an abstract entity. In the case of Jesus Christ, as we shall see, it applies to both the spirit or ghost of His human body (spirit or ghost spelled with a small "s" or "g") as well as the divine Spirit or Ghost which *dwelt* in His human body (Spirit or Ghost spelled with a capital "S" or "G"); His divine Spirit or Ghost, of course, being God.

"Ghost," in the presentation of death, is seen in each of the four gospels when the Christ voluntarily sacrifices His human life for us. That is, the sacrifice of His life is expressed in a way that stresses His own volition:

> Jesus...yielded up the ghost (Matthew 27:50);
> And Jesus cried with a loud voice, and gave up the ghost (Mark 15:37);
> And when Jesus had cried out with a loud voice, he said, Father, into thy hands I commend my spirit: and having said thus, he gave up the ghost (Luke 23:46);
> When Jesus therefore had received the vinegar, he...gave up the ghost (John 19:30).

To the seventeenth century reader, "to give up the ghost" rendered the idea that Jesus gave up His life and soul of His own will, by His own choice. Indeed, the Bible tells us that He had the power and authority to lay down His life (as a human being) and to take it up again (as God).

> For this the Father loves Me, because I lay down My [own] life to take it back again. No one takes it away from Me. On the contrary, I lay it down voluntarily - I put it from Myself. I am authorized *and* have the power to lay it down - to resign it; and I am authorized *and* have power to take it back again. These are the instructions (orders) which I have received [as My charge] from My Father (John 10:17,18, Amp).

On the other hand, Ghost, in the presentation of life, is seen in each of the four gospels when John the Baptist announces that the Spirit of Jesus, God, will baptize with the Holy Ghost; that is, with His Holy Spirit. (The Spirit of Jesus, God, *is* the Holy Ghost of Jesus.) Here are the declarations in the KJV of the Spirit giving life:

I indeed baptize you with water unto repentance: but he that cometh after me is mightier than I, whose shoes I am not worthy to bear: he shall baptize you with the Holy Ghost...(Matthew 3:11);

I indeed have baptized you with water: but he shall baptize you with the Holy Ghost (Mark 1:8);

I indeed baptize you with water; but one mightier than I cometh, the latchet of whose shoes I am not worthy to unloose: he shall baptize you with the Holy Ghost...(Luke 3:16);

...he that sent me to baptize with water, the same said unto me, Upon whom thou shalt see the Spirit descending, and remaining on him, the same is he which baptizeth with the Holy Ghost (John 1:33).

John the Baptist recognized that the Spirit of God, the Holy Ghost, dwelt in the Man Christ Jesus. Moreover, he prophesied that God dwelling in the Christ would come back 50 days after the Christ's resurrection and baptize belivers with the Holy Ghost. (Pentecost occurs 50 days after the Christ's resurrection - see Leviticus 23:16 - and commemorates the distinction between the Lord's earthly ministry and the ministry of His Spirit from heaven.) In short, the baptism of the Holy Ghost is the same as sending the influences of God Himself to convict, convert, purify, strengthen, encourage, comfort, and guide the soul.

On the evening of the first day of His resurrection, before He had ascended to His Father, before the outpouring of His Spirit at Pentecost, Jesus appeared to the disciples who were locked in a room for fear of the Jews. He greeted them with "Peace be unto you" and showed them His hands and His side. Then, "...he breathed on them, and saith unto them, Receive ye the Holy Ghost" (John 20:22, KJV).

This was to symbolically strengthen them for the task He was about to assign them at Pentecost, and to remind them of the source of that strength. The act of breathing on the disciples was used to represent the nature of the influence that would come upon them and the source of that influence - Jesus' Spirit. It was an act similar to God breathing into Adam the breath of life (Genesis 2:7). On the first day of the resurrection the act of breathing on the disciples for strength and authority was symbolic. The breathing was not that of the personal Holy Ghost but rather an earnest of that gift to be breathed onto the disciples by the mouth of Jesus' Spirit at Pentecost.

In addition, writing to Timothy, Paul said, "That good thing which was committed unto thee, keep by the Holy Ghost which dwelleth in us" (2 Timothy 1:14, KJV). In the phrase "that good thing committed to thee" the reference is to sound Christian doctrine which Paul had entrusted to Timothy, and which he was required to transmit to others. By the aid of the Holy Ghost of Jesus, which indwells Christians, Timothy was admonished to keep and preserve the knowledge and the love of truth brought about by the influences of Jesus' Spirit.

In short, there are many scriptural references that clarify the indwelling of the Holy Ghost. It can mean the Spirit of God (the Father) in the believer (Romans 8:9, 11), or the Spirit of the Christ in the believer (Romans 8:9). Or, it can mean the Spirit of God in the Church or in the believer (1 Corinthians 3:16; 2 Corinthians 6:16). Or, it may mean that the Christ "dwell in your hearts through faith" (Ephesians 3:17). Or, It may mean "the Word of God richly dwell within you" (Colossians 3:16). The Holy Ghost *is* God, God the Father, the Spirit of the Christ, and the Word of God. Indeed, both the Son and the Father dwell in the believer (John 14:23) since the Holy Ghost includes the Son and the Father: the Son embodied the Father who is the Holy Ghost, i.e., Spirit (John 4:24).

DEITY 7

LAW

Conscience, because it comes from God consciousness, provides a person with an intuitive sense of Jehovah's moral law and is therefore a decent (but limited) moral guide. Though of divine origin, conscience is not the voice of God. It's the voice of the person's soul and comes from within. And because it comes from within it is easily corrupted. Though the roots of conscience have a divine beginning the fruits of conscience are not in God's control.

When Jehovah instituted His moral law on Mount Sinai He began to re-assert divine control in the affairs of the world. Before giving the law to Moses He allowed the nations to do their own thing (Acts 14:16). Though "the law brings about wrath" (Romans 4:15) it began to re- establish Jehovah's presence in His creation. Nonetheless, the written law was limited: When transgressed it condemned the sinner but provided no way out of the condem-nation of sin. There was no release from sin.

Indeed, Jehovah's written moral law was not designed to justify the guilty sinner: "By the works of the law no flesh will be justified" (Romans 3:20a, NASB), meaning no one is released from the guilt of sin by such works that the law requires. Obedience to the law is simply one's moral obligation. Obedience to the law carries no rewards.

Why then did Jehovah institute the written moral law? To expose sin. That is, to reveal the divine definition of sin as opposed to the hazy definition of sin which comes through conscience. Before Jehovah gave Moses the law, sin was without a definite meaning. Indeed, prior to the law, sin against God was unknown: "Through the law comes the knowledge of sin" (Romans 3:20b, NASB). By His law Jehovah tells us what sin is. Hence, besides revealing the will of God, the law uncovers sin.

SIN

God's law is a set of rules governing human conduct. If no such rules are given or known, there is no transgression of them. Hence, no sin: "Where there is no law, neither is there violation" (Romans 4:15, NASB). If there is no command to pursue a certain course, if there is no injunction to forbid certain behavior, all action is innocent. Before the advent of God's law men were not charged with sin: "Sin is not imputed when there is no law" (Romans 5:13, NASB).

Indeed, Paul writes, "Apart from the law sin is dead" (Romans 7:8b, NASB). Here, Paul speaks of a time before he applied the true purpose of the law to his heart. Before his conversion sin was inactive and inoperative in Paul's life. Sin existed but in his heart it was dead. He was a self-righteous Pharisee. His self-righteousness protected him from the accusations of the law. He considered himself blameless. (See Philippians 3:4-6; Acts 23:1; 26:4,5.) In Paul's religious walk the law was an external discipline leading to external righteousness. Because he considered himself outwardly righteous the idea of sin in his heart was a dead issue.

After the Damascus road experience, however, the true meaning of the law came into Paul's heart: "Sin became alive and I died" (Romans 7:9b, NASB). When Paul applied the law to his heart, and no longer to his outward actions, sin became active and operational and convicted his soul. With a new vision Paul gained a new understanding of just how sinful he really was. Guilt and misery took on life and he suffered the pains of death. Sin reigned and raged in his soul. Paul was humiliated and shamed. In this sense the awareness of sin in his heart killed Paul.

LAW AND SIN

In giving the law it was Jehovah's plan to expose the hidden feelings of the heart; not to condemn but to turn the sinner to God. No man really knows his own heart until God's law crosses his path and shows him what sin is. Designed to reveal the true nature of sin Jehovah instituted His law to induce the sinner to look for salvation from his sin. Consequently, the New Testament says, the law is a guide, appointed by God, to lead a person's spirit in the right direction (Galatians 3:24). First, however, the problem created by the law - sin - must be resolved to allow God to pour out His Spirit, for His Spirit's purity cannot abide with sin's impurity.

GOD CANCELS SIN

God's written law and sin are intertwined. God's law and sin go hand in hand. You can't have one without the other. Without the law there is no sin and sin doesn't exist without the law.

To reconcile the world to Himself God had to deal with sin. The barrier that existed between God and His people had to be eliminated. Sin had to be taken out of the world because God, the purity of God's Spirit, cannot associate with the impurity of sin. Indeed, sin is what caused God to withdraw His Spirit from the world in the first place. God and sin are incompatible.

Yet, while dealing with sin, God had to, at the same time, keep His law intact. The law is good. It came from God's heart.

To arbitrarily cancel sin from the world was out of the question. God's law created sin. Then, to cancel it, would destroy God's credibility. No one would trust Him. Besides, the cancellation of sin would demand the cancellation of the law since sin and the law are inseparable. One depends on the other.

How, then, did God dissolve the sin-problem? The answer is that He did not do it alone. He and His Son did it, acting in conjunction. Humanity worked with (obeyed) Deity to resolve the issue.

Reconciliation, resolution of the sin-problem, was accomplished by the Christ's surrender to God's will. Reconciliation comes to us from God through His Son: "God reconciled us to Himself through Christ" (2 Corinthians 5:18, NASB). Then, in the next verse (2 Corinthians 5:19, NASB), further explaining the plan of reconciliation, Paul writes, "God was in Christ [the Man] reconciling the world to Himself."

This verse, 2 Corinthians 5:19, clarifies the nature of the plan of reconciliation. God, the fulness of God's Spirit, was in the Man Christ Jesus reconciling the world to Himself. God was intimately united to the Man Christ Jesus and revealed Himself to the world in His Son. The message Paul wants to convey is that God and the Man Christ Jesus - together - fulfilled God's plan of reconciliation.

Reconciliation between God and mankind could not have been accomplished by God alone. There had to be a Mediator, a sinless Man who was mystically connected, through the virgin birth, to God's heart (John 7:29).

God reconciled us to Himself through His Son. God dwelt in His Son, manifesting His grace through a Man. Christ the Man was the Mediator through whom God was enabled to provide reconciliation. Through the Man Christ Jesus God freed the world of sin.

That God reconciled Himself to the world through the work of a human being is verified in other verses of Scripture. Romans 5:10 says we are reconciled to God by *the death of His Son*. Ephesians 2:15 says the Christ abolished the enmity between God and man by *His own crucified flesh*. Colossians 1:20 says peace was made by *the blood shed on the cross*. Hebrews 2:17 makes it clear: In order to make reconciliation for the sins of the people, God assumed a body; He dwelt in a body made by the virgin birth, a body with soul and spirit like everybody else's body. As a Man God's Son suffered and died in our stead.

The following verse is most important in understanding the cancellation of sin. 2 Corinthians 5:21 stipulates how God accomplished reconciliation, how God resolved the sin-problem. The Message Bible says, "God put the wrong on him who never did anything wrong." NASB puts it this way: "He [God] made Him [the Christ] who knew no sin to be sin." Here, Paul presents the fact that the Christ has been made sin for our benefit. Thus, God cancelled sin by laying all sin on His Son, the Man Christ Jesus.

A CLOSER LOOK AT 2 CORINTHIANS 5:21

God made His Son to be sin. He made Him to be sin on our behalf. For our sake He laid all sin on His Son.

But what is meant by this? What is its *real* meaning? It cannot mean the Son of God was literally made sin and consequently deserving of hell. No one can claim this. In no way was the Lord Jesus guilty of sin. The expression must therefore be, in some sense, figurative.

The declaration that God made the Messiah to be sin is a Hebraic figure of speech. It represents the idea of an Old Testament sin-offering. In the Old Testament a lamb was a sin-offering that a sinner presented to the priest as a sacrifice for his own sin. Jehovah accepted the sacrifice and forgave the sinner. In other words the lamb was a substitute for sin. The lamb's blood covered the sinner's sin.

Jesus Christ was God's Lamb (John 1:29). He gave his own sinless life for sin. He "rescued us from this evil world we're in by offering himself as a sacrifice for our sins" (Galatians 1:4, Msg). "Christ redeemed us from that self-defeating, cursed life by absorbing it completely into himself. Do you remember the Scripture that says, 'cursed is everyone who hangs on a tree'? That is what happened when Jesus was nailed to the cross: He became a curse, and at the same time dissolved the curse [of the law]" (Galatians 3:13, Msg).

The Christ "gave Himself up for us, an offering and a sacrifice to God..." (Ephesians 5:2, NASB).

"He offered himself as a sacrifice to free us from a dark, rebellious life into this good, pure life, making us a people he can be proud of, energetic in goodness" (Titus 2:14, Msg).

"In that death, by God's grace, he fully experienced death in every person's place" (Hebrews 2:9, Msg).

"He used his servant body to carry our sins to the Cross so we could be rid of sin" (1 Peter 2:24, Msg).

The Man Christ Jesus offered Himself a sacrifice for sin. As the head of mankind He voluntarily assumed the place of mankind and intentionally presented Himself to God as a living sacrifice for the sins of mankind. God accepted that sacrifice and made His Son to be answerable for all sin. He paid the price for sin though He didn't have to die. He was sin-free. By raising Him from the dead God made Him the final sin-offering. Animal sacrifice for sin was over.

In short, when Paul writes that God made His Son to be sin he graphically represents God's grace. The sin He laid on His Son was our sin - everybody's sin. Our sin was cancelled and transferred to God's Son. By imputing our sin to His Son, God sovereignly delivers those "in Christ" from the consequences of sin. As a result of God's grace, in gratitude, those "in Christ" will no longer *indulge* in sin.

GOD'S CONDEMNATION OF OUR SINS

The sin of Adam and Eve (transgression of Jehovah's spoken command) brought enmity between God and mankind. Their sin alienated us from God. As a result of their sin we have inherited a sinful nature by genetic transmission. Their tendency to sin has been handed down to us.

Adam and Eve sold us as slaves to sin (Romans 7:14). They delivered us into the hands of the devil. No one is free of sin (Romans 3:23). Our native depravity, under which we struggle, and which brings us grief and despair, confirms that we are inherently sinful. And there is nothing we can do about it. Because of Adam and Eve's sin we are condemned to sin.

But, two thousand years ago, God revealed His grace and showed us mercy. To restore harmony and communion, God removed our sins from His memory. He took us under His wings and protected us from the consequences of our sins. He condemned our sins to oblivion, i.e., to eternal forgetfulness (Romans 8:3). He sovereignly censured our sins. He weakened sin's power over us and destroyed sin's influence on our lives. By neutralizing our sins God freed us from sin's bondage, the bondage we were under on account of Adam and Eve's disobedience.

It should be noted that, since sin is transgression of God's written law, only God is in a position to deal with the consequences of transgression. No one other than God can bring about sin's demise. He has the final say-so. Only God has the authority to judge sin. Only God can manage the consequences of disobedience to His law. Only God is in control of sin's fate. Only God can finally settle the sin-problem since sin ultimately concerns Him only. He has the final word regarding the disposition of our sins.

How did God dispose of our sins? He took them from us and laid them all on His Son, the Man of Calvary. God transferred our sins to His Son just as He conveyed the sins of an Old Testament sinner to a lamb. But in the New Testament He removed our sins from our shoulders and placed them on a Man, a sinless Man.

The prophet Isaiah, in chapter 53, shows that God imputed our sins to the Christ, the Man who God appointed to be the sin-bearer. "...[I]t was *our* pains he carried, *our* disfigurements, all the things wrong with us (v.4)...it was our sins...that ripped and tore and crushed him - *our sins*! He took the punishment that made us whole (v.5)...God has piled all our sins, everything we've done wrong, on him, on him (v.6)...beaten bloody for the sins of my people (v.8)...The plan [of God] was that he [the Christ] gave himself as an offering for sin (v.10)...he himself carries the burden of their sins (v.11)...He took on his shoulders the sin of many" (v.12).

God put all our sins on His Son. The Christ was a full-blooded but sinless human being. Yet, He put Himself in the place of sinners and bore that which our sins deserved - death. He made Himself a sin-offering. God accepted that offering and to show us the measure of His grace He placed all our sins on His Son. "He used his servant body to carry our sins to the Cross so we could be rid of sin..." (1 Peter 2:24, Msg).

Because of the Christ's work on the cross God condemned all our sins to oblivion. The work was done on earth by a Man but the decision to cancel our sins was made by God in heaven. The Father (Deity) transferred our sins to His Son (humanity). He placed our sins on the human body of the Christ.

When the Father transferred our sins to the Son, the Father was obligated to forsake His Son. "My God, My God, why have you abandoned Me - leaving Me helpless, forsaking and failing Me..." (Matthew 27:46, Amp). Why was the Father obligated to abandon His Son? Because God can have nothing to do with sin. He can sovereignly do away with sin but He cannot associate with sin. Without the work of the Christ (humanity) on the cross, God (Deity) could not have cancelled sin.

"You know the story of how Adam landed us in the dilemma we're in - first sin, then death...Sin disturbed relations with God in everything and everyone" (Romans 5:12, Msg). In other words, when Adam sinned it threw our relation with God into disorder. God had to turn His back on everything and everyone in the world. Sin entered the world when Adam sinned and God cannot fellowship with a sinful world (Genesis 3:16-24). At the fall, when sin entered the world, God withdrew His Holy Spirit.

Likewise, God's Spirit had to withdraw from the Messiah when Deity transferred our sins to His Son. Like light and darkness, the pureness of Spirit and the pollution of sin do not mix. There is nothing in common between holiness and sin. So Spirit, God that dwelt in the Christ, left the Son of Man.

It is certain that the Christ was innocent. It is certain that the Father approved the work of His Son. The Christ had done nothing to forfeit the

favor of His Father. As His own obedient Son, God loved Him. For His inno-
cence, for His sacrifice, for His obedience, God did not forsake His Son. He
forsook His Son because He had to. His grace demanded it.

He had to abandon His Son because His Son was made a sin-offering. The
consequence of sin is death. God is a living God. He cannot inhabit a dead
man.

It was the Father's hatred of sin that caused the Son to cry out, "My God,
My God, why have you abandoned Me?" Because of His hatred of sin (and
His love for us) God left His Son helpless on the cross. But it is vital to rec-
ognize that the object of God's hatred was sin, that is the abolition of sin, not
His Son.

Therefore, having cancelled sin, having fulfilled the plan of reconciliation, God raised His Son from an ignominious death. The Man Christ Jesus
now dwells in heaven at the right hand of His Father in a glorified body interceding on our behalf. Moreover, the glorified body of the Christ in heaven is
of the same nature that our "spiritual body" (1 Corinthians 15:44) will be
when we are resurrected.

THE EFFECT OF SIN'S CONDEMNATION

God's grace begins in the New Testament. He first pours out His heart of
compassion, His Spirit, into the womb of the virgin Mary (Luke 1:35). The
fruit of her womb is the birth of the God-Man who brings about the resolution of the sin-problem. The sin-problem resolved, God next pours out His
heart, His Spirit, at Pentecost (Acts 2:17). The result is the spread of the God-
Man's Spirit throughout the world.

The God-Man's Spirit is Jesus' Spirit. The Spirit that now covers the earth
is the same Spirit that dwelt in the Man Christ Jesus, and the same Spirit that
communicated with Adam. It is Jesus' Spirit, God, that founded His Church,
the Man Christ Jesus being the chief cornerstone (Ephesians 2:20).

Keep in mind that the God-Man had two natures. He was fully God, or
Spirit (John 4:24), and He was fully Man, or flesh (1 John 4:2). From His
mother He got full humanity. From His Father He got full Deity. Humanity
is flesh, Deity is Spirit.

Deity (Spirit) dwelt in humanity (flesh). Deity inhabited Christ the Man.

All the fulness of God was *in* Christ (Colossians 1:19). Human nature and the fulness of divine nature lived together in one body (Colossians 2:9).

Furthermore, the nature of Deity does not change. God's nature is always the same. That is to say that God did not *become* a Man but *dwelt* in the Man Christ Jesus.

The God-Man's message is twofold. First is the condemnation of sin and its result -reconciliation - which was taken care of by the Man Christ Jesus (Romans 8:3). Second is the outpouring of the God-Man's Spirit which was prophesied in the Old Testament. "I [Jehovah] will pour out my Spirit on every kind of people" (Joel 2:28, Msg). The outpouring of God's Spirit occurred in the New Testament at Pentecost. Romans chapter eight throws light on the *new* operation of God's Holy Spirit.

Romans 8:2 (Msg), summarizes the effect of sin's condemnation. "A new power is in operation. The Spirit of life in Christ, like a strong wind, has magnificently cleared the air...". The new power in operation is Spirit, the Spirit of life in Christ Jesus. In addition, the condemnation of sin cleansed the world's atmosphere ("cleared the air") to receive the purity of Jesus' Spirit.

Jesus' Spirit comes alive in Romans chapter eight. Indeed, Paul begins his treatise on the operation of the Spirit at the end of chapter seven. He asks the question, "Who will set me free from this body of death?" (Romans 7:24, NASB). He answers the question and says, "Thanks be to God through Jesus Christ our Lord!" (v.25). "Through Jesus Christ" refers to both the work of the Man Christ Jesus on the cross and the subsequent operation of His Spirit from heaven. Paul thanks the Man Christ Jesus as well as Jesus' Spirit for deliverance from sin, Paul's body of death being the source of sin.

Jesus' Spirit is referred to no less than 18 times in Romans chapter eight. That includes two times each in verses 5 and 26, and three times in verse 9. By contrast Spirit is mentioned only once in the seven preceding chapters of Romans and only twice in the following eight chapters.

Following is a verse by verse commentary on Romans chapter eight as it regards the operation of Jesus' Spirit in our lives as Christians. It should be kept in mind that reference to "Jesus' Spirit" includes the work of His flesh on the cross as well as the operation of His Spirit among believers. The two, flesh and Spirit, do not function separately. Spirit and flesh worked together to save us.

- There is no condemnation for those who are in Christ Jesus (v.1). To be "in" Christ Jesus is to be spiritually united to Him. This union is consummated by joining our human spirit with His divine Spirit. The result is that, through Him, our human soul is freed from the guilt and condemnation of sin, that is, Old Testament law.
- In opposition to Old Testament law the gospel of Jesus Christ establishes a new law which sets us free. We are no longer governed by the written law - which convicts and condemns - but by Jesus' Spirit. Paul calls this new law the law of the Spirit of life in Christ Jesus (v.2). The Spirit of life in Christ Jesus means God gives us a second chance.
- Those who conduct their lives in accordance with Jesus' Spirit are made righteous (released from the guilt of sin) by God (v.4).
- Surrender to Jesus' Spirit brings peace to the soul (vss.5 & 6).
- There is no pleasing God apart from Jesus' Spirit (v.8). God is not pleased with those who ignore His Son.
- God's Spirit *is* Jesus' Spirit. Apart from Jesus' Spirit there is no (re)connection to God (v.9).
- In Christ Jesus the believer's spirit comes alive because of righteousness imputed by Jesus' Spirit (v.10).
- In Christ Jesus even the believer's *mortal* body comes alive (v.11).
- God grants eternal life through Jesus' Spirit (v.13).
- Believers, led by Jesus' Spirit, become sons and daughters of God (v.14).
- By Jesus' Spirit we receive a "Spirit of adoption" and are made children of God (v.15).
- Because Jesus is the Son of God, Jesus' Spirit assures the believer that he or she is a child of God (v.16).
- By accepting Jesus' Spirit into our hearts we become God's children and share in His inheritance (v.17).
- Jesus' Spirit provides the first fruits of heavenly inheritance even while on earth, even though we may groan inwardly waiting for the redemption of our bodies, redemption that finally delivers us from the sinful nature we live in (v.23).
- Jesus' Spirit bears us up in our weaknesses. And we all have weaknesses. Our depravity exposes them (v.26).
- Jesus' Spirit intercedes for us (vss. 27,34; see also Hebrews 7:25).

In short, after God condemned sin by the work of His Son's flesh, Jesus' Spirit came down to earth on the day of Pentecost and inaugurated His Church. Now the Church operates under the guidance of His Spirit. His Spirit helps His disciples along the way to resurrected life.

In the introductory chapters of Romans Paul describes the condemnation of sin, the legal condemnation of sin. Though sin still exists in the world God sovereignly and judicially condemns it. Because of the work of the Christ on the cross God annihilates the existence of sin in those who believe. In the first seven chapters of Romans Paul explains the gospel that frees those in Christ from the condemning sentence of God's law.

Then, in chapter eight, Paul immediately proceeds to the operation of Jesus' Spirit in our lives as believers. In one breath, so to speak, he goes from the cancellation of sin to the things of Jesus' Spirit. Why the sudden change - from sin to Spirit? Why does Paul emphasize Spirit after sin had been condemned?

Because, according to Paul, that is the way God set things up. There is a godly order - first the natural (in this case sin), then the spiritual (or Spirit). "The spiritual did not come first, but the natural, and after that the spiritual" (1 Corinthians 15:46, NIV). First the decadence of sin (embodied by Adam) then the perfection of Spirit (embodied by the Christ). (See Paul's reasoning, 1 Corinthians 15:35-58.)

It goes without saying that the two, sin and Spirit, are not compatible. They cannot exist together in harmony. Sin and Spirit cannot operate consonantly in the same environment. Sin is too aggressive and domineering.

So, for those who believe in the miraculous birth, life, death, and resurrection of Christ Jesus, God condemned their sins to oblivion. God erased the sins of those in Christ from His remembrance. God forgot the sins of those who put their trust in the sacrificial death of His Son. God destroyed the sins of those who believe that the Son of Man died for them.

So, what really happened when God condemned sin? What was the effect of sin's condemnation? God's condemnation of sin purified the spiritual atmosphere of the world and made possible the return of Jesus - manifested by His Spirit. Sin's condemnation made room for Jesus' Spirit. The spiritual and judicial cleansing of the world's environment allowed the purity of Jesus' Spirit to return to earth.

EPILOGUE

Imagine, simply as an intellectual exercise, the condition of the world if God had *not* given us His Son and had not placed our sins on Hm. His Spirit could not have come to earth. It would have no place to go and no heart to enter. Sin dominates the world of human experience. Sin would not have allowed Jesus' Spirit into its territory. If God had not condemned sin, sin would have overwhelmed Jesus' Spirit. Sin is powerful. Indeed, the power of sin crushed the purity of God's written law (Romans 8:3). If God had not relegated our sins to His Son, His Spirit would have no dwelling place on earth and the New Testament would not have been written.

DEITY 8

BIRTH BY SPIRIT

Spirit brings life. A good example is God (Spirit) giving life to Adam. New Testament examples of God giving life are the virgin birth of Jesus and the born-again experience brought about by Jesus' Spirit, which is God. Because of the Messiah's birth, resurrection, the outpouring of His Spirit, and the born-again experience, birth by the Spirit is a New Testament reality that was unclear in the Old Testament.

For the believer in Christ, Jesus' Spirit brings new life. Jesus' Spirit does not restore the old life but makes the believer a new creature, creature meaning *creation*, denoting the act of morally creating a new being. "Anyone united with the Messiah gets a fresh start, is created new. The old life is gone; a new life burgeons!" (2 Corinthians 5:17, Msg). God, Jesus' Spirit, makes the believer a new (regenerated) creature by setting him or her free from the corruption of the fall - just as the Messiah was born free from the corruption of the fall because God was His Father.

Jesus, speaking to His disciples, said, "The Spirit can make life" (John 6:63, Msg). He was referring to His own Spirit, the fulness of God's Spirit that dwelt in His physical body. The New Testament dispensation of Spirit, Jesus' Spirit, is a new covenant that grants new life to the soul dead in sin. Jesus' Spirit made Paul a servant "of a new covenant, not of the letter, but of the Spirit; for the letter [of the law] kills, but the Spirit gives life" (2 Corinthians 3:6, NASB).

There is a remarkable resemblance between the Messiah's birth by God's Spirit and the believer's birth by Jesus' Spirit. (God, who is Spirit, dwelt in Jesus. Therefore Jesus' Spirit is God's Spirit.) God's Spirit caused the conception of new life in the virgin Mary's womb just as Jesus' Spirit begins the development of a new life in the beliver.

Matthew said, "Mary's pregnancy is Spirit - conceived" (Matthew 1:18, Msg). In Luke the angel Gabriel told Mary that God's Spirit "will come upon you...Therefore the child you bring forth will be called Holy, Son of God" (Luke 1:35, Msg).

The Messiah's flesh and blood was developed in the womb of the virgin Mary by the power of God's Spirit. The Christ's human nature was not made by ordinary generation. God, who is Spirit, prepared Himself a body through the virgin birth. "You don't want sacrifice and offerings year after year; you've prepared a body for me for a sacrifice" (Hebrews 10:5, Msg). (There is no record of the Messiah speaking these words but it is language that appropriately expresses the nature of His work as a Man.) God prepared Himself a body to do His will. His will was accomplished by His Son on Calvary.

Similarly, a body of believers, the Church, is being prepared to do God's will on earth, to take care of the needs of the needy, both physical and spiritual, and to be a light to the world by raising up the name of Jesus. The Christ's Church is being made by Jesus' Spirit. (When Jesus said, "I will put together my Church" (Matthew 16:18) He meant His Spirit will build His Church - not His flesh.)

Just as the Messiah's birth was effected by God's Spirit, so the Church's birth is being accomplished by Jesus' Spirit. Both the generation of the Christ's physical body and the creation of His spiritual body - the Church - were carried out, not by human agency, but by God. Through the Christ and His Church God's will is being accomplished on earth.

NICODEMUS

Nicodemus, a prominent leader of the Jews, came to Jesus by night cautiously seeking a private interview. He looked favorably on the Savior's cause and came to inquire more fully of Jesus' teachings. "Rabbi, we all know you're a teacher straight from God. No one could do all the God-pointing, God-revealing acts you do if God weren't in on it" (John 3:2, Msg).

Jesus knew Nicodemus' heart. He surmised what Nicodemus should know about spiritual things. Jesus did not beat about the bush but came right to the point. He replied, "Unless a person is born from above, it's not possible to see what I'm pointing to - to God's kingdom" (v.3).

Here, Jesus states one of the fundamental and indispensable doctrines of Christianity. To be born from above, from heaven, is spiritual birth, the emergence of a new heart and a new mind, the birth of a new soul. Jesus wants Nicodemus to know that following the law is our moral obligation, but not the way of pleasing God.

Contrary to the law, spiritual regeneration is not outward but inward. It is not of the body but of the soul. It is the result of the heart being impregnated by Jesus' Spirit. Just as God is the real agent in the birth of the body, so also is He the creator of a person's new spirit. "But the person who takes shape within is formed by something you cannot see and touch - the Spirit - and becomes a living spirit" (v.6).

Jesus wants Nicodemus to know that the heart must be changed by God - from above - by the agency of His Spirit. This great change is ascribed to Jesus' Spirit. "It wasn't so long ago that we ourselves were stupid and stubborn, dupes of sin, ordered every which way by our glands, going around with a chip on our shoulder, hated and hating back. But when God, our kind and loving Savior God, stepped in, he saved us from all that. It was his doing; we had nothing to do with it. He gave us a good bath, and we came out of it new people..." (Titus 3:3-5, Msg).

Indeed, the new life in Christ is a cleansing. "Now that you've cleaned up your lives by following the truth, love one another as if your lives depended on it. Your new life is not like your old life. Your old birth came from mortal sperm; your new birth comes from God's living Word. Just think: a life conceived by God himself" (1 Peter 1:22, Msg).

Paul expands on the new life:

And so I [Paul] insist - and God backs me up on this - that there be no going along with the crowd, the empty-headed, mindless crowd. They've refused for so long to deal with God that they've lost touch not only with God but with reality itself. They can't think straight anymore. Feeling no pain, they let themselves go in sexual obsession, addicted to every sort of perversion.

But that's no life for you. You learned Christ! My assumption is that you have paid careful attention to him, been well instructed in the truth precisely as we have it in Jesus. Since, then, we do not have the excuse of ignorance, everything - and I do mean everything - connected with that old way of life has to go. It's rotten through and through. Get rid of it! And then take on an entirely new way of life - a God-fashioned life, a life renewed from the inside and working itself into your conduct as God accurately reproduces his character in you.

What this adds up to, then, is this: no more lies, no more pretense. Tell your neighbor the truth. In Christ's body we're all connected to each other, after all. When you lie to others, you end up lying to yourself.

Go ahead and be angry. You do well to be angry - but don't use your anger as fuel for revenge. And don't stay angry. Don't go to bed angry. Don't give the Devil that kind of foothold in your life.

Watch the way you talk. Let nothing foul or dirty come out of your mouth. Say only what helps, each word a gift (Ephesians 4:17-29, Msg).

Jesus goes on to explain to Nicodemus that everyone who is born of the Spirit is, in some respects, like the effect of the wind. You don't see it but you see its effects in changed lives, and you know, therefore, that it is there and is operating. But because Nicodemus was an Old Testament Jew, and Jesus' Spirit had not yet been diffused, he objected to Jesus' doctrine. He could not perceive how it could be, and asked, "What do you mean by this? How does this happen?" (John 3:9, Msg).

Nicodemus, no doubt, shared the common notion among the Jews that the Messianic kingdom was to be a political kingdom in which the nation of Israel would be freed from foreign domination. He could not understand how he, a good man, one of the rulers of Israel, a strict Jew, would not be welcomed into the Messianic kingdom with open arms, just as he was. He could not see that. He did not understand that he would have to allow Jesus' Spirit to reconstruct his mind and heart.

Jesus admonishes Nicodemus for his doubting and questioning attitude and assures him the doctrine of being born-again is from heaven. In support of this doctrine Jesus makes a remarkable statement. He says the doctrine of being born-again is from heaven and He is qualified and authorized to speak of heavenly things because He comes from there. "No one has ever gone up into the presence of God except the one who came down from that Presence, the Son of Man" (John 3:13, Msg). The literal translation of the Westcott and Hort Greek text reads as follows: "And no one has ascended into the heaven if not the one out of heaven having descended, the Son of Man."

In other words, no man can speak of heavenly things because no man has ever ascended into heaven and returned. Jesus spoke of heavenly things with authority because He was God who clothed Himself in a human nature. The Christ, on earth, as the Son (humanity), represented the Father (Deity) in heaven. As the Son of God *and* the Son of Man He was competent to do and declare the will of God.

It is clear that Jesus' human nature was not in heaven. There are no human natures in heaven. Spiritual natures yes, but no human natures. The Son of Man's human nature was generated in the womb of the virgin Mary. It was Jesus' divine nature, God, who came down to earth and assumed a human body.

That God (the Father) came to earth and dwelt in a Man (the Son) is a clear indication of the fact that Jesus Christ had two natures. He was Spirit as well as flesh. Nicodemus, because of his distorted idea of the office of the Messiah, probably thought Jesus was a prophet - not God manifested in the flesh (1 Timothy 3:16).

THE SPIRIT OF JESUS IN THE BOOK OF ACTS

Luke begins the book of Acts with the resurrection of Jesus Christ. He gives an account of the forty days Jesus spent with the disciples talking about the things of the kingdom of God. Then, on the mount of olives, "As they watched, he was taken up and disappeared in a cloud" (Acts 1:9, Msg). The disciples stood there, staring into space. Suddenly two men appeared in white robes. They said, "You Galileans! - why do you just stand here looking up at an empty sky? This very Jesus who was taken up from among you to heaven will come as certainly - and mysteriously - as he left" (Acts 1:11, Msg).

It was not Jesus' body that would come back. His Spirit would come back ten days later at Pentecost.

Jesus' Spirit, the Spirit of God residing in the Man Christ Jesus, had not yet been made manifest to the world when He walked the earth. It was not until Pentecost that God poured out His Spirit. Before the death and resurrection of the Man Christ Jesus, God's Spirit was silently communicated by Jesus' miracles.

In the third chapter of the book of Acts Luke tells of the healing of a forty year old man who had been crippled from birth. Every morning he was carried to the entrance gate of the temple to beg for money to buy food. When he saw Peter and John about to enter the temple he asked for a handout. Peter responded, "I don't have a nickel to my name, but what I do have, I give to you: In the name of Jesus Christ of Nazareth, walk!" (Acts 3:6, Msg). And the man walked and danced for joy. "In the name of Jesus" is the same as saying "In the name of God" - who is Spirit.

The significance of prayer "in the name of Jesus" deserves special notice. The expression means, *by His authority*, or, *by virtue of the power derived from Him*. Jesus wrought miracles because He was God manifested in the flesh. He claimed dominion over disease and death. Peter, on the other hand, drew upon God's authority and God's power by calling on the name of Jesus. It was God who healed the man, not Peter.

The name of Jesus, then, is God's name. Because God is Spirit, it was Jesus' Spirit that healed the cripple. "In the name of Jesus" is the only way of calling on the power and authority of God.

Shortly after Pentecost "The whole congregation of believers was united as one - one heart, one mind!...They shared everything" (Acts 4:32, Msg). "Joseph, called by the apostles 'Barnabas' (which means "Son of Comfort"), a Levite born in Cyprus, sold a field that he owned, brought the money, and made an offering of it to the apostles" (Acts 4:36,37, Msg).

But Ananias sold a piece of property and lied to the apostles, secretly keeping part of the price for himself. When confronted by Peter, of the deception, Ananias immediately fell down dead. Later, Ananias' wife, Sapphira, came in and she lied about the price, too. Peter asked, "What's going on here that you connived to conspire against the Spirit of the Master?" (Acts 5:9, Msg). When she heard these words she too fell over dead.

The point is that "Spirit of the Master" is the Spirit of Jesus, the Holy Spirit of God.

After revealing Himself to the disciples at Pentecost, Jesus revealed Himself to Paul. On the way to Damascus to persecute believers Paul was struck blind by a flash of bright light and heard a voice, "Saul, Saul, why are you out to get me?" (Acts 9:4, Msg). Surprised, Paul asked, "Who are you Master?" The reply was, "I AM Jesus..." (Acts 9:5). Of course, it was Jesus' Spirit, God, who spoke to Paul (Acts 9:15).

When Peter visited the church in Lydda he met a man named Aeneas who had been in bed eight years, paralyzed. Peter said, "Aeneas, Jesus Christ heals you. Get up and make your bed!" (Acts 9:34, Msg). And he got out of bed, healed. "Everybody who lived in Lydda and Sharon saw him walking around and woke up to the fact that God was alive and active among them" (Acts 9:35, Msg). Thus, Jesus Christ's Spirit, God, healed Aeneas.

While living as a guest of Simon the tanner in Joppa, Peter received a vision from Jesus' Spirit. Jesus told Peter to eat food that was not kosher. Peter objected. But what Jesus meant by this command was that Peter was to go to a Roman centurion, who was a Gentile, and present the gospel. In other words, Jesus' Spirit, through Peter, brought the good news of reconciliation, regeneration, and resurrection to the (non-kosher) Gentiles, too (Acts 10:11- 15).

Jesus' Spirit warned Agabus, a prophet from Jerusalem, that a severe famine was about to devastate the country. (The famine actually came during the rule of the Roman emperor Claudius, A.D. 41.) So the disciples gathered food and money to send to their brethren in Judea (Acts 11:28-30).

When King Herod had Peter arrested and put in jail, Jesus' Spirit sent an angel to free him. When the angel came Peter was sleeping. The angel woke Peter up and told him to get up and leave the jail. Peter thought he was dreaming but when he got outside he realized it was not a dream and went to the house where the disciples were gathered, praying (Acts 12:7-12; see also v.17).

The Holy Spirit of Jesus led Paul and his traveling companions on their missionary journeys to Asia Minor and Greece. On the second journey "They went to Phrygia, and then on through the region of Galatia. Their plan was to turn west into Asia province, but *the Holy Spirit* blocked that route. So they went to Mysia and tried to go north to Bithynia, but *the Spirit of Jesus* wouldn't let them go there either" (Acts 16:6,7, Msg - emphasis added to show the Holy Spirit and the Spirit of Jesus are two ways of expressing the same Spirit).

In Philippi, a Roman colony in Greece, Paul and his traveling companions came across a prayer meeting. "We took our place with the women who had gathered there and talked to them. One woman, Lydia, was from Thyatira and a dealer in expensive textiles, known to be a God-fearing woman. As she listened with intensity to what was being said, [the Spirit of] the Master [Jesus] gave her a trusting heart - and she believed!" (Acts 16:14, Msg).

In Corinth, a well known city in Greece, speaking to the Jews about the Messiah, Paul got discouraged with their constant arguing and contradictions. He threw up his hands and said he was going to preach the gospel to the Gentiles. That night he received a word of encouragement from the Lord. Jesus' Spirit came to him and said, "Keep it up, and don't let anyone intimidate or silence you" (Acts 18:9, Msg).

Finally, back in Jerusalem, after Paul's trial in front of the high council of Pharisees and Sadducees, Jesus' Spirit appeared and said, "It's going to be all right. Everything is going to turn out for the best. You've been a good witness for me here in Jerusalem. Now you're going to be my witness in Rome!" (Acts 23:11, Msg).

THE MISSING LINK
When Jesus walked the earth He was both Man and God. Through the God-Man the world came to know God's heart. Today, Jesus' Spirit, emanating from the pages of the Bible and from the firmament, governs the lives of believers.

By his Spirit Jesus calls us to worship Him - as Man and as God. We are called to worship Him as Man because He is pure and undefiled - sinless. As a Man He is our example to follow. We are called to worship Him as God because He (God) chose to join Himself with our condition. It was God Himself who came to earth and assumed a body like ours.

Jesus' Spirit puts us in touch with the Christ's humanity (body, soul, spirit) as well as Jesus' Deity (God). Jesus' Spirit provides the means of communication between God and humanity. We are connected to God by Jesus' Holy Spirit. The Spirit of the Man Christ Jesus supplies the spiritual link between God and man that was missing from the time of the fall to Pentecost.

MORE ON THE SPIRIT OF JESUS

The phrase "Spirit of Jesus" directs attention to the divine nature of Jesus. That is, "Spirit" spelled with a capital "S" refers to God who is Spirit (John 4:24), whose Spirit is holy. When "spirit" is spelled with a small "s" it refers to the human nature of the Christ - His body, soul, spirit.

This section deals with the Spirit of Jesus - God - residing in your heart. The following verses from Scripture, substantiating Jesus' Spirit in your heart, are presented in short, concise form so the reader won't be distracted.

- God is Spirit (John 4:24). All the fulness of God's Spirit resided in Jesus (Colossians 2:9). Hence, the Spirit of Jesus is the Holy Spirit of God residing in the believer.
- "You realize, don't you, that you are the temple of God, and God himself is present in you" (1 Corinthians 3:16, Msg).
- "I'll live in them, move into them; I'll be their God and they'll be my people" (2 Corinthians 6:16, Msg). It is Jesus' Spirit that lives in us and is our God.
- When Paul says, "Jesus Christ is in you" (2 Corinthians 13:5) he means the Spirit of Jesus in your heart, not His flesh.
- We are being made into "a holy temple built by God, all of us built into it, a temple in which God is quite at home" (Ephesians 2:22, Msg).
- When Paul prays "that Christ will live in you..." (Ephesians 3:17) he asks that Jesus' Spirit dwell in your heart.
- "Let the Word of Christ - the Message - have the run of the house" (Colossians 3:16, Msg). This verse assumes the Word of God, which became flesh, dwell in your heart (house).
- "The Spirit which He has made to dwell in us jealously desires us" (James 4:5, NASB). Here the apostle simply says the Spirit of Jesus, God in us, loves us.
- "As we keep his commands, we live deeply and surely in him, and he lives in us. And this is how we experience his deep and abiding presence in us: by the Spirit he gave us" (1 John 3:24, Msg). The Spirit God gave us is Jesus' Spirit.

- From heaven an angel thundered, "Look! Look! God has moved into the neighborhood, making his home with men and women!" This is the Message Bible's version of Revelation 21:3 meaning God - Jesus - came to earth and dwelled in and among His people.

Fine things happen when we allow the Spirit of Jesus to work in our lives. Love, joy, peace, patience, kindness, goodness, faithfulness, gentleness, self-control (Galatians 5:22,23) are evident when we trust Jesus' Spirit to conduct our behavior. Inner strength comes from the Spirit of Jesus. The mind is enlightened and the consciousness is elevated. Our resolve is sustained in times of trial by the Spirit of Jesus. Jesus' Spirit silently persuades and succors. In short, we are introduced to the Character of God by the Holy Spirit of Jesus.

DEITY 9

HIS SPIRIT IN HIS CHURCH

It is not by might nor by power but by His Spirit that the Lord subtly accomplishes His work (Zechariah 4:6). He built - and is building - His Church by His Spirit, the Man Christ Jesus being the cornerstone (Ephesians 2:20). That is, the Christ's human nature provided the basic principles of His Church while Jesus' divine nature, His Spirit, builds His Church, and indeed, holds the superstructure together. Through the baptism of His Spirit, God places each member of His Church "in Christ," meaning each member is in union with Jesus Christ's human nature as well as His divine nature - God.

God designed His Church to be a special residence of His Spirit. His Church is a temple where God's Holy Spirit dwells. In reality, there is no other Spirit than the Holy Spirit of Christ Jesus, "For in Him all the fulness of Deity dwells in bodily form" (Colossians 2:9, NASB). "Spirit" is a term that embraces "all the fulness of Deity."

Holy is the heart where that Spirit dwells because it is a temple where Jesus dwells, not in the flesh but by His Spirit. To house such a guest is a divine privilege. With what anxious care should we cherish the presence of such a guest; with what concern should we guard our conduct so we may not grieve His Spirit away!

As Christians we must always have special regard for the Lord Jesus Christ. Because He is the cornerstone upon which all of Christianity is founded, upon which the whole spiritual temple is raised, upon whom the Church rests, He deserves our constant consideration. How important, then, that the Church should have correct views of the God-Man. How important that the doctrine respecting His divine nature (Spirit) and His human nature (flesh) should be maintained. In Christianity Jesus Christ is all there is. There can be no other person of God.

Jesus Christ is both Father and Son. The Father (Spirit) dwelt in the Son (humanity). And His Spirit is Holy and acting in the world today. When Philip asked Jesus to show Him the Father, Jesus replied, "To see me is to see the Father" (John 14:9, Msg). Of course, this reply is not literal since the Father is invisible. No man has seen God at any time. What is meant by Jesus' reply is that He is the incarnate manifestation of God the Father. Seeing the Son is to see the Father because of the intimate spiritual and physical union of the two natures - humanity *and* Deity.

The Christ, speaking as the Son of God, goes on to tell Philip, "Do you not believe that I am in the Father and the Father is in Me? The words that I say to you I do not speak on My own initiative, but the Father abiding in Me does His works" (John 14:10, NASB). When Jesus says, "the Father abiding in Me," He makes clear reference to the mystical union of Father and Son made possible by the virgin birth.

It is not a matter of indifference that Jesus Christ is both God and Man. Indeed, it should be a matter of deep concern to His Church. A proper view of who Jesus Christ really is brings us into intimate relationship with God's Spirit. There can be no other person of God to diminish the power and authority and dignity and integrity and reputation of the Lord Jesus Christ. It is only through the Messiah that we come to know God's heart. The only Spirit that puts us in touch with God is the Spirit of Jesus Christ.

Jesus is God who is Spirit; and, of course, God's Spirit is Holy. It is God, the divine nature of Jesus, the Spirit of the Christ, that changes hearts. As God, Jesus' Spirit is eternal, without beginning and without end, omniscient, omnipotent, and omnipresent. And because there is only one Spirit, Jesus' Spirit is the only Spirit of God operating in the world today.

Everything regarding the welfare of the Church and the peace of its members depends on proper views of the Christ: God in the Christ and the Christ in God. It is faith in Jesus Christ alone that unites an individual to God. Connection to God, His being, His personality, to all He says and promises, is by faith in Jesus Christ. Faith in any other entity is fictitious. Union with Jesus Christ, whether His divine nature or His human nature, is by believing that He is God's Holy Spirit manifested in the flesh (1 Timothy 3:16).

The Son of Man declares that He and God's Spirit are indivisible. Speaking to the Jews He says, "Then perhaps things will come together for you, and you'll see that not only are we doing the same thing, we *are* the same - Father and Son. He is in me, and I am in him" (John 10:30, Msg). In His final prayer, before being crucified, He asks His Father that His disciples might be united, "Just as you Father, are in me and I in you, so they might be one heart and mind with us" (John 17:21, Msg). "Us" includes humanity and Deity.

In the above verses, the Christ, speaking as Man, affirms He is also God. By His own words He validates His dual nature. The Jews understood the meaning of the Christ's words because they took up stones to kill Him for blasphemy. He, being a Man, called Himself God (John 10:33).

The only spiritual authority that comes from heaven and permeates the world is the Holy Spirit of Jesus Christ. Two thousand years ago He was a Man who walked the earth. Now, since Pentecost, by His Spirit, He provides the animating and vital principle that gives life to born again believers. How? By the influence of His Holy Spirit.

It is the Christ's Holy Spirit flowing from heaven that holds the body of Christ together. Jesus Christ's divine nature - Spirit - is the binding agent that keeps the Church intact. In spite of man-made doctrines that tend to divide different denominations, it is the Spirit of the Christ that enables believers to fellowship with one another.

And what is Christian fellowship? It may be described as a mystical (SPIRITual) union of those who are in Christ, those who are brought together by the work He accomplished as a Man on earth and bonded together by His Spirit from heaven. Jesus' Holy Spirit from heaven, His divine nature, controls the destiny of the Christian Church.

SPIRIT

Terms in the Bible used to describe the divine nature of the Man Christ Jesus include the Old Testament name Yahweh as well as the titles LORD, Lord, God. New Testament appellations include Father, Spirit, and Holy Spirit.

These terms represent the incorporeal, invisible, spiritual Being of God, the one God of the Old and New Testaments who dwelt in the Christ when He sojourned on earth. All these terms and titles relate to the Spirit resident in the Christ's human nature.

That there is a difference between the two natures of Jesus Christ should be clear. The human nature is not divine and the divine nature is not human. They are two different natures: the Christ's divine nature is pure Spirit (John 4:24) while His human nature was made up of body, soul, and spirit (1 Thessalonians 5:23).

Because the descriptive title "Spirit" is all-inclusive, it best represents the invisible, omnipotent, omnipresent, omniscient, spiritual nature of Deity. Spirit also transmits the idea of supernatural eternalness. In the following verses the word "Spirit" is used as a handle to grab hold of the divine nature residing in the Christ's human nature.

- When imprisoned Paul called upon the "Spirit of Christ" (Philippians 1:19) for sustenance. That is, Paul called upon Deity, the same Deity (God, Father) that Christ the Man called upon to bear His trials.
- God sent the Spirit of His Son into our lives (Galatians 4:6). The phrase "Spirit of His Son" refers to the Christ's divine nature - God. So God sends His own Spirit, the Spirit of Jesus, into our hearts.
- "Now the Lord is the Spirit" (2 Corinthians 3:17, NASB). "The Lord" refers to the Christ. "Spirit" refers to Deity. That is, the Christ's human nature embodied the Spirit - God.

That the Spirit of the Christ signifies the Spirit of God is made clear in a number of parallel passages. Indeed, Jesus' Spirit and God's Spirit perform the same function throughout the New Testament. That is, God works in His creation by His Holy Spirit, The Spirit of Jesus Christ.

- Just as God's Spirit gave life to Adam so the Christ's Spirit gives new life. Thus, the Spirit of God who gave life to Adam and the Spirit of the Christ, a life-giving Spirit (1 Corinthians 15:45) are the same Spirit.
- Peter wrote, "the Spirit of Christ" was working in the prophets of the Old Testament (1 Peter 1:11). In another place Peter wrote, "the Holy Spirit"

moved on the prophets (2 Peter 1:21). These two verses show the two expressions, Spirit of Christ and Holy Spirit, refer to the same Spirit.

- Speaking as God, Jesus said He will raise up the believer on the last day (John 6:40). Paul said the Spirit raises the dead (Romans 8:11). Thus, Jesus' divine nature, God, is the Spirit that provides eternal life.

- Along the same lines Paul said the Spirit raised the Christ from the dead (Romans 8:11). Yet Jesus, speaking as God, said He will raise Himself up from the dead after three days (John 2:19). Again, Jesus reveals that His divine nature is the Spirit that raises the dead.

- Similarly, Jesus said the Father raises the dead (John 5:21) while in another verse Jesus said He, as God, will raise the dead (John 6:54). Thus, to recognize a difference between Father, Jesus' Spirit, and Holy Spirit goes against Scripture.

Examples abound in the New Testament of the Christ's Spirit, God's Spirit, and Holy Spirit fulfilling the same office, role, purpose, and function. Why? Because all three expressions refer to the same spiritual Being - a Being that cannot be divided. That is, Spirit cannot be divided. How can you divide Spirit? There is one Spirit: "One and the same Spirit works in all these things, distributing to each one individually just as He [the Holy Spirit of Jesus] wills" (1 Corinthians 12:11, NASB).

God is Spirit (John 4:24) whether the Christ's Spirit, God's Spirit, or Holy Spirit. The Christ's Spirit refers to the Christ's divine nature which is God. Clearly, God's Spirit is God because God is Spirit. And God's Spirit is Holy (Leviticus 11:44 and 1 Peter 1:16). Moreover, that God is Spirit, whether the Christ's Spirit or Holy Spirit, is evident from a comparison of Acts 5:3 with Acts 5:4 and from a comparison of 1 Corinthians 3:16 with 1 Corinthians 6:19.

In a single verse Paul shows that the Spirit of God and the Spirit of the Christ are the same Spirit: "However, you are not in the flesh but in the Spirit, if indeed the Spirit of God dwells in you. But if anyone does not have the Spirit of Christ, he does not belong to Him" (Romans 8:9, NASB).

Another example: "Do you not know that you are the temple of God, and that the Spirit of God dwells in you?" (1 Corinthians 3:16, NASB). Yet, by faith the Spirit of the Christ dwells in our hearts (Ephesians 3:17).

In 2 Corinthians 6:16 Paul said, "We are the temple of the living God." In Galatians 4:6 (NASB), Paul said, "God has sent forth the Spirit of His Son into our hearts." The Spirit of His Son is God Himself who dwells in the temple of our hearts.

The Spirit of God and the Spirit of the Christ are two expressions describing the same Spirit that dwells in the believer's heart. Yet, Paul admonishes Timothy to "Guard, through the Holy Spirit *who dwells in you* [emphasis added], the treasure that has been entrusted to you" (2 Timothy 1:14, NASB). Thus, the term "Holy Spirit" also applies to "Spirit of God" and "Spirit of Christ" dwelling in the believer.

At Pentecost the believers were filled with the Holy Ghost of Jesus (the Holy Spirit - Acts 2:4). Yet in other verses already cited (Romans 8:9; Galatians 4:6; Philippians 1:19; etc.) we are filled with the Spirit of the Christ or the Spirit of God. That is, the Christ in us (Colossians 1:27). Hence, the Holy Spirit is the Holy Ghost of the Christ as well as the Holy Spirit of God.

Parakletos is a Greek word translated as Intercessor, Counselor, Advocate, and Comforter. The Holy Spirit is the *Parakletos* in John 14:26 as well as the Spirit of Jesus Christ in 1 John 2:1. Here there is no discrepancy. The Spirit of Jesus Christ (Spirit spelled with a capital "S") is the Holy Spirit of God.

In Luke 12:12 Jesus said the Holy Spirit will provide words of defense in times of persecution. But in Luke 21:15 (NASB), Jesus said, "I [by my Spirit] will give you utterance and wisdom which none of your opponents will be able to resist or refute." Again, there is no discrepancy. The Holy Spirit and the Spirit of Jesus are two expressions for the same Spirit.

Paul led a missionary group into what is now Turkey. Luke, describing the trip, wrote, "And they passed through the Phrygian and Galatian region, having been forbidden by the Holy Spirit to speak the word in Asia" (Acts 16:6, NASB). However, in the next verse, Luke wrote, "And when they had come to Mysia they were trying to go into Bithynia and the Spirit of Jesus did not permit them" (Acts 16:7, NASB). In verse 6 the Holy Spirit prevented them from going in one direction and in verse 7 the Spirit of Jesus did not permit them to go in another direction. Here it is clear that the Spirit of Jesus is the Holy Spirit.

The Spirit intercedes for us in Romans 8:26. Jesus, our High Priest, intercedes for us in Hebrews 7:25. According to these verses both the Spirit and

Jesus intercede for us. Yet, there is but one Intercessor.

In short, "We know that we abide in Him and He in us because He has given us of His Spirit" (1 John 4:13, NASB). Jesus has imparted the influences of His Holy Spirit to our souls. That He would give us His Spirit is one of the promises the Lord Jesus made to His disciples after letting them know He would go away (John 14:16, 17, 26; 15:26; 16:7). The Son of God has placed His Holy Spirit on our hearts (Romans 8:16).

GOD, SPIRIT, FATHER

God is Spirit (John 4:24). The Christ's Father is the eternal Spirit, the Holy Spirit that came upon and inseminated the womb of the virgin Mary (Luke 1:35). As a result of this miraculous conception the child that was born embraced all the fulness of Deity: God, Spirit, Father (Colossians 1:19).

As believers we become sons and daughters of God by adoption (Romans 8:15), united to the Christ as brothers and sisters (Matthew 25:40), and, through Him, united to God as His children. That is, by means of the Spirit of Jesus Christ, God "predestined us to adoption as sons" (Ephesians 1:5, NASB), His Spirit bearing witness with our spirit that we are children of God (Romans 8:16). Thus, because we are adopted by the agency of the Christ's Spirit into the family of God, His Spirit is our Father.

On sending out His disciples to preach the gospel the Christ said, "It is not you who speak, but it is the Spirit of your Father who speaks in you" (Matthew 10:20, NASB). On another occasion, regarding the anxiety of being persecuted, the Christ told His disciples, "The Holy Spirit will teach you in that very hour what you ought to say" (Luke 12:12, NASB). Thus, because there are not two Spirits telling the disciples what to say, the Spirit of the Father and the Holy Spirit are the same Spirit.

In like manner the Father raised Jesus Christ from the dead (Ephesians 1:17-20). Yet, Romans 8:11 says the Spirit raised Jesus Christ from the dead. Thus, no distinction can be made between the Father and the Spirit.

The "Spirit of truth" abides in us (John 14:17). Yet, according to John 14:23, it is the Father who lives in us. Hence, the Father is the Spirit of truth.

The Holy Spirit is the *Parakletos* (John 14:26). Yet, in another verse, the "Father of our Lord" is the *Parakletos* (2 Corinthians 1:3). Though different expressions, both "Holy Spirit" and "Father of our Lord" refer to the same *Parakletos.*

Parallel to the above observation, "the Spirit" sanctifies (1 Peter 1:2) while the "Holy Father" sanctifies (John 17:11-17), meaning the Spirit and Holy Father are the same Being who sanctifies.

Since God, Spirit, and Father perform the same operation it can be concluded that each expression, though voicing a different view of God's nature and presenting a different notion of who God is, pertains to the one God of the Old and New Testaments.

God, Spirit, Father are three titles (not names) that trigger the idea of an all-powerful, all-knowing, everywhere present supreme Being - who is an invisible (Holy) Spirit. Given that there is one Spirit, each of the three expressions invokes the concept of one divine Being. Each term expresses one of an infinite number of attributes. The word God recalls and records the idea of ultimate reality: God is real and everything else is passing. From the term Spirit arises the idea of an immaterial and activating principle: God is operational in the affairs of men and not disinterested. Father, as applied to Deity, brings to mind that God is Creator and Progenitor of everything.

In short, the descriptive expressions - God, Spirit, Father - imply that God is infinitely manifold. And because He is infinite He has other attributes and manifestations as well. For example, God is love (1 John 4:16), God is one (Deuteronomy 6:4), God is Savior (1 Timothy 1:1), God is immutable (James 1:17), God is righteous (Jeremiah 23:6), God is holy (Leviticus 11:44), God is all-powerful (Genesis 17:1), God revealed Himself in a Man (1 Timothy 3:16), God is life (1 John 5:20), God is light (1 John 1:5), God is eternal (Romans 16:26), God IS...(Exodus 3:14; Hebrews 11:6). Moreover, God is the bread of life, a rock, fortress, shield, exalted, shepherd, perfect, just, truth, merciful, gracious. As ruler of His kingdom, God is King. There is no list that could contain all that God is. Because He is infinite, God's inherent characteristics and outward manifestations are infinite. Spirit and Father are only two of God's manifestations.

CONCLUSION

Father (who is Spirit), Spirit of God, Holy Spirit, and Spirit of Christ are four expressions that describe one spiritual Being. The term "Spirit" is used to convey the idea inherent in each expression. Unlike the Hebrew Scriptures, the operation of the Spirit, which began in the New Testament at Pentecost, plays a leading role in bringing men into the kingdom of God and nurturing them along the way to heaven. The Spirit, of course, is the Holy Spirit of Jesus Christ.

The name Yahewh (I AM), and the titles Lord (sovereign King), God (goodness and supreme, ultimate reality), Father (intelligent designer, Creator) describe Deity in more or less material terms, terms that the human mind can grasp. The title "Spirit," however, best describes Deity because God is omniscient, omnipotent, and omnipresent, qualities that are unseen, beyond comprehension, but perceived by the human spirit. The human spirit can, more or less, relate to the divine Spirit although no one can fathom what is all-knowing, all-powerful, and everywhere present. And, no human mind is able to penetrate and understand the notion of an infinite, eternal, living Spirit. Yet, the history of Christianity reveals that Jesus' Spirit regenerates man's fallen nature and fills men's hearts with new life.

Jesus' Spirit comes to us by the sacrificial death of Christ the Man. Until He performed His great sacrificial work, the way was not open for Him, as God, to pour out His Spirit, the Spirt of Jesus Christ, to continue the work of Christ the Man. Indeed, who else but the Spirit of the Christ, the Christ's divine nature, could carry on the work of the Christ?

Because the terms Spirit, God, and Father are neutral titles of recognition, they cause no controversy. But the name of Jesus causes emotional problems among non-believers. The name of God the Father in the New Testament is Jesus, whose Spirit is holy.

DEITY 10

BOTH NATURES IN HIS CHURCH

When He ministered on earth as a Man, the Christ told His disciples that He would not leave them orphans (John 14:18). So, by His Spirit, Jesus came back at Pentecost and established His Church. Jesus is Head of His Church not only according to His divine nature but also according to that nature which is akin to ours, His human nature, a nature that died, a nature that we can relate to. Through the Christ's human nature the Church has access to Deity, Jesus' divine nature.

Paul says, "And He [God] put all things in subjection under His feet, and gave Him [the Christ] as Head over all things to the Church..." (Ephesians 1:22, NASB). This verse declares Jesus Christ to be Head of the Church according to both natures: His resurrected human nature that sits on the right hand of God and His divine nature which is God. God appoints the Christ, the resurrected Man, to have dominion over all things regarding the welfare of God's people. That is, God's heart leads the Christ and the Christ shows the Church the way to God's heart.

(Here it is implied that when the necessity for the Son's peculiar work of mediation should cease, when the consequences of sin have been abolished, when God's original purpose for His creation has been restored, when there is a new heaven and a new earth free of sin (Revelation 21:1), God would resume His absolute authority and dominion as it was before the fall.)

The Head of the Church must be related to its members, and of the same substance - body, soul, spirit. So, to give the Church the authority it needed, God Himself came to earth and assumed our flesh by way of the virgin birth. The Man that was born called Himself the Son of God as well as the Son of Man, Son of God signifying Deity and Son of Man signifying humanity. God appointed the Son of Man to be Head of the Church. God governs the Church's agenda through His Son, the resurrected Man. Thus, both natures of Jesus Christ are engaged in the direction of the Church. "We look at this Son and see the God who cannot be seen. We look at this Son and see God's original purpose in everything created...And when it comes to the church, he organizes and holds it together, like a head does the body" (Colossians 1:15-18, Msg).

Paul uses the word "Head" to denote Lord and Master. "Head" also implies that the head possesses within itself all the fulness of those things necessary for the functioning of the Church: edification of self as well as others, thinking, attitude, activity, proper relationships, intercourse, etc. God, through the Christ, supplies the individual members of His Church with all things necessary to sustain His Church.

Conscience (which is not a good guide because it is easily disobeyed and offers no recourse) was the only agent that governed the affairs of men before the Christ came into the world. Prior to the Christ's ministry men were unforgiven sinners, separated from God; and, because of willful sin, opposed God. Before the Christ's advent men were unwilling to be restrained and sought their own pleasure and were proud and vain and in conflict with God's law and government.

What was God to do to change men's hearts and bring them back to Himself? He assumed a body and "...reconciled us to Himself through Christ..." (2 Corinthians 5:18, NASB). Now, by His Spirit, the Christ serves as the Church's head, the Church's guide.

Because God took the initiative and lived in a body like ours and worked through His Son to reconcile Himself to us, the Christ is present in His Church according to both natures, divine and human. As the God-Man He shared the feelings of both man and God. And He knew what had to be done to resolve the conflict between God and man (refer to Matthew 11:27 with John 2:25). The Christ was acquainted with the views, desires, needs, claims, and prejudices of God as well as man. Because the Christ sought and fulfilled the welfare and honor of both parties in conflict, God righteously seated Him at His right hand and made Him the head of the Church.

(RE)UNION WITH GOD

The word "religion" comes from two Latin words: "re" (again) and "ligar" (to connect). "Religion," then, means "to connect again." The re-connection, of course, is understood to mean reconciliation with God.

The (re)union of God and His people is made clear in the New Testament. In fact, that's what the New Testament is all about. This real and vital (re)union is especially emphasized by the apostles John and Paul. The peculiar phraseology they employ (dwell in, abide in, dwelling of God, Christ in you) highlights the (re)union and conveys the idea of the most intimate possible connection between God and His people. Both John and Paul tell of Jesus' Spirit being in our hearts. Here are some examples.

- Quoting Jesus, John writes, "...you will know absolutely that I'm in my Father, and you're in me, and I'm in you" (John 14:20, Msg).
- Again, quoting Jesus, John writes, "Live in me. Make your home in me just as I do in you" (John 15:4, Msg).
- "Do you not recognize this about yourselves, that Jesus Christ is in you" (2 Corinthians 13:5, NASB).
- "...it is no longer I who live, but Christ the Messiah, lives in me..." (Galatians 2:20, Amp).
- Paul prays, "I ask him to strengthen you by his Spirit - not brute strength but a glorious inner strength - that Christ will live in you as you open the door and invite him in" (Ephesians 3:17, Msg).
- John tells his readers, "All who keep His commandments...abide in Him, and He in them. They let Christ be a home to them and they are the home of Christ. And by this we know *and* understand *and* have the proof that He [really] lives *and* makes His home in us, by His (holy) Spirit Whom He has given us"(1 John 3:24, Amp).

Further illustrations provide evidence of this (re)connection. Each example, even from the Old Testament, highlights the reality of Jesus' Spirit (Ghost) being spiritually bonded to our fleshly nature.

- Speaking through Isaiah, Jehovah declares, "I will pour my Spirit into your descendants and my blessing on your children" (Isaiah 44:3, Msg).

Here, Jehovah addresses the nation of Israel. Reference to the descendants of Israel includes spiritual Israel - Christians.

- Jehovah says the same thing through Ezekiel. "I'll put my Spirit in you and make it possible for you to do what I tell you and live by my commands" (Ezekiel 36:27, Msg). Jehovah's Spirit is Jesus' Spirit.

- Through the prophet Joel, Jehovah declares He will show pity and favor to the descendants of Israel. "I will pour out my Spirit on all mankind" (Joel 2:28, NASB).

- "But if God himself has taken up residence in your life, you can hardly be thinking more of yourself than of him. Anyone, of course, who has not welcomed this invisible but clearly present God, the Spirit of Christ, won't know what we're talking about. But for you who welcome him, in whom he dwells - even though you still experience all the limitations of sin - you yourself experience life on God's terms. It stands to reason, doesn't it, that if the alive-and-present God who raised Jesus from the dead moves into your life, he'll do the same thing in you that he did in Jesus, bringing you alive to himself? When God lives and breathes in you (and he does, as surely as he did in Jesus), you are delivered from that dead life. With his Spirit living in you, your body will be as alive as Christ's!" (Romans 8:9-11, Msg).

- "You realize, don't you, that you are the temple of God, and God himself is present in you?" (1 Corinthians 3:16, Msg). God's presence is the presence of Jesus' Spirit.

- "And in him you too are being built together to become a dwelling in which God lives by his Spirit" (Ephesians 2:22, NIV). That is, "in which *Jesus* lives by his Spirit."

Christians are (re)united to God by faith in Jesus Christ. This bond with God is sealed by Jesus' Spirit. "This is how we know we're living steadily and deeply in him, and he in us: He's given us life from his life, from his very own Spirit" (1 John 4:13, Msg).

MORE ON JESUS' SPIRIT

Jesus in heaven governs His Church on earth by His Spirit. Jesus' Spirit animates His mystical body and controls its activities. By His Spirit Jesus determines the direction of the Church and establishes its goals - to glorify God and to plant and cultivate the seed of the gospel.

Christians are mystically united to the Christ and are being transformed into His likeness (Romans 8:29). By Jesus' Spirit alone is the heart changed and purified. Were it not for Jesus' human life on earth and the agency of His Spirit from heaven, the truths and workings of the Christ's gospel would not be known and the human race would still be lost - there would be no Church.

Is it possible, then, that another Spirit, other than the Spirit of the Lord Jesus Christ, might be instrumental in presenting the gospel to the world? No. By His work on earth as a Man and by His Spirit from heaven, Jesus Christ's Spirit alone comforts those who live in a sick and dying world.

Three times in chapter 14 of the book of John, Jesus promises to return to earth after His death: "I'll come back..." (v.3); "I will not leave you orphaned. I'm coming back" (v.18); "I'm going away, and I'm coming back" (v.28).

Though He was going away He assured His disciples He would return to help them in their Christian walk. Of course He did not come back as a Man but by His Spirit. He came back at Pentecost to continue the work He began as a Man and to produce in His people the views and feelings He established as a Man and to spiritually incorporate Himself into His people so *they* might manifest His Spirit.

The New Testament reveals that all the fulness of God's Spirit resided in the Man Christ Jesus. Then, when Christ the Man died and was resurrected, Jesus (God) sent back His holy Spirit at Pentecost to minister to a world that had been cleansed of sin by the Christ's defeat of the devil - victory over death. And, by His Spirit, He established His Church, and indeed, dwells in His Church.

The sense of "to dwell in" means Jesus - as God - takes up residence in the believer's heart and produces the fruit of His Spirit (Galatians 5:22,23). These attributes - sacrificial love, inner joy, peace, patience, kindness, goodness, faithfulness, gentleness, self-control - do not flow from our own nature but come to us from Jesus' Spirit.

The nature of our hearts is wicked and self-centered. The virtues listed in Galatians are not natural and do not come from our hearts but are produced by a foreign influence - the agency of Jesus' Spirit operating on the soul. Jesus' Spirit from heaven influences, motivates, directs, guides, and nourishes His body of believers.

The word "spirit" (spelled with a small "s") is used in a variety of significations - ghost, temper, mental vigor, vivacity, a prevailing tone. That is, spirit is a quality in a person's actions. It even has something to do with alcohol.

In the Bible, spelled with a capital "S," Spirit means God because God is Spirit (John 4:24). The phrase "Spirit of Christ" (Romans 8:9) also means God because it refers to the Christ's divine nature. In His Church and in the world God operates through His Spirit, that is, the Spirit of Jesus Christ.

"You, however, are controlled not by the sinful nature but by the Spirit, if the Spirit of God lives in you. And if anyone does not have the Spirit of Christ, he does not belong to Christ" (Romans 8:9, NIV). In this verse the connection of the two phrases "Spirit of God" and "Spirit of Christ" in one breath, so to speak, demands that these two expressions be understood as referring to the same spiritual Being - God - since there is only one Spirit. By making reference to the Spirit of God alongside the Spirit of Christ, Paul emphasizes the spiritual reality that the Spirit of God is indeed the Spirit of Christ.

Paul poses the same spiritual reality in another verse. "And if the Spirit of him who raised Jesus from the dead is living in you, he who raised Christ from the dead will also give life to your mortal bodies through his Spirit, who lives in you" (Romans 8:11, NIV). Here, the reality is that the Spirit who raised the Christ from the dead - God - lives in you. At the same time the Spirit who lives in you is the Spirit of the Christ (John 17:23; Galatians 2:20; Ephesians 3:17; Colossians 1:27). Given that there is but one Spirit, the Spirit of God is the Spirit of Christ. And Christ's Spirit is holy.

The Christ's Spirit occupies a special presence in the Christian's heart. Jesus' divine nature, God in the believer, guarantees the security of an actual nearness to God, a real communion with Him that may be enjoyed everywhere and at all times. For this reason the Christ's Spirit is omnipresent. The Christ's Spirit in the believer takes the form of a continuous flowing fountain of spiritual influence that comforts, supports, and strengthens. (See John 7:37,38.)

We see God at work in the world through the Christ's Spirit. It was the Christ's Spirit that founded the Church. His Spirit is made manifest by the worldwide Church. Moreover, the very existence of the Church assures the believer that God is at hand and is eternally present to save the non-believer. The Christ's Spirit operating in the world expresses the redemptive presence of God to the world and reveals the gracious presence of God's concern for fallen humanity.

SPIRITUAL GIFTS

Chapter twelve of Paul's first letter to the Corinthians begins the discussion of spiritual things - or gifts. The general scope of this chapter is to show that spiritual things (gifts) are diverse but they all have their origin in one Spirit, which is, of course, the Spirit of Jesus Christ. There is no other divine influence that regulates and determines what Christians do.

The purpose of spiritual gifts is to edify the Church and build it into a spiritually functioning body. In the Church of Christ there is a necessity for different gifts to deal with the various challenges the Christian encounters in his walk in an evil world. To diversify the operation of the one Spirit of Jesus that produces the gifts, various gifts are needed to confront the various provocations Christians meet during their sojourn on earth.

"God's various gifts are handed out everywhere; but they all originate in God's Spirit...Each person [in the Church] is given something to do that shows who God is" (1 Corinthians 12:4,7, Msg). The gifts are diverse. Some are listed in 1 Corinthians 12.

Wise counsel,
Clear understanding,
Simple trust,
Healing the sick,
Miraculous acts,
Proclamation of God's word,
Distinguishing between spirits,
Prayer to God in a language you never learned,
Interpretation of a strange language when it's a message from God.

Other gifts are listed in the book of Romans, chapter twelve.

Prophecy,
Practical service,
Teaching,
Encouraging guidance,
Financial giving,
Leadership,
Acts of mercy.

"All these gifts have a common origin, but are handed out one by one by the Spirit of God. He decides who gets what, and when. You can easily enough see how this kind of thing works by looking no further than your own body. Your body has many parts - limbs, organs, cells - but no matter how many parts you can name, you're still one body. It's exactly the same with Christ. By means of his one Spirit, we all said good-bye to our partial and piecemeal lives" (1 Corinthians 12:11,12, Msg). Paul's point is that, though varied, all God's gifts come from one source - the Spirit of Jesus Christ.

The "common origin" of "all these gifts" can be traced to the Lord Jesus Christ for His Spirit is the "one Spirit of God." His Spirit - His divine nature - is God who hands out His gifts. To create another Spirit to distribute the gifts of God is to reveal a misunderstanding of the biblical truth that God the Father, who is Spirit and originator of the gifts, dwelt in His Son, the Man Christ Jesus.

All spiritual things in the Church (gifts as they are called in most Bible versions), are derived from Jesus Christ. His sacrificial work on earth paved the way for the things of His Spirit to be poured out from heaven. All spiritual endowments, whether charismatic or otherwise, are determined and distinguished by the special influences of the Christ's Spirit. No other divine influence edifies His Church. His Holy Spirit from heaven enriches all activities in the Church. To recognize any Spirit that influences the behavior of Christians - other than the Holy Spirit of Jesus Christ - is foreign and contrary to the plan and work that God began in Him.

REGENERATION

Asking Jesus to be the Master of your life is the best decision you'll ever make. Immediately upon asking Him to be your Lord and Savior, His Spirit rushes to dwell in your heart and you enter His kingdom, the kingdom of God, and your spiritual sojourn on earth begins. You are as good as dead before asking Jesus to come into your heart. You are living in a contaminated world in accordance with the unbridled dictates of your flesh. On opening your soul to the Lord, His Spirit takes up residence in your soul and the juices of His Spirit start to vitalize the duration of your new spiritual existence.

The Holy Spirit of the Christ becomes the source of your inner spiritual strength. By His Holy Spirit nourishing your human spirit you depart from the temporal kingdom of the world and pass into an eternal kingdom of heaven, a new spiritual existence that transcends physical death. His Holy Spirit helps you endure transient life on earth which can be troubling. His Spirit flowing into your spirit replenishes your soul as well as your body according to God's word. For you, the Christian sojourner, regeneration is a process of Jesus Christ's Holy Spirit working on your human spirit and your human spirit yielding to His Holy Spirit until your earthly sojourn ends.

From beginning to end, from regeneration to resurrection, you, the Christian sojourner, are under the influence of Jesus Christ's Holy Spirit. By supernatural wavelengths He sends His Spirit to assist you during your stay on earth. As a believing sojourner His Holy Spirit influences your every step along the way to heaven. Even when you step out of the way His Spirit guides you back into the way.

The divine influences in your new life, fellow sojourner, come from the Holy Spirit of the Lord Jesus Christ. Those divine influences, which control the actions of your new life, are written on the pages of your heart by the finger of God. He, by His Spirit, produces and provides new life on earth, giving inner peace and joy while you are passing through a sick, decaying, dying, and frightening world.

Regeneration, new life, comes to you, dear sojourner, as a result of the operation and influence of Jesus Christ's Holy Spirit. Because no one else made the sacrifice He made, no other divine influence provides the foundation for a new life of liberty and freedom from the guilt and shame of sin. Jesus Christ's Spirit subtly rules, commands, controls and influences all Christianity, the religion that is spiritually derived from the work of the Man Christ Jesus.

By the agency of His Spirit the defilements of the world are washed away and you are sanctified by God and justified in God's eyes. Hence, you are spiritually, and as a result, physically rejuvenated. And because Christianity has no other foundation than Jesus Christ there is no other Spirit than His Spirit that provides a new and regenerated life. Your new life in Christ, dear sojourner, begins as a spiritual trip on earth and will continue as a spiritual trip, with all its glory and excitement, throughout eternity.

"Unjust people who don't care about God will not be joining his kingdom.

Those who use and abuse each other, use and abuse sex, use and abuse the earth and everything in it, don't qualify as citizens in God's kingdom" (1 Corinthians 6:9,10, Msg). And, fellow sojourner, "A number of you know from experience what I'm talking about, for not so long ago you were on that list. Since then, you've been cleaned up and given a fresh start by Jesus, our Master, our Messiah, and by our God present in us, the Spirit [of Jesus Christ]" (1 Corinthians 6:11, Msg).

You, the Christian sojourner, are spiritually minded when you are under the direction and influence of Jesus Christ's Spirit. But the mind of a man or woman outside the influence of His Spirit is easily swayed by the lies of the devil. Indeed, he or she has no way of recognizing the devil's deceptions. It is only the Spirit of the Christ that makes the mind of the Christ visible.

Thanks to the influence of the Christ's Spirit - God's grace - you, dear believer, are born again - regenerated. Everyone has sinned, "but you were washed, but you were sanctified, but you were justified in the name of the Lord Jesus Christ, and in the Spirit of our God" (1 Corinthians 6:11, NASB). Here, in three words - washed, sanctified, justified - Paul discloses the meaning of regeneration.

When God's word says you were "washed" what does He mean? He means it is a spiritual washing. God means He cancels every one of your sins - past, present, future. He means, by your trust in the work of the Man Christ Jesus, your soul has been totally purified by His Spirit. To be washed is to be cleansed of the dirtiness of sin. You, beloved believer, can walk confidently knowing you are free of sin and its consequences - guilt, shame, death. "[L]et us draw near with a sincere heart in full assurance of faith, having [had] our hearts sprinkled clean from an evil conscience and our bodies washed with pure water" (Hebrews 10:22, NASB).

Immediately upon being washed by Jesus' Spirit at conversion, fellow traveler, your soul is sanctified by His Spirit. Now He begins the process of changing your heart. While God's Spirit washes your soul in one clean sweep, sanctification follows spiritual cleansing. Sanctification is a successive, advancing process of regeneration. God sets you apart and begins a progressive work of holiness in your heart. Then, the completion of sanctification, death of the body, introduces the Christian traveler to the reality of eternal life in heaven. Sanctification, from beginning to end, is a spiritual adventure in becoming more like the Christ and less attached to the world. Of course, to become like the Christ is to yield to the influences of His Holy Spirit, that is, God.

On being washed and sanctified by God's Spirit you are justified by His Spirit. This means God declares you *not guilty* of transgressing His law. On believing in the work of the Man Christ Jesus, God affirms that you are innocent because the Christ brought an end to the curse of the law. (The curse of the law is automatic condemnation since everyone is guilty of transgressing God's law; moreover, the law provides no hope of acquittal.)

But you are pardoned and treated as if you had never sinned against God. Your sins are forgiven. You are accepted by God as an upright citizen in His kingdom. In short, your faith in Jesus Christ admits you to God's favor. And, as you probably know, dear believer, it was the influence of Jesus' Holy Spirit that convicted you and brought you to believe. By His Spirit you are made a righteous person in God's eyes.

Regeneration is accomplished by the merits of Christ the Man (humanity) and by His Holy Spirit (all the fulness of divinity) working in your heart. When men recognize that they are by nature polluted and depraved sinners without merit before God and without hope, when they realize that they are not the center of the universe, and when they are convicted of sin and depravity and look for help and finally turn to Jesus Christ and place their trust in Him, His grace and holiness renew their soul and they are washed clean and sanctified and justified by His Spirit.

That is, by the Holy Spirit of Jesus Christ men and women are led to lead a holy life, their faith making them fit for heaven. By faith men and women are cleansed, pardoned, and accepted by God as righteous - by and through the qualities and actions of Jesus Christ alone. Being washed, sanctified, and justified is done by the agency of Jesus' Holy Spirit. There is no other agent, spiritual being, or heavenly power that accomplishes the plans of God.

Conclusion

Worship Of Both Natures

INTRODUCTION

Worship, the noun, comes from worthiness to receive reverence and honor. Worship, the verb, is defined as the spontaneous expression of devotion and thanks. To whom, then, should honor and thanks be given? To the Father for giving us His Son? Or to the Son for giving His life (God cannot die) for our sins? Or to both Father and Son? To both Deity and sinless humanity?

Without the Man Christ Jesus' sacrificial death as payment for sin there would be neither redemption nor salvation. God's grace would be incomplete without the Son of Man's work on the cross. Hence, the person of Jesus Christ, who embodied both divinity and humanity - God and Man - is to be worshiped. Indeed, the Word of God tells us to honor and thank the God-Man. "Moreover, the Father judges no one, but has entrusted all judgement to the Son, that all may honor the Son just as they honor the Father. He who does not honor the Son does not honor the Father, who sent [begot] him" (John 5:22,23, NIV).

Needless to say, the God-Man, Jesus, is the only person of God worthy of worship. In the New Testament the name of Jesus is the only name that designates God. Father and Holy Spirit are titles that serve to describe certain aspects of God but they are not names of God. The name of Jesus embodies God's reputation, all that God is, and God's spiritual nature. "And everyone who calls on the name of the Lord will be saved" (Acts 2:21, NIV). "Salvation comes no other way; no other name has been or will be given to us by which we can be saved, only this one" (Acts 4:12, Msg). "Of Him all the prophets bear witness that through His name everyone who believes in Him receives forgiveness of sins" (Acts 10:43, NASB). We receive forgiveness of sins from the Father based on the sacrificial death of His Son, the God-Man.

THE FATHER (SPIRIT) ACCOMPLISHES HIS MANDATE THROUGH THE SON (FLESH)

God's Holy Spirit and His assumed nature, the Man Christ Jesus - both Deity and humanity - acted in conjunction to achieve mankind's salvation. Each nature performed, in communion with the other, that which was proper to it to save the world from the consequences of sin. They did not act separately. The Father gave the world His Son and the Son cleansed the world of sin by His blood. The Father crushed the devil's headship by the work of His Son. Indeed, "The Father abiding in Me," Jesus said, "does His works" (John 14:10, NASB).

There is no way Deity can die for sin. Deity cannot die. And there is no way humanity can destroy the guilt and condemnation of sin. Humanity cannot get rid of sin and restore life. Humanity cannot eliminate the lies of the devil. These are gifts and blessings that come from the Father (Deity) through the work of the Son (humanity).

The New Testament gifts and blessings of God did not occur outside the works of the flesh. The extraordinary influences of the Father's Spirit dwelling in the Son brought about the Christ's sacrificial death. "Through the Spirit, Christ offered himself as an unblemished sacrifice, freeing us from all those dead-end efforts to make ourselves respectable, so that we can live all out for God" (Hebrews 9:14, Msg). The Son by His willingness to obey, suffered death in accordance with the Father's will.

The Christ's work to achieve redemption was not a work of humanity alone. Scripture says God redeemed His Church by His *own* blood (Acts 20:28). God, who is Spirit and has no blood, redeemed His Church through the work of a Man, His only begotten Son. That is, Spirit influenced humanity to achieve God's redemption. The Father, Spirit, provided the world with redemption based upon the work of the Redeemer, God's *own* blood.

Redemption of our souls came about by the God-Man's two natures working together. However, the difference between the two natures remained intact. God was God and Man was Man. There was a difference but no separation. They (Deity and humanity) were one, united for one purpose (John 10:30): To renew mankind. That is, Deity redeemed mankind on account of what the Redeemer (humanity) did for us. The Man Christ Jesus sacrificed His life for our sins. God accepted the sacrifice and set us free from the shackles of sin.

But we must not think Spirit was inactive because humanity did all the work. On the contrary, each nature performed that which was proper to it. Redemption was not accomplished by human nature alone. For then the power and honor of redemption would be taken from the divine nature and our redemption would not be sufficiently sure and firm if it rested solely on the work of the human nature, for, in the case of redemption, flesh cannot do what Spirit did, and vice versa.

Suffering and death are not properties of Spirit. Yet, through suffering and death the wrath of God was placated. Thanks to the Man Christ Jesus' suffering and dying for us, God crushed the headship of the devil, destroyed death, restored life, and liberated the devil's captives. These are divine powers put into effect by the works of the flesh.

The work of both natures - the power of both natures working together for the benefit of mankind - can be described as a big fishhook covered by human flesh. When it was swallowed by the serpent, Leviathan, it spelled his doom. By way of explanation the fishhook represents God. The bait God used to lure Leviathan was the person of Christ. Now, God has delegated us to be the fishermen.

SPIRIT'S RESPONSE TO HUMANITY'S SUFFERING AND DEATH

The union and communion of Spirit and flesh in the Son of God was intimate. Both natures acted in communion to produce and accomplish the effects of the Christ's work. Also, in the death and suffering of the Christ's human nature, the divine nature was not inactive. While it is true that God willed that the Christ suffer, and permitted Him to die as prophesied, God's Spirit was not idle but always present, strengthening and sustaining, helping His Son bear the burden and emerge victorious. God knew all along He had every right to sovereignly raise His sinless Son from the dead.

The Son, knowing He was sinless and did not have to die, obediently submitted to the Father's will and chose death. He did not follow the call of His flesh but surrendered to the influence of the Spirit that dwelt in Him. The Son yielded to what the Father had willed.

Because the union of the two natures was intimate we can be sure the Father did not stand idly by while the Son faced death. Without a doubt the Spirit fortified the flesh in the face of suffering and death. Given that God's Spirit tore the veil of the temple in two from top to bottom, split rocks, caused an earthquake, opened tombs, raised the dead, and brought darkness for three hours at the Christ's crucifixion, we can be sure the Father was ministering to His Son's human spirit.

Yet, under the pressure of intense suffering the Christ cried out, "My God, My God, why hast Thou forsaken Me?" (Matthew 27:46, NASB). This was clearly His flesh crying out. Since there can be no communion between God's eternal Spirit and death, the Son's indwelling Holy Spirit was compelled to leave Him. Because He took upon Himself the curse of the law, being made a curse for us (Galatians 3:13), because He was made a sin offering (2 Corinthians 5:21), because His death was our death, and because our sins were placed on Him, the eternal Spirit was obliged to withdraw from Him, for God's Holy Spirit can have nothing to do with sin and death. Then the Christ yielded up His human spirit (Matthew 27:50).

THE SON OF MAN AT THE RIGHT HAND OF GOD

Now, apart from the law, the righteousness of God is appropriated, acquired, and possessed by faith in the resurrection of the Christ (Romans 3:21). God instituted His plan of justification by faith in the resurrected Savior. The resurrection inaugurated God's scheme of acquitting men in the sight of His law, permitting them to enter into God's grace.

Now, having become the first Man to be born again from the dead (Colossians 1:18), the Christ sits at the right hand of God (Psalm 110:1), being restored a life-giving Spirit (1 Corinthians 15:45), interceding on our behalf (Romans 8:34), paving the way for believers to follow (Romans 6:5).

Being seated at the right hand of God (Ephesians 1:20) does not mean God has hands or a right and left side, but that God glorified the Son of Man and raised Him to the highest honor and appointed Him as head of the Church (Ephesians 1:22). In other words the Son of Man was God's right hand Man in bringing about restoration.

The Son of Man was no longer a human being with vital functions and an animated human nature after His death and resurrection. Now He is restored a vivifying Spirit in heaven with the power of imparting life to sick and dying human beings. He is now what He said He was: The source of life. "For just as the Father raises the dead and gives them life, even so the Son [of God] also gives life to whom He wishes" (John 5:21, NASB).

The Son of Man now represents His Church before the mercy seat of God in heaven (Romans 8:34). The resurrected Christ now lives in heaven making intercession for us. He constantly presents the merits of His death before God as cause for believers to be saved from death (Hebrews 7:25; 9:24).

God judges no man (John 5:22). The Father has given the Son authority to judge mankind because He is the Son of Man (John 5:27). That is, God gave the risen human nature of the Man Christ Jesus the power to execute judgment since it is only proper that one of our own nature should judge the world (Acts 17:31).

Just before Stephen was stoned to death he looked up and saw the Son of Man standing at the right hand of God (Acts 7:56; see also Daniel 7:13f). Being positioned at the right hand of God simply means the Christ was given ultimate power to judge all flesh (John 17:2), the righteous as well as the unrighteous. All mankind is under His control (Matthew 25:31-46). And because He has been given all authority over God's creation, the Church, which is His body (1 Corinthians 12:27), is safe and will endure forever.

BOTH NATURES DEMAND WORSHIP

Both natures of the God-Man demand worship because both natures were involved in our redemption and our salvation: Humanity sacrificed His life for us, and, because of humanity's death, Deity provides our salvation. Salvation is a divine blessing that humanity cannot provide. The Church sees Deity in the Son of God as God, creator of all things (Colossians 1:16). The Church also sees the Son of God as Redeemer, Substitute, Savior, Mediator, High Priest - His human qualities. The Church worships Jesus Christ as God manifested in the flesh (1 Timothy 3:16) who worked on our behalf in order that God save our souls. And, by His resurrection, the Church looks to the Christ as the guarantee of eternal life in heaven (Ephesians 1:14). The Church's only object of worship and adoration is the God-Man.

In the name of Jesus Christ the Church is baptized to receive the gifts of God's Holy Spirit (Acts 2:38) as well as being baptized into Christ Jesus' death (Romans 6:3); that is, death to self to walk in newness of life. We are justified "in the Spirit of our God" (1 Corinthians 6:11) and we are justified by the Christ's blood (Romans 5:9). We are justified by the work of both Spirit and flesh, by the work of both Deity and humanity.

Indeed, the truth that both natures demand worship is made clear by Jesus Himself. "So that all will honor the Son," Jesus said, "in the same way as they honor the Father. Whoever does not honor the Son does not honor the Father who sent [begot] him" (John 5:23, GNNT). In other words, whoever denies the one denies the other. That is, whoever worships one worships the other. One nature without the other affords neither redemption nor salvation.

"WE"

"If anyone loves me," Jesus said, speaking for Himself (humanity) and His Father (Deity), "he will obey my teaching. My Father will love him, and *we* will come to him and make *our* home with him" (John 14:23, NIV, emphasis added). This is figurative language meaning "we will come to live in his heart." "We" includes the Son who died for our sins and the Father who forgives our sins.

These two truths, liberating the world of sin by the sin-bearer and pardoning the world's sins by the Father, emphasized by the pronoun "we," establishes a proper view of the relation between Father and Son that is effected among Christians: Humanity gave His life for our sins while Deity guarantees salvation from sin. Thus, the Christian is under the influence of the Holy Spirit of the Father as well as the flesh of the Son. Consequently, both natures are worthy of worship.

"I and the Father," Jesus said, "one (thing) we are" (John 10:30, Westcott and Hort, Interlinear Translation). The phrase translated "one (thing) we are" expresses union. That is, more than union of purpose, design, plan, and counsel. It expresses the oneness or unity of nature between Father and Son which includes the power of sinlessness - an attribute of the God-Man. God joined Himself to the embryo in the womb of a virgin and dwelt in the Manchild that was born. "For the full content of divine nature lives in Christ, in his humanity" (Colossians 2:9, GNNT). Thus, because of the unique union of Spirit and flesh in the God-Man, worship of both natures in Jesus Christ brings us closer to ultimate reality.

DEITY IS INACCESSIBLE APART FROM THE CHRIST'S HUMANITY

Because the Son came to us from the Father's heart of grace ("I came forth from the Father...", John 16:28, KJV) by way of the virgin birth, we must particularly beware that we do not artificially separate the union of the two natures when in fact there is a oneness of nature in Father and Son. That is, both humanity and Deity, besides being sinless, had the same plan for the earthly and spiritual state of human existence. Unlike fallen humanity's relationship with God, which was inconsonant and shameful, the Son's relationship with the Father was harmonious and shameless. Consequently, both natures deserve honor: The Father because He devised the plan of redemption and the Son because He fulfilled God's plan of redemption.

In the design and objective of redemption each nature did that which was proper to it. By His grace the Father (Deity) gave us His Son (humanity). By His sacrificial death the Son bought back our souls from the devil's captivity.

Is it only God's divine nature, His Holy Spirit, that leads us in our Christian walk toward maturity? Or is His assumed nature, the Christ's flesh, also *symbolically* leading us when we give our life to the Lord? After all, God's Word is our guide to heaven and it was God's Word that became flesh (John 1:14). Just as the Christ's body and blood are symbolically with us at communion, is it not possible that the sacrificial death of His flesh is also included when Paul admonishes us to be filled with His Spirit (Ephesians 5:18)?

Paul, in Romans 8:2, speaks of "the Spirit of life in Christ Jesus." Under the principles of the Christian religion Jesus Christ sends His Holy Spirit from heaven to earth to apply His work to the hearts of men and women. The work and influence of His flesh, which come to us by His Spirit, and bring us the Spirit of life in Christ, are part of the Christian scheme. Had God's Holy Spirit not intervened in world affairs the Christ would not have been born. Had the Christ not been born His Spirit would not have been poured out onto a sick and dying world. "Whoever does not have the Spirit of Christ does not belong to him [God]" (Romans 8:9, GNNT).

In our church services, in our prayers, in our daily life we seek God through the Son of Man. We seek Deity through humanity. God is inaccessible apart from the Christ's humanity. Speaking as Man, not as God, Jesus said, "I am the way...no one comes to the Father but through Me" (John 14:6, NASB). "Anyone who acknowledges that Jesus Christ came as a human being has the Spirit who comes from God" (1 John 4:2, GNNT). Thus, the God-seeker cannot separate Jesus Christ's humanity from His Deity.

SUMMARY

Reason enough to worship the Man Christ Jesus as well as God the Father is the fact that our only access to God is through the humanity of the Christ who sacrificed His life and paid the penalty for our sins. Only a sinless Man of our own nature could do such a thing for us. God did not pay the price. God did not die for our sins. God is infinite and eternal and cannot die.

God was not born. He was the Father of the Christ and dwelt in His Son (Colossians 2:9), the Man who was born. If Christian worship is to be acceptable to God the worship of both natures in Jesus Christ - Deity and humanity - is essential since one nature without the other does not, indeed, cannot provide either salvation or forgiveness of sin.

Clearly, God wants both natures to be present in His Church. Both presences are seen by the eyes of faith. We see, thank, and worship God who remits our sins, symbolized by the sacrament of water baptism; and, we see the Man Christ Jesus through the cup of wine and unleavened bread which represent His body and blood. God's Spirit is seen by the spread of His Church worldwide, and the Lord's body is invisibly present in each Church each time the Lord's Last Supper is celebrated.

Not only are both natures of Jesus Christ present in the Church but each nature also dwells in its individual members. "Whoever loves me," Jesus said, "will obey my teaching. My Father will love him, and my Father and I will come to him and live with him" (John 14:23, GNNT). John also wrote, "If what you heard from the first dwells *and* remains in you, then you will dwell in the Son and in the Father (always)" (1 John 2:24, Amp).

By faith both the Father (Deity) and the Son (humanity) dwell in the believer. And after death, at the resurrection, the believer dwells in the Son and in the Father. Indeed, the divine nature of the Son, The Spirit of the Christ, *is* the Father. "Anyone, of course, who has not welcomed this invisible but clearly present God, the Spirit of Christ, won't know what we're talking about" (Romans 8:9, Msg).

God's name in the New Testament is Jesus. The name "Jesus" refers to Deity: "God provides salvation." The title "Christ" refers to humanity: The anointed one or the Savior. Paul emphasizes that both natures are in the believer. "Do you not yourselves realize *and* know (thoroughly by an ever-increasing experience) that Jesus Christ is in you?" (2 Corinthians 13:5, Amp). Both the experience of God's salvation and the experience of the Christ as Savior are in us.

Jesus Christ is both God and Man, both Spirit and flesh in one person. And because the right hand of God, where the Christ is seated, is everywhere present, the resurrected Christ is everywhere present since, in reality, God has no right side. Presently the Christ is not limited to a body in one particular place. Both natures merit our worship because both natures took part in our salvation: God, Spirit, Deity providing salvation; the main ingredient in salvation being the Savior's (humanity's) sacrificial death.

Thus, through the Son (humanity) we fellowship with the Father (Deity). Apart from the Son we cannot fellowship with the Father who is Spirit (John 4:24). "And [this] fellowship that we have (which is a distinguishing mark of Christians) is with the Father and with His Son Jesus Christ, the Messiah" (1 John 1:3, Amp).

Along the same lines, in His final prayer on earth, praying as a Man, praying to His Father in heaven, Jesus pleaded,

Father, it's time.

Display the bright splendor of your Son

So the Son in turn may show your bright splendor.

You put him in charge of everything human

So he might give real and eternal life to all in his charge.

And this is the real and eternal life:

That they know you,

The one and only true God,

And Jesus Christ, whom you sent [begot] (John 17:1-3, Msg).

Here, "to know" expresses more than a mere acquaintance with the character of God. "To know" includes an especially marked influence on the mind and heart that the Father (Deity) and the Son (humanity) produce. That is, knowledge of the Father's role and the Son's role in the plan of salvation offers inner peace and joy, "real and eternal life."

Finally, Paul writes, "Every tongue should confess that Jesus Christ is Lord, to the glory of God the Father" (Philippians 2:11, KJV). Here, the Greek word translated "Lord" supports the idea that Jesus Christ is proprietor and owner as well as ruler over all God's creation. God appointed the Son of Man to that office. He exercises dominion over all the universe God created - to the glory of God the Father. To honor the Son (humanity) is to glorify the Father (Deity).

About Pentecostal Publishers

Christianity has experienced a number of organizational changes since its beginnings. Starting with the original disciples it began to develop into an institutional body. First came the papacy, Roman Catholicism, and religious councils in the middle ages. Second came Martin Luther, Protestantism, and the revelation of God's grace. Then, in the twentieth century, Pentecostalism was born again after two thousand years.

Pentecostalism celebrates the descent of Jesus Christ's Holy Spirit into the world. Pentecostalism reveals new truths about the Man Christ Jesus. Specifically, when He walked the earth He was fully God and fully Man. He embodied two natures. In short, Jesus Christ is the only person of God; all the fulness of God *dwelt* in the Man Christ Jesus. God did not "become" a Man (God does not change from one form to another) but God, whose Spirit (John 4:24) is Holy, *dwelt* in a Man (Colossians 2:9).

The mission of Pentecostal Publishers is to present this truth to quicken love and respect for Jesus Christ as our only God and Savior. God's Holy Spirit provides salvation based upon the shed blood of the Man Christ Jesus. To introduce any other person of God into the Godhead tends to divert attention away from the absolute deity of the Lord Jesus Christ.

When the Bible makes reference to the Holy Spirit it refers to the Holy Spirit of Jesus Christ dwelling in and activating His people, influencing the world's moral direction. When, in the last of the end times, Jesus Christ's Holy Spirit is withdrawn from the world (2 Thessalonians 2:7) and the devil is allowed to reign freely, the world will have no moral direction.

The goal of Pentecostal Publishers is to magnify the name of Jesus Christ and to explore the contradiction between multiple personalities in the Godhead and the absolute humanity/deity of the Lord Jesus Christ.